D1602045

Jack London

JACK LONDON

One Hundred Years a Writer

EDITED BY

Sara S. Hodson

AND

Jeanne Campbell Reesman

HUNTINGTON LIBRARY · SAN MARINO, CALIFORNIA

Printed in the United States of America

Published by the Huntington Library Press
1151 Oxford Road, San Marino, California 91108
www.huntington.org/HLPress/HEHPubs.html

LIBRARY OF CONGRESS CATALOGING-IN-PUBLICATION DATA

Jack London : one hundred years a writer / edited by
Jeanne Campbell Reesman and Sara Suzanne Hodson.
        p. cm.
    Includes bibliographical references and index.
    ISBN 0-87328-195-0 (alk. paper)
        1. London, Jack, 1876–1916—Criticism and interpretation.
    I. Reesman, Jeanne Campbell.   II. Hodson, Sara Suzanne, 1949–
        PS3523.046 Z654   2002
        813'.52—dc21   2002000763

CONTENTS

List of Illustrations vii

Acknowledgments ix

Preface xi

Introduction I
Sara S. Hodson

Jack London and Anna Strunsky 21
    Lovers at Cross-Purposes
Jacqueline Tavernier-Courbin

Fathers and Sons in Jack London's "The House of Pride" . . 44
Gary Riedl and Thomas R. Tietze

Jack London's "Second Thoughts" 60
    The Short Fiction of His Late Period
Lawrence I. Berkove

Jack London's *Martin Eden* 77
    The Multiple Dimensions of a Literary Masterpiece
Joseph R. McElrath Jr.

Algebra of Twisted Figures 98
   Transvaluation in *Martin Eden*
María DeGuzmán and Debbie López

Jack London "In the Midst of It All" 123
Sam S. Baskett

Jack London and "the Sex Problem" 147
Bert Bender

"The (American) Muse's Tragedy" 189
   Jack London, Edith Wharton,
   and *The Little Lady of the Big House*
Donna M. Campbell

   Contributors' Notes 213
   Index 217

ILLUSTRATIONS

Figure 1 104
  "Swinburne! That fellow had eyes and he had certainly
  seen color and flashing light. But who was Swinburne?"
  The Pacific Monthly 20, no. 3 (September 1908), 237

Figure 2 107
  "She shook hands, frankly, like a man . . . Never had he seen
  such a woman." *The Pacific Monthly* 20, no. 3 (September
  1908), 239

Figure 3 108
  " 'But I'm goin' to make it my class' . . . His voice was
  determined, his eyes flashing, the lines of his face had grown
  harsh." *The Pacific Monthly* 20, no. 3 (September 1908), 241

Figure 4 111
  "That bunch of hoodlums was lookin' for trouble, an' Arthur
  was n't botherin' 'em none. They butted in on 'm an' then I
  butted in on them an' poked a few!" *The Pacific Monthly* 20,
  no. 3 (September 1908), 242

Figure 5 112
  Drop cap. *The Pacific Monthly* 21, no. 2 (February 1909), 166

PLATES .   .   .   .   *following page* 132

Anna Strunsky, ca. 1900.

Bess Maddern, Jack London's first wife, ca. 1900.

"Bert" and Jack London, ready for hop-picking,
England, 1902.

Jack London, in the East End, London, 1902.

Jack London as proponent of the physical culture
movement, ca. 1904.

Charmian and Jack London on the bow of the partially
completed *Snark*, 1906.

The *Snark*, Hawaii, 1907.

Jack London aboard a dinghy alongside the *Snark*, ca. 1907.

Jack London at work, Pearl Harbor, 1907.

Charmian London, Hawaii, 1915.

Jack London at Waikiki, 1915.

Jack London, ca. 1900–1905.

Charmian London on Sonoma Boy, ca. 1915.

Jack London with his Shire stallion, Neuadd
Hillside, ca. 1915.

Jack London, ca. 1914.

Jack and Charmian London at the ranch cottage, ca. 1915.

ACKNOWLEDGMENTS

The editors would like to thank all the participants in the Fourth Biennial Jack London Society Symposium. The editors also warmly acknowledge the friends and colleagues who helped make the book possible, especially Milo Shepard of the Jack London Ranch, who was, as always, generous with his time and encouragement, and Earle Labor and Earl Wilcox, who offered insightful readings of the manuscript. Shannon Cotrell served as research assistant at the University of Texas at San Antonio, which also lent support through a faculty awards program administered by the College of Liberal and Fine Arts. For their help and support, the editors wish to thank the following at the Huntington: Robert C. Ritchie, W. M. Keck Foundation Director of Research; David S. Zeidberg, Avery Director of the Library; Peggy Bernal, Director of the Huntington Press; Romaine Ahlstrom, Head of Reader Services; Lauren Tawa, Exhibitions Preparator; Mona Noureldin and Ann Mar of the Ahmanson Reading Room; Mary Robertson and Lita Garcia in the Manuscripts Department; Christine Fagan and Kristin Cooper in the Manuscripts Stacks; Tom Canterbury and his staff in the Rare Books Stacks; and the Photographic Department. Finally, we thank the distinguished scholars whose essays appear in this volume.

PREFACE

The essays presented in this volume commemorate the centenary of Jack London's beginnings as a writer by marking the maturity of Jack London scholarship. The contributors address questions that have long preoccupied readers of London's diverse canon and students of his life, from his relationship with his collaborator Anna Strunsky to the competing crosscurrents of *Martin Eden*. Seeming contradictions between London's use of naturalism and romanticism and between his avowed socialism and unmistakable belief in individualism have long been debated, but here too are insights into new areas such as his literary experimentation, his handling of race, and his foray into a feminine point of view in his last novel, *The Little Lady of the Big House*. London is a mercurial figure who has consistently refused definition, and that will probably continue to be the case. But the eight essays of *Jack London: One Hundred Years a Writer* represent the finest in critical thought on the subject and furnish the reader with both a broad sense of the meaning of London's career and brilliant readings of his remarkable prose. It has been a great pleasure to work with Sara S. Hodson on this milestone collection.

Jeanne Campbell Reesman
University of Texas at San Antonio

Jack London

SARA S. HODSON

Introduction

N A GENERAL, vaguely general way, you know my
aspirations; but of the real Jack, his thoughts, feelings,
etc., you are positively ignorant. . . . If I had followed
what [my sister] would have advised, had I sought her
I would to-day be a clerk at forty dollars a month, a railroad
man, or similar. . . . Do you know my childhood? When I
was seven years old, at the country school of San Pedro's, this
happened. Meat, I was that hungry for it I once opened a
girl's basket and stole a piece of meat—a little piece the size
of my two fingers. I ate it but I never repeated it. In those
days, like Esau, I would have literally sold my birthright
for a mess of pottage, a piece of meat. . . .

You cannot understand, nor ever will.

Nor has anybody understood. The whole thing has been
by itself. Duty said "do not go on; go to work." . . . Every

body looked askance; though they did not speak, I knew
what they thought. Not a word of approval, but much of
disapproval. . . .

So be it. The end is not yet. If I die I shall die hard, fighting to the last, and hell shall receive no fitter inmate than
myself. . . . I don't care if the whole present, all I possess, were
swept away from me—I will build a new present; If I am left
naked and hungry to-morrow—before I give in I will go
on naked and hungry; if I were a woman I would prostitute
myself to all men but that I would succeed—in short, I will.[1]

On 30 November 1898, Jack London wrote to Mabel Applegarth this bold assertion of his will and determination to escape
the life of a "work beast" and to succeed as a writer in the face of
overwhelming odds. Recently returned from a year seeking gold
in the Klondike, and enriched, not with gold dust, but with nug-
gets of experience and observations that would inspire his stories
of the North, London was still months away from his first real
successes in the profession he would call "the writing game."

By the turn of the century, London would see his writing career take root, following a two-year apprenticeship sitting at his
frequently pawned typewriter, subsisting on the income from odd
jobs, and collecting a dispiriting quantity of rejection notices that
he impaled on a tall spindle. Finally, in January 1899, his story
"To the Man on Trail" was published in the *Overland Monthly*, and
"A Thousand Deaths" appeared in a magazine called *The Black
Cat* in May 1899, earning him the sum of $40. He achieved na-
tional exposure when the *Atlantic Monthly* published "An Odyssey of the North" in its January 1900 issue. Most significant and
heartening for the young writer, in November 1899, Houghton
Mifflin accepted a volume of his short stories, *The Son of the Wolf*,
and it appeared the following year. By December 1900, London could write to Charles Warren Stoddard (the man he consid-

ered a surrogate father and addressed as "Dad") with calm self-assurance, "I once thought, when I was a little more callow than I am now, that I should like, above all else, to be a professor of English literature . . . now I do not care to be a professor at all. Life is so short. I would rather sing the one song than interpret the thousand."[2] Now a newly established author with the status of a professional, he no longer needed to assert aggressively his obligation and responsibility to his mind and soul, as he had in his letter to Mabel Applegarth.

Over the next four years, London became one of the most famous and successful authors of his day with the publication of his vastly popular novels *The Call of the Wild* (1903) and *The Sea-Wolf* (1904), as well as several volumes of short stories, and other books including his sociological study of poverty in Britain, *The People of the Abyss* (1903).

Thus began the professional literary life of one of the most astonishing authors in America and, indeed, in the world. Over his brief life of just forty years, London wrote at least fifty books while pursuing a host of other careers as adventurer, sailor, prospector, explorer, journalist, war correspondent, sociologist, and rancher—careers that for decades dominated both critical and public perceptions of London, often diverting attention from, and even eclipsing, his achievements as a writer. Before the concept was known, London became a best-selling author, both at home in the United States and abroad, where he quickly became, and remains to this day, one of the most popular authors in the world.

Today, a century after London's initial literary successes, the passage of the centennial anniversaries of his first professional publications presents an opportune moment to examine his writing career and to assess the state of critical London scholarship. This volume of essays by major London scholars offers insightful studies and analyses of the author and his works that not only build on previous scholarship, but also provide new interpretations, thus extending ever further our understanding of London's stories and novels.

For several decades after his death, scholars uniformly dismissed London's writings either as second-rate hack work or as adventure and animal stories for juveniles. Several factors contributed to these perceptions. First, London often insisted that he disliked writing and pursued the occupation only for money, especially to support his other careers. For example, writing in May 1900 to another aspiring writer, his friend and admirer Cloudesley Johns, "At the moment I get a good phrase I am not thinking of how much it will fetch in the market, but when I sit down to write I am; and all the time I am writing, deep down, underneath the whole business, is that same commercial spirit. I don't think I would write very much if I didn't have to."[3] Similarly, London's 9 April 1913 letter to neophyte writer Cordie Webb Ingram is equally emphatic about his distaste for writing: "And please remember . . . that I do not like to write for a living, even; that if I had my way I should not write a single line."[4]

What are we to make from protestations such as these, and why should we not take them literally as the entire story about London's motives? Jeanne Campbell Reesman perceptively proposes that such statements arose from his basic honesty and capacity to question his own behavior, as well as his willingness to hold inconsistent views in the course of his developing self and beliefs: "Thus, London entertained seemingly contradictory philosophies, but he could claim sincerity in his writing at the same time that he announced his willingness—indeed, desire— to play the 'writing game' and be well paid for it."[5] Jacqueline Tavernier-Courbin offers a closely related interpretation, noting that London "claimed a little too loudly that he was writing for money, thus projecting the image of a mercenary writer that did not tally with an idealized vision of a writer's vocation."[6] In addition, it seems that London was adopting a pose, perhaps because he wished to be perceived as working hard at his writing craft, making sacrifices for it, or because he was aware of his image as a manly adventurer, and knew this image was better represented to the public by daring escapades than by writing.

Another contributing factor to the perception of London as a hack writer was the enormous popularity of his works, both during and after his lifetime. For many critics and scholars, popular books and best-sellers by definition could not be "literary" but instead must be merely light books of little intellectual content and of no consequence. Indeed, London fueled these perceptions by referring to himself as a hack writer on at least one occasion. Replying to Houghton Mifflin's request for a biographical sketch before publishing *The Son of the Wolf* in 1900, London, perhaps merely assuming a pose of false modesty from the security of his new stature as a professional writer, offers up this assessment of his work:

> As to literary work: My first magazine article (I had done no newspaper work), was published in January, 1899; it is now the sixth story in the *Son of the Wolf.* Since then I have done work for the *Overland Monthly*, the *Atlantic*, the *Wave*, the *Arena*, the *Youth's Companion*, the *Review of Reviews*, etc., etc., besides a host of lesser publications, and to say nothing of newspaper and syndicate work. Hackwork all, or nearly so, from a comic joke or triolet to pseudo-scientific disquisitions upon things about which I knew nothing. Hackwork for dollars, that's all.[7]

Even recognizing the lesser writing efforts London managed to sell before the successes of his more serious and accomplished efforts in major publications, one finds it difficult to put much credence in London's assertion, given the litany he provides in his biographical sketch of prestigious journals in which his articles and stories have appeared. Rather, London seems to be hiding, in a feigned cloak of modesty, an impressive array of credits of which he feels justifiably quite proud.

Far more revealing of London's own philosophy and approach to writing is the advice he gave to would-be writers, in a variety of settings. In a well-known, frequently quoted letter to Cloudesley Johns, London admonishes his correspondent to enliven his prose, to make his writing throb with life and energy:

> Don't you tell the reader. Don't. Don't. Don't. But HAVE YOUR CHARACTERS TELL IT BY THEIR DEEDS, ACTIONS, TALK, ETC. . . . . And get the atmosphere. Get the breadth and thickness to your stories, and not only the length (which is the mere narration). . . . And get your good strong phrases, fresh, and vivid. And write intensively, not exhaustively or lengthily. Don't narrate—paint! draw! build!—CREATE! Better one thousand words which are builded, than a whole book of mediocre, spun-out, dashed-off stuff. . . . Pour all yourself into your work, until your work becomes you, but no where let yourself be apparent.[8]

In an essay entitled "Getting into Print," London similarly exhorts novice authors to abjure the easy route in pursuing their craft: "Don't dash off a six-thousand-word story before breakfast. Don't write too much. Concentrate your sweat on one story, rather than dissipate it over a dozen. Don't loaf and invite inspiration; light out after it with a club, and if you don't get it you will nonetheless get something that looks remarkably like it." He goes further, enjoining writers to "find out about this earth, this universe; this force and matter, and the spirit that glimmers up through force and matter from the magnet to Godhead. And by all this I mean WORK for a philosophy of life. It does not hurt how wrong your philosophy of life may be, so long as you have one and have it well."[9]

Obviously, an author's espousal of such an approach cannot be taken at face value as assurance that he has successfully adopted it (and, indeed, in response to London's advice not to write too much, not to "dash off a six-thousand-word story before breakfast," one inevitably thinks of his one thousand words per day, producing fifty books over a period of less than twenty years). However, we don't need to rely solely on London's word. Scholarship in recent decades has confirmed that London fully lived up to his own authorial advice. London's tales display not only the vigorously muscular style he advocated, but also abundant evidence that he worked hard for his own philosophy of life. Examining the stories and novels below their surface richly rewards scholars and thoughtful readers alike with the fruits of an agile and complex mind at work exploring ways of interpreting and understanding people and their worlds.

Modern scholars who now come to London's works free of earlier dismissive attitudes have emphatically placed London among the best American authors and have moved steadily forward in reassessing the earlier disparaging assessments of his work and in disproving some old assumptions about London that had long been legend among both scholars and the general public. The extent of these legends is formidable, particularly when gathered together, as Susan Nuernberg has, in a thorough yet admirably economical treatment:

> The prevailing myths are that London was one of the most autobiographical of American writers, that he committed suicide, that he wrote obsessively about his own illegitimacy, that he was a writer of dog stories and adventure tales for adolescent boys, that he was a racist, a womanizer, an alcoholic, and a hack writer, and that he contradicted himself and was confused in his thinking about socialism, individualism, scientific materialism, and idealism.[10]

Over the last thirty to forty years, scholars have faced a daunting task but have made significant progress toward critiquing these myths and replacing them with solid, well-documented analyses of London's life and works. Much of the credit for laying the foundation for this process belongs to scholars like Sam Baskett and Earle Labor, who were among the first to study seriously the author whose legacy was burdened by such profound misapprehension. Theirs was a lonely "calling in the wild" in the years when the academy viewed Jack London with scorn; indeed, Labor tells of being introduced by Baskett at a 1963 conference as "the other Jack London scholar."[11]

In the intervening years, London scholarship has entered full maturity and continues to advance on many fronts. The *Jack London Journal* is well established by editor James Williams; in addition to panels held at MLA and other scholarly conferences, the Jack London Society, under the leadership of executive coordinator Jeanne Campbell Reesman, has held five biennial symposia and has sponsored many panels at the American Literature Association and other conferences; and a Jack London list over the Internet (jack_london@listhost.uchicago.edu), managed by James Williams, offers fans and scholars a forum for discussion and sharing information. The increase in scholarly enterprise has been astonishing. In his "Afterword" to Cassuto and Reesman's *Rereading Jack London*, Earle Labor provides an overview of the impressive array of publications over the last few decades—important reading for anyone seeking an understanding of London scholarship and how far it has advanced.[12] Without rehearsing Labor's work, let us mention only a few of the titles to appear just in the last decade. Stanford University Press published in 1993 a three-volume edition of London's complete short stories, edited by Earle Labor, Robert C. Leitz III, and I. Milo Shepard, as a companion to its 1988 edition of London's letters; Jacqueline Tavernier-Courbin's *The Call of the Wild: A Naturalistic Romance* is an excellent study of the novel; an edition of the novel, *The Call of the Wild, by Jack London, with an Illustrated Reader's Companion*, incorporates editor Dan Dyer's extensive research in Alaska; *The Criti-*

cal Response to Jack London, edited by Susan Nuernberg, gathers together critical essays; Jeanne Campbell Reesman's *Jack London: A Study of the Short Fiction* offers important interpretations; Dale Walker and Reesman edited *No Mentor But Myself,* a collection of London's works about writers and writing; Twayne issued *Jack London: Revised Edition,* a critical introduction by Labor and Reesman; and Leonard Cassuto and Reesman compiled their edition of essays, *Rereading Jack London.*[13]

Even with the surge in London scholarship, no satisfactory scholarly biography exists. Andrew Sinclair's *Jack* (1977) and Alex Kershaw's *Jack London: A Life* (1998) contain errors of fact and of interpretation. A happy contrast is Russ Kingman's readable and mostly reliable *A Pictorial Life of Jack London* (1979), which remains the best narrative of the author's life.[14] Earle Labor is currently at work on a scholarly biography for Farrar Strauss and Giroux.

As to the future of London research, the outlook is richly promising. With extensive archival material available in repositories, much of it still unused or barely examined, the research opportunities are great, as Reesman has discussed in her essay "Prospects for the Study of Jack London."[15] Among the many possibilities she sees are the as-yet-unpublished story notes, plus several hundred story and novel ideas that London never used. Caches of correspondence are untapped, and much remains to be done with the vast array of photographs. There is no complete set of the works, so one of the biggest needs is for authoritative texts of all of London's writings, with full scholarly apparatus. These, and many more needs and opportunities, are outlined in Reesman's essay, making it an essential resource for any scholar casting about for the next project or confronting an archival finding aid at one of the repositories holding original London materials, like the Huntington Library.

The Huntington Library stands at the center of London scholarship, with its enormous archive of his papers that lures scores of researchers through the reading room door each year. The acquisition of the London archive began soon after London's death in 1916 and after retired businessman and collector Henry E. Huntington endowed in 1919 the research and cultural institution that would bear his name. In 1924, learning that London's widow Charmian sought an appropriate repository for his papers, and displaying impressive foresight concerning the lasting importance of the California author, Huntington dispatched his librarian Leslie Bliss to the Beauty Ranch to examine the papers. Receiving a favorable report, Huntington authorized the purchase of London's literary drafts, which soon arrived in the stacks and became but the first of a raft of further material that followed over the ensuing seventy-five years. Additions for the collection came to the Huntington by purchase and also by gift, due to the extraordinary generosity of Irving Shepard and the Irving Shepard Trust, and of his son I. Milo Shepard. Thanks to their selfless commitment to London scholarship, London's papers are preserved together and made available to scholars through the research library and to the general public via an exhibitions program. As recently as the mid-1980s, a gift of 130 original photograph albums ensured the preservation of these remarkable images as historical artifacts and as resources for original research, and in early 2000, I. Milo Shepard donated a large set of files concerning the posthumous publication of London's books, of significant value for the study of the bibliographic and publishing history of the author.

The Huntington's archive of London's papers, numbering about sixty thousand items, is the largest London collection in the world and also by far the largest literary archive of personal papers in the library (the next largest collection for an author contains about eight thousand pieces). The collection includes more than one thousand drafts (sometimes multiple versions, in autograph and/or typescript) and notes for nearly all of London's writings. A notable exception is the autograph manuscript for *The Call of the Wild*, which London discarded after its first publication. Among the many exceptional literary manuscripts are the complete autograph manuscripts of *Martin Eden* and "To Build a Fire," and drafts of portions of *Cherry*, the incomplete, unpublished novel London was working on when he died. Also present is the manuscript of *The Sea-Wolf*, a charred and congealed hunk tragically burned in the conflagration that followed the San Francisco earthquake of 1906 and therefore relegated to artifact status.

The extensive correspondence files include London's revealing, affectionate letters to Cloudesley Johns, his early love letters to Charmian London, and the letters he wrote to Anna Strunsky Walling while they were jointly writing *The Kempton-Wace Letters*. A long series of letters from London's beloved stepsister Eliza London Shepard contains numerous details of running the Beauty Ranch, and correspondence between London and such other authors as Mary Austin, Upton Sinclair, and George Sterling includes discussion of literary and political matters. Other correspondence documents London's extensive interests and endeavors, including socialism, the ranch, the genesis of story ideas, films made from his books, advice and encouragement for young writers, and such enterprises as the cruise of the *Snark* and other trips and adventures.

A series of documents contains agreements, book contracts, and royalty statements. London's extensive subject file, retained in his own ordering and arrangement, holds hundreds of offprints and clipped articles that he gathered on topics of interest, ranging from Alaska to yachts and, in between, such topics as copyright, dogs, fiction, gonorrhea, Jung, Molokai, plots, sea fiction, socialism, trade unionism, and women. Also in the ephemera files are boxes filled with magazine printings of London's tales, comic books based on the stories, magazine ads incorporating images from London's works, and other items. A superb set of more than a dozen enormous scrapbooks, attesting to the active life of Charmian's scissors and paste pot, contains thousands of news clippings about London and his works, abundantly documenting the extent to which the media-savvy author promoted himself and his writings in an age before the emergence of the cult of Madison Avenue advertising. Approximately sixty broadsides include posters, as well as oversize clippings, many covering his days as a war correspondent in Korea in 1904. One of the most exciting sections of the collection contains about ten thousand photographs, including snapshots, high-quality interpositives, and contact prints of images from the photograph albums, prepared for reference use and reproduction in order to protect and preserve the fragile albums. Finally, London's personal library of several thousand volumes includes his annotations in some of the books that most influenced him.

This vast archive continues to grow, as the Huntington adds to it whenever possible. Highlights of new acquisitions in the last decade include a stunning, large-format, full-color theater exhibitor's book for *The Call of the Wild*, showing how the film was used to entice local businesses to advertise in the theater. Also acquired at auctions are a set of notes for the novel *Adventure*, to supplement the autograph manuscript of the novel already in the collection, and a characteristically vigorous letter by London concerning the story "To Build a Fire" that emphasizes the veracity of certain details in the story to convince a doubting editor at the *Youth's Companion*. In late 1998, again at auction, the library placed the winning bid on a group of fifty-six letters from Charmian London to Harvey Taylor, dating from 1931 to 1932, augmenting a large series of similar letters already in the collection that deal with Taylor's friendship with Charmian and his efforts to act as her agent. Ironically, and representative of how the acquisitions game often works, the letters arrived in the old manila envelope in which they had been stored, annotated with a pencil note by Taylor, "Give to Huntington Library."

In the last two years, the Huntington has purchased two important groups of material, both from private collectors. In early 1999, the library acquired an impressive set of fourteen autograph and typewritten letters, dating from 1900 to 1906, from London to Charles Warren Stoddard, an early editor of the *Overland Monthly* and the man whose travel books inspired London's voyage on the *Snark*. Addressed to "Dad," the letters (which include the one quoted above) are unusually confiding in tone and reveal many details about London's personal life, including his doubts and fears but also his conviction of his own "right conduct" in separating from his first wife, Bess, as well as his comments about the relationship of his first marriage to his collaboration with Anna Strunsky Walling on *The Kempton-Wace Letters*. The following year, the library purchased a fine group of twenty-five letters by London and Charmian to various addressees. Six letters from London to Benjamin De Casseres deal with literary matters, and one especially interesting letter from the just-widowed Charmian to the same addressee, dated 29 November 1916, firmly disputes De Casseres's apparent assertion that London was now "star-roving" after death. Among this group is also a 13 January 1909 note from London to "Miss Goldstein," quoting his famous credo ("I would rather be ashes than dust.") and remarking that he had said it seven years before. This item, though small, offers important partial documentation for this London epigram of great popularity but elusive origin.

The Huntington, then, possessing superb resources for the study of Jack London, together with the fine (but underutilized) London collection at Utah State University, the material at the Bancroft Library, Sonoma State University and the Jack London Research Center in Glen Ellen, and small caches of manuscripts in other repositories, offers extraordinary opportunities for researchers, and these opportunities have been abundantly exploited by a steady stream of scholars, working both in the library and via correspondence.

Committed as it is to furthering scholarship through its research collections, the Huntington also adheres to a mission of education for the general public via its exhibitions. In honor of the Fourth Biennial Jack London Society Symposium, held at the library in 1998, the Huntington mounted a major exhibit on London's life and works. Entitled "The Wisdom of the Trail: Jack London, Author and Adventurer," the exhibit ran from September 1998 through early January 1999 and was viewed by about sixty thousand visitors, as well as nearly three thousand children in school groups led by docent tour guides. Consisting of more than sixty original items, including letters, inscribed first editions, diaries, annotated books, photographs, and ephemera, plus illustrations and wall reproductions, drawn primarily from the library's own collection, the display also included a few select items borrowed from a pair of private collections. In planning the exhibit, I was the fortunate beneficiary of several decades of scholarship, and especially the recent work of those whose contributions are mentioned earlier in this essay. Knowing that, for many people, a good deal of the fascination with London centers on his life of adventure, and exploiting those adventures for the splendid related visual material, I still wanted to concentrate on London's writings. Thus, the exhibit sought to present his multifaceted careers and adventures, yet to root them firmly on a central focus of his literary works, which are the output of his primary career. A major goal for the exhibit was to introduce (or reintroduce) visitors to the stories and novels, and to entice or inspire them to discover (or rediscover) the wonderful tales of this still-neglected writer. This emphasis on the writing and the works inspired the introductory text placed at the beginning of the exhibit:

> Jack London is known to people the world over as the author of such novels as *The Call of the Wild* and *White Fang.* In his short life of just forty years (1876–1916), he pursued a course of larger-than-life adventure as a sailor, tramp, com-

mon laborer, journalist, war correspondent, sociologist, and rancher.

This life of adventure has often overshadowed London's primary calling—writing an astonishing total of fifty books, including novels, short story collections, and nonfiction work. In his adventures, he found many of the characters, settings, and situations that would inspire and inform the tales he would write, but he also looked to the scores of books he read throughout his life for the ideas and systems of thought that would shape the raw material gleaned from his own life and adventures. Armed both with life experiences and with the fruits of his extensive reading, he sought in his own writings to find the answers to life's great questions. In his adventures and in his own writing, Jack London searched for the wisdom of the trail.

In display cases with such themes as "The Klondike," "Man of the People," "Journalist," "The Cruise of the *Snark*," "Tales of the South Pacific," "The Valley of the Moon," and "Novelist of Ideas," the exhibit presented such items as early letters from London to his friends Mabel Applegarth and Cloudesley Johns setting forth his authorial hopes and ambitions; letters that reiterate the intentions of his partly autobiographical novel *Martin Eden* and explain the meaning of the novels *The Star Rover* and *The Iron Heel*; literary correspondence with fellow authors Joseph Conrad, Mary Austin, Upton Sinclair, and Sinclair Lewis; autograph manuscripts of London's important stories "All Gold Canyon" and "Water Baby" and his futuristic novel *The Iron Heel*, along with galley proofs, photographs, an editor's letter, and a full-color illustration for "Koolau the Leper," all of which show the author's creative process; first editions of *The Call of the Wild*, *The Sea-Wolf*, *The People of the Abyss*, *The Star Rover*, *Martin Eden*, *The Cruise of the "Snark,"* and *The Son of the Wolf*; and photographs taken by London and Charmian depicting scenes from the San Francisco earthquake, the Russo-Japanese War, ports of call in the South Pacific, and life on the Beauty Ranch.

The Huntington expected the exhibit to be very popular with visitors, but the intensely direct and emotional bond that people felt with London was astonishing. I had placed a three-hundred-page volume of blank pages at the end of the exhibit and invited people's comments by posing the question "What does Jack London mean to you?" By the time the exhibit closed, the volume was filled, capturing for the library a permanent record of the profound influence exerted by the life and works of the man people think of simply as "Jack." That influence is vividly expressed in selected comments culled from the book:

> Jack, you are one heck of a man. Thanks for sharing your adventures and life with others and me. You gave me the courage to adventure out in the world! Thanks!

> As an English teacher, I appreciate London because he, more than any other author I have taught, gets kids "hooked" on literature. I find success here where other writers have failed to "reach" their minds. Thanks for the exhibit.

> This exhibit brought back the memory of "the first" book I read. Of course, I had read books assigned by teachers, at five pages per day. One day, when I was about twelve years old, I picked up *The Sea-Wolf* on a Saturday morning. I read the entire book before the sun set. I still remember that day in 1945. Thanks.

> I want to go back & re-read Jack London. The exhibit makes him real.

> Seeing London's hand on these pages of manuscript is like the completion of a thought: the boldness is there in every

stroke, and the compassion, and above all, the testing of the limits of what can be written about.

He's intililligent [*sic*]. Emma, 8 yrs.

How could such a nice and calm looking man write such a harsh book as *The Sea-Wolf*? Zoe, age 10.

Jack London—A reminder of the responsibility we all bear to think for ourselves, as deeply as we can, and to feel for others, as deeply as we can. An excellent introduction to his life, this exhibit, thanks.

Jack, you warmed my blood in the cold Canadian winters.

May the fire in the spirit of this adventurous man burn forever for all to see and feel—that they too find inspiration from him.

I owe my existence to Jack London. This is because my father, a young (Jewish) boy in Warsaw, was so inspired by Jack London's novels that he saved his pennies and earned passage to America and finally Oakland, in 1928–29. Thus, London saved *his* life—he escaped Poland before the Nazi invasion. P.S. Thank you for a *fine* exhibition.

As an addendum to the comments book, a phone call that came in during the run of the exhibit brought a request for the full text of London's credo, which was reproduced alongside a portrait of London on the main title wall. The caller acted at the request of friends, a couple who had visited the exhibit a day or two before and returned home to learn that the woman's mother had suddenly passed away while they were viewing the exhibit. They had been struck by London's "I would rather be ashes than dust" philosophy and how well it captured the mother's vigorous life, and now they wished their friend to read the credo during the memorial service.

This vignette and the visitor comments point up London's extraordinary capacity to connect with readers from all walks of life, whether they be scholars, informed general readers, or just those who enjoy losing themselves in a good yarn. Earle Labor has called London not only a major figure in American literature, but "perhaps our greatest Folk Hero," noting that no other writer has so completely enthralled Americans of every age. Labor turns to Ralph Waldo Emerson for description of this phenomenon: "In his essay 'Greatness,' Emerson remarks, 'Whilst degrees of intellect interest only classes of men who pursue the same studies, as chemists or astronomers, mathematicians or linguists, and have no attraction for the crowd, there are always men who have a more catholic genius, are really great as men, and inspire universal enthusiasm. A great style of hero draws equally all classes, all the extremes of society, till we say the very dogs believe in him.' " Labor adds his own coda to Emerson: "This comment, better than any I know, explains Jack London's extraordinary universal appeal."[16]

The essays that Jeanne Campbell Reesman and I have chosen for this volume to commemorate one hundred years of London's writing career, while reflecting a variety of approaches suitable to a writer of London's wide range, nonetheless form distinct groups, dealing with London's life, his short stories, and two of his novels. Jacqueline Tavernier-Courbin unveils new complexities and cross-purposes in the accepted story of Jack's relationship with his first love, Anna Strunsky Walling. Gary Riedl and Thomas R. Tietze examine the psychological dualities of the father-son and half-sibling relationships in the short story "The House of Pride." In "Jack London's 'Second Thoughts': The Short Fiction of His Late Period," Lawrence I. Berkove demonstrates that, in contradiction to the conventional view that many of London's late works are potboilers, these tales are actually complex "second thoughts," in which London reexamined and modified or even reversed many of his ideas and beliefs.

Martin Eden is the focus of a trio of essays. Joseph R. McElrath Jr. considers the novel in the context of other literary masterpieces and asserts that, like these masterpieces, it rewards repeated readings and analyses because it possesses multiple dimensions, to a far greater degree than even London himself recognized. For María DeGuzmán and Debbie López, those multiple dimensions become twisted figures, in which complexity is created by a variety of paired opposites. In "Jack London 'In the Midst of It All,'" Sam S. Baskett explores the problematic relationship between the author and his main character, analyzing the ways in which qualities of the self in the novel present a portrait of London as a young artist.

The final two essays concentrate on the late novel *The Little Lady of the Big House.* Looking at the novel as a study of sexuality, Bert Bender explores it in the contexts of London's other novels and of Darwin's theory of sexual selection. Donna M. Campbell draws illuminating parallels between London and Edith Wharton and specifically compares London's novel with Wharton's short story "The Muse's Tragedy."

As these essays show us so well, Jack London's inspiration came, again and again, even when he had to light out after it. The philosophies for which he worked so hard served him well in creating richly layered, complex stories and novels that challenge and reward us in the first reading, and all the more each time we return to them. A century ago he persevered, against the advice of friends and family, and prevailed in his powerful determination to escape the life of the common "work beast," as he called it, and to follow his heart and mind to become a writer. In the one hundred years of his writing career, recognition of his authorial stature has grown and matured, and he has come into his own as one of the greatest and most remarkable American authors.

NOTES

1. Earle Labor, Robert C. Leitz III, and I. Milo Shepard, eds., *The Letters of Jack London* (Stanford, Calif.: Stanford University Press, 1988), 23–26.

2. Jack London to Charles Warren Stoddard, 6 December 1900, Acquisition no. 1938, The Henry E. Huntington Library.

3. *Letters*, 182.

4. Ibid., 1149.

5. Jeanne Campbell Reesman, "Prospects for the Study of Jack London," *Resources for American Literary Scholarship* 25, no. 2 (2000): 133–58.

6. Jacqueline Tavernier-Courbin, "Introduction," *Critical Essays on Jack London*, ed. Jacqueline Tavernier-Courbin (Boston: G. K. Hall, 1983), 2.

7. *Letters*, 149–50.

8. *Letters*, 191–92.

9. Jack London, "Getting into Print," *The Editor* (March 1903): 57; reprint in Dale L. Walker and Jeanne Campbell Reesman, eds., *No Mentor But Myself: Jack London on Writers and Writing* (Stanford, Calif.: Stanford University Press, 1999).

10. Susan Nuernberg, ed., *The Critical Response to Jack London* (Westport, Conn.: Greenwood Press, 1995), xxiii.

11. Earle Labor, "Afterword," in *Rereading Jack London*, ed. Leonard Cassuto and Jeanne Campbell Reesman (Stanford, Calif.: Stanford University Press, 1996), 218.

12. Ibid., 217–23.

13. Earle Labor, Robert C. Leitz III, and I. Milo Shepard, eds., *The Complete Short Stories of Jack London* (Stanford, Calif.: Stanford University Press, 1993); Jacqueline Tavernier-Courbin, *The Call of the Wild: A Naturalistic Romance* (New York: Twayne Publishers, 1994); Dan Dyer, *The Call of the Wild, by Jack London, with an Illustrated Reader's Companion* (Norman: University of Oklahoma Press, 1995); Nuernberg, *The Critical Response to Jack London*; Jeanne Campbell Reesman, *Jack London: A Study of the Short Fiction* (New York: Twayne Publishers, 1999); Walker and Reesman, *No Mentor But Myself: Jack London on Writers and Writing*; Labor and Reesman, *Jack London: Revised Edition* (New York: Twayne Publishers, 1994); Cassuto and Reesman, *Rereading Jack London*.

14. Andrew Sinclair, *Jack: A Biography of Jack London* (New York: Harper and Row, 1977); Alex Kershaw, *Jack London: A Life* (New York: St. Martin's Press, 1998); Russ Kingman, *A Pictorial Life of Jack London* (New York: Crown, 1979; reprint, Middletown, Calif.: David Rejl, 1992).

15. Reesman, "Prospects," 133–58.

16. Labor, "Afterword," 223.

JACQUELINE TAVERNIER-COURBIN

Jack London and Anna Strunsky
Lovers at Cross-Purposes

J ACK LONDON AND Anna Strunsky met in March
1899 in San Francisco in the Turk Street Temple at a
meeting of the American Branch of the Socialist Labor Party commemorating the Paris Commune.[1] He was
twenty-three and she twenty. They had listened to the speaker,
Austin Lewis, "a London University man, who brought something of the old-world culture to [their] Western movement. It
was as if [they] were there in that Paris which [they] had never
seen, in a time before [they] were born. In that hour [they] re-
lived those days and nights of conflict and tragedy" (393, 1). Jack
rose from his seat well toward the front to speak to Austin Lewis;
Anna was also on her way to the speaker, and Frank Strawn
Hamilton introduced them. Anna fell immediately under Jack's
spell, feeling that "there was that about him that made one feel
that one would always remember him. He seemed the incarna-

tion of the Platonic ideal of man, the body of an athlete and the mind of a thinker" (393, 2). "He had large blue eyes, dark lashes, a broad forehead over which a lock of brown hair fell and which he often brushed aside with his small, finely shaped hand. He was deep-chested, [and] wide shouldered" (392, 17). "His smile was warm and bright and his mouth opening in its ready laugh revealed an absence of two or three upper front teeth which only accentuated . . . the boyishness of his appearance" (393, 3). Anna herself was lovely, with a tiny waist (which was never restrained in a corset), "soft brown eyes, a kindly smile and a throaty little voice that did things to your spine."[2] She was a wonderful dresser and had exquisite taste, as well as a slight Russian accent that gave charm to her precise English.

Within a few days, Jack visited her in her home bringing "something of the far places in which he had been." They sat in front of an open fire and spoke of the socialist meeting where they had met and of the socialist movement. Many such meetings would follow. They spoke of literature and read together Dante, Swinburne, Kipling, Wordsworth, Browning, Conrad, and many others. Jack spoke of his own reading of Darwin, Spencer, and Haeckel, which he called getting his scientific basis: "he was getting himself a university education—in bed, between the hours of eleven and two in the morning" (393, 3). This was the beginning of a deep friendship between them that could easily have matured into romance had she been less coy and he less impulsive.

Jack visited Anna's home regularly; they would go out for long walks on the beach and in the hills; they worked together on the business of the "American Friends of Russian Freedom" of which he was president (393, 21); they read fiction, socialist essays, and poetry together; he wrote to her daily, and she waited for his letters, receiving them with rapture in her heart from the smiling letter carrier on the doorstep (393, 97). Jack confided in her, telling her about his boyhood, his first love for Mabel Applegarth, his belief in a better world and in his writing, showing her his manuscripts—even the rejected ones, "like a beggar exposing his sores"—to encourage her in her own writing career. He wooed her, called her the All-Desired, Protean, or just You—Dear You (393, 97); he gave her flowers and books, "identified her with the poems she recited to him on their walks. . . . He thought his love for her was the measure of all he was" (394, 62). He was infatuated with her, but at the same time he felt that she "would be throwing herself away on him. Even as he thought this, he wondered about himself being able to think it. It came from a habit of doing the hard thing and of refusing to be the dupe of a too easy optimism. He could not take her along into the struggle and the turmoil that would be his, or the narrow life in a suburban cottage. 'Remember always that a man will protect a woman from every other man in the world except himself!' He smiled tenderly" (393, 98).

Then, on a certain Wednesday at the end of March 1900, when the romantic tension between them had reached a peak, on the grounds of the University of California at Berkeley, which she attended, Anna withdrew in coyness, never realizing that it would prompt a much more violent withdrawal on his part:

> [T]hey had climbed the slopes, slippery with pine needles and sun-parched grass, still warm to the touch. The first star shone. The bicycle which had brought him from Piedmont had been left standing against one of the walls of North hall. Roses bloomed in the college gardens. Hedges flamed with pink and red geraniums.
>
> They would remember that day, the clear sky, the breeze stirring the leaves of the red-wood under which they sat, with the book open to the chapter on Kant with which her review in class would deal the following morning—the Categorical

Imperative. They felt the call of youth to youth, the hunger of
the heart for the beautiful and good which each was to the
other.

There was a feeling of crisis between them—of something
nearer, sweeter about to be born.

This was love, he thought.

Then he heard her say that she would go away—when
her studies were done, to Europe, to Russia to share the
revolution beginning there.

On Saturday, three days later, he was married in Church
to another. (393, 63)

The other woman was Bessie Maddern, with whom he was not in
love and to whom he had only referred once in a casual way in his
conversations with Anna.[3]

If ever a gesture was miscalculated, Anna's was. Fearing she
had given her emotions away, she had pulled back in an attempt
to convince him that "the fluttering of her hand as it lay in his, the
color racing in her cheeks, the too great brightness of her smile,
the something unsteady in her voice breaking with eager happiness, had nothing to do with him. Heaven forbid he should think
it concerned him!" (393, 99)—and she was indeed more successful than she ever expected or wanted to be. In that moment "on a
hilltop in California, his hand straying over her loosened hair,
she threw a vista of distance and struggle between them, and
made the lovely moment stagger off and away" (393, 99).

[Her] soul followed the fashion and was wrapt securely from
her own view and his in many impenetrable swathings of
indirection and over-elaborateness [i.e., she flirted, hoping
to egg on, not discourage]. She had taken refuge in a remark
about going to Russia, fearing she had been overbold, fearing
that he might feel she had made some demand upon him.

One says one thing and means another, says the first thing that comes into the mind. She feared he might think that she was wooing him, that she was "invading his personality" (a phrase she had learned from her Anarchist friends). (393, 99)

Thus their first chance of marriage was crushed, notwithstanding the fact, as she acknowledged later, that she might well have accepted him had he asked: "If he had asked her to marry him, sitting there on that knoll, the book on her lap, she might have thrown her young arms around his neck, pressing her head against his shoulder which it hardly reached" (393, 99–100). But his reaction to perceived rejection was violent, and he virtually turned around and married the first woman his eyes fell upon, no matter how he would rationalize it to himself, Anna, his friends, and in *The Kempton-Wace Letters*. Given his reaction to Anna's coy flutter it is hardly surprising that, years later, he should have welcomed with relief and joy Charmian Kittredge's emotional and sexual frankness during their first romantic encounter: "Had you failed by a hair's breadth in anything, had you made but the one coy flutter of the average woman, or displayed the fear or shock of the average woman, we should have struggled, and somewhat sordidly. . . . But you were so frank, so honest, and, not least, so unafraid."[4]

Anna would probably have had no reason to foresee Jack's reaction to her "coy flutter," since flirting was their normal way of interacting, as it often was between adults who found each other attractive at a time when proper young women could not consider any physical intimacy before marriage. It was an enjoyable and slightly risky "game played on top of the table between [usually] evenly matched players, and it [ended] in a draw"[5]—at least, it was expected to. It acknowledged physical attraction and sometimes romantic love while accepting and understanding the necessity of distance; it titillated sensuality and imagination without overstepping the bounds of proper behavior. Thus, Jack's reaction appears to have been a measure not only of his frustrated desire for her but also of his fear of being rejected by a loved one —a fear probably resulting both from the pain of his having felt unloved by his mother and of his having been outspokenly rejected by Chaney, the man he presumed to be his father. After this fiasco, Jack and Anna nevertheless continued flirting with each other[6]—something that Bessie found difficult to deal with, but that Charmian, Jack's second, more playful and worldly wife, had no problem accepting.

Jack's marriage to Bessie proved a failure from the outset, as they were incompatible in almost every way, particularly in the departments of romance and sensuality. Frustrated, hungry for love and affection, Jack turned again to Anna, writing to her in July 1900:

> For all the petty surface turmoil which marked our coming to know each other, really, deep down, there was no confusion at all. Did you notice it? To me, while I said "You do not understand," I none the less felt the happiness of satisfaction —how shall I say?—felt, rather, that there was no inner conflict; that we were attuned somehow; that a real unity underlaid everything. . . . Comrades! Ay, world without end![7]

By the end of August, they had begun writing *The Kempton-Wace Letters*.[8]

The idea of writing the *Letters* came to Jack and Anna on a day when they and Bessie were sailing together on the Bay in his little boat, *The Spray*. They were becalmed and discussing eugenics. "Jack was saying that love was a madness, a fever that passes, a trick. One should marry for qualities and not for love. Before marrying one should make sure one is not in love. Love is the danger signal" (392, 24). There is much bitter irony in Jack's arguing for loveless marriages in the presence of both the woman he loved and the one he had married without love, and who were both well aware of the situation. Moreover, if, as both Jack and Anna suggested, they had worked out the whole plot for the book before they began writing it,[9] they clearly forecasted the failure of London's loveless marriage. It is also incongruous that in *The Kempton-Wace Letters*, Anna, the romantic who had rejected the man she was in love with for essentially bourgeois reasons, should extol the overwhelming power of love, while Jack should keep punishing himself for the love he felt for Anna by glorifying the very kind of marriage in which he was himself already unhappy. Anna may have been right when she fantasized that he had married "stolidly without love" because he was "hopeless of being loved" and that he had proposed to her whom he loved, fully expecting her rejection, because he "wanted to kill all chance of hoping."[10]

On 15 January 1901, Jack and Bessie's first daughter, Joan, was born. Although Jack turned into a doting father, he was nevertheless aware that the child tied him more tightly to a marriage he was unhappy in, as he had written to Anna on 29 December 1900:

> [J]ust when freedom seems opening up to me, I feel the bands tightening and the rivetting of the gyves. I remember now when I was free. When there was no restraint, and I did what the heart willed. . . . But now, one's hands are tied, one may not fight, but only yield and bow the neck. After all, the sailor on the sea and the workers in the shop are not so burdened. To break or be broken, there they stand. But to be broken, while not daring to break, there's the rub.[11]

Jack and Anna worked on *The Kempton-Wace Letters* throughout 1901. However, 1901 was a fairly depressing time for Anna, as suggested by her notebook, which is pervaded with the idea of death, and where she sketched a series of stories entitled "Studies in Suicide."[12] James Boylan partly attributes her sadness to her feelings of guilt at having had to reject an unwanted suitor—perhaps "Cameron King, a lawyer who had attended Stanford with Anna and had been infatuated with her since."[13] It may well also have had something to do with her continuing involvement with Jack, her knowledge of his unhappiness, and the unavoidable question of what might have been had she not implicitly rejected him on that spring day of 1900, just a few months past. Their correspondence and their get-togethers involving the writing of the *Letters* kept them in close contact, and he started courting her again through the mail, confessing his love for her in muted terms:

> Why you have been a delight to me, dear, and a glory. Need I add, a trouble? For the things we love are the things which hurt us as well as the things we hurt. . . . What you have been to me? I am not great enough or brave enough to say. This false thing, which the world would call my conscience, will not permit me.[14]

Late in February 1902, Anna went to the little resort town of San Rafael, and Jack kept thinking of her—"Day by day I look out across the bay to a nook in the Marin shore where I know San Rafael clusters, and I wonder how it fares with you and how you are doing"—and wishing her a new year "empty of heartache, and soul sickness, and the many trials which [had] been [hers] in the past twelve months"—and which had been his, too, he might well have added. *The Kempton-Wace Letters* project was drawing to a close and, as Anna was finding it hard to work in San Rafael, Jack pressed her to come and live in his new house: "What ho! now, for the revision! You must come & live with us during that momentous period. It's glorious here, more like a poppy dream than real living."[15] Anna did eventually accept, and arrived in either late April or early May. How long she stayed in the house is unclear. According to James Boylan, she may have stayed as long as three weeks.[16] In an interview two years later, after the scandal of Jack's divorce was in the newspapers, she described the visit in guarded terms:

> During the first few days of my stay Mrs. London was very cordial and manifested great interest in our work, but, after a stay of five days, I became convinced that, for some reason, Mrs. London had begun to dislike me. She said nothing of any importance to make me feel out of place, but, judging from several little occurrences, I decided it was best for me to leave the London home. I carried out my resolve and left Piedmont, much against Mr. London's will, and, apparently, Mrs. London's also. Both husband and wife accompanied me to the train, and the farewell between Mrs. London and myself was that of two acquaintances between whom existed a mutual liking.[17]

Whether Anna did stay three weeks or whether she made a few shorter stays, the situation must have been fairly tense, even if Jack did not notice it.

It was then, at the beginning of May 1902, that Jack and Anna had another chance at love and marriage, but again she rejected him. Alone in his house with her, Jack declared his love and proposed: "[He] told her that his marriage was *dissolved*, as it would have been if he had never seen her or if she had never been born,"[18] and he asked her to marry him (393, 100). At first, Anna refused, feeling that "it was one thing to be in love with him when he was free like herself" and another when he was married to another woman and had a child, thinking that she could never regain "that lovely feeling she had had that they belonged together." But Jack insisted, urging her to accept his love; and she did—"with a tumult of joy in her heart . . . she promised to marry him." But she could not live with the idea that she was achieving happiness at the expense of Bessie's, and "within two weeks, she took a trip across the Bay back to his house to break [her] promise," telling him that she did not want to begin her life by hurting another and that she did not love him enough to become his wife (393, 100).

Strangely enough, London does not seem to have been convinced by this second rejection—perhaps having learned from his reaction to the first one that rashness did not pay off—and he kept on writing her love letters. In July 1902, on his way to London, crossing the American continent on a train, he wrote to her from all the states, picturing their future together (393, 100).[19] The day before sailing, he wrote to her that he had received her "ink-beteared letter" and that he loved her.[20] Clearly, neither of them seems to have truly believed in the reality of their breakup. However, Anna's discovery of Bessie's second pregnancy brought out her anger, jealousy, and frustrated passion: she wrote to him, trying to appear indifferent, but "in the middle of a page came her words like a torrent of tears, stormy as her heart" (393, 101), accusing him of having lied to her concerning his relations with his wife.

Anna's angry accusations severed the bond that her refusal to marry him almost four months earlier had failed to do. When he received her letter, London was exhausted from an all-night walk on Saturday with the homeless of the East End of London and from spending Sunday with them under the pouring rain "in the fierce struggle for something to eat." Still, he defended himself with some energy:

> I have insulted your love by lying to you. I try to follow your mind processes to see where you develop that lie. . . . I expect a child to be born to me shortly. Work back nine months. Come ahead again to the time at the Bungalow when we held speech upon a very kindred subject. Bearing these two periods in mind, if you have a superficial knowledge of things

sexual and physiological, you will fail to discover any lie. If you have not this knowledge, & I do not think you have, consult some woman who has.

Shall I tell you what I have been guilty of? Not of lying, but of keeping my word . . . I promised that I would not tell you of any expected child. I promised, that is all. I promised, & I kept my word.[21]

London referred to Anna's accusations again in at least two more letters to her, eventually apologizing for not having taken "the knock out clean & not put up any defense." While they remained friends—their friendship rather strained for a while—their romance was over, and London resigned himself to "dream[ing] romances for other people and transmut[ing] them into bread & butter."[22] Anna was terribly upset when she received his letter. She realized the measure of his unhappiness, commenting later that the way he had dug his pen into the paper showed his anger and despair, and that she had feared he might do something terrible.[23] She "would come to realize her cruelty later and be overwhelmed with remorse. . . . She would be able to reconcile his statement that all was over between himself and his wife, and the coming of the child. Time is a relative thing. It had seemed long to him and the separation had seemed absolute" (393, 101). Indeed, despite her and Jack's differing perceptions of time, she could not but have realized that Becky, London's second daughter, born on 20 October 1902, had to have been conceived before May 1902. There was no doubt, though, that Anna was deeply hurt and shocked by the discovery of Bessie's pregnancy. Anna was a thorough romantic who believed that marriage was sacred and that both men and women could only have one true love in their lives. While intellectually and emotionally passionate, she was also sexually naive and believed that one could only be physically intimate with the loved one. Not only was she unable to understand Jack's complaints about his and Bessie's sexual incompatibility, but she was also clearly deeply disturbed by the discovery that Jack had continued having sex with his wife despite his lack of love for her and his unhappiness in the marriage—and that not only a few short months before he proposed to her, but also probably even later. Much later in life, when she had grown-up daughters of her own, she would come to envy the sexual freedom of modern young women.[24]

Anna's motivations for rejecting Jack were probably rather obscure, even to herself. He was indeed from a very different world from hers, and, although she was a dreamer and worshipped romance ("Romance is true—highest truth and highest good"[25]), she was also worldly, her impulses to break away from her social class never amounting to more than vague desires. Her despair when she lost another incipient lover, Robert Wilson, who died by "accidental gas asphyxiation" on 8 February 1905, may help understand her. Upon learning the news of his death on 18 February, Anna discovered that she loved this man whom she had known since she was eight, and who was twelve years her senior, and confided her sorrow and regrets to her diary during the next few days:

> Robert Wilson is dead. . . . I wish I had died before this news came to me. . . .
>
> I refused myself to him. I was blind with worldliness. I chose the more fortunate, the gayer, and they in turn refused me so that we suffered together and in the same way my lover and I. . . . He was all I have tried to be, all I have loved, and I knew it for I loved him—but I placed others so far above him in my world, desired others. . . . I am a materialist.[26]

She would later comment that she had awakened to true love twice in her life, "once when Robert died . . . and again to English [Walling] in St. Petersburg" in February 1906:

What have I to do with love?

I have waited for love to take me up to the high places, to take me down to the depths. I have looked to love with pleading tear-filled eyes. Now love is here and I cry out in anguish, what is it to me? What does it require at my hands?

Henceforth I am no longer alone. I am more afraid of this than a sick child alone in the dark.[27]

This same fear, but greatly magnified, probably prevented her from making a commitment to Jack London—greatly amplified because he was very different from her, both temperamentally and socially. London was neither Jewish nor wealthy; unlike Walling, who was already a millionaire, London was outspokenly materialistic and bent on making money, which shocked Anna despite her own reluctantly acknowledged materialism. While Anna and English's brand of socialism was an idealized mental construct based on no personal experience of want, London's was more bitter and skeptical, grounded in a young lifetime of struggle in the lower classes and the underworld. Both Anna and London were dreamers, but London wanted to turn dreams into facts through hard work and perseverance, and Anna was more indecisive and dilatory. Thus the idea of marrying a Jack London who was both charismatic and relentlessly determined to succeed, socially inferior but intellectually more mature, must have appeared a frightening challenge to Anna.

Anna, too, wanted to be a writer, but she had neither the urgent need nor the self-discipline required. As she would note in 1934, while looking over her notes for stories and novels in her 1901 diary, "It is with me as it has always been. Nothing finished, only begun, only hopes, that is."[28] Indeed, Anna's fictional output remained tiny compared to Jack's, including mostly her share of *The Kempton-Wace Letters* and *Violette of Père Lachaise*—a short, fictionalized subjective autobiography. In February 1935, while she and English were separated because of his affair with another woman, but still on friendly terms, she took stock of her life:

> [It] is not a question of forgiving English at all. I love him, always have loved him. I am only sorry he has had to suffer through me. I love him and I have devoted my life to him, since 1906. Only I would have done better if I had written, been effective, dynamically effective, in the world of literature and social progress. I would have spared him the feeling of disillusionment in the woman he chose to be his companion, his wife, Comrade, and the Mother of his adored children.[29]

Indeed, English had expected that she would accomplish more, and Anna herself believed that she had proved a victim of her own idealism, "plagued by standards so high as to find herself unable to attach herself to any movement, to undertake for long any task."

> It was so easy not to work, to contemplate, dream, plan, and not to move towards one's goal. It was so difficult to keep the brain and the nerves tense. Ideas hovered above her head, and did not quite descend within her reach. Something irked and tormented her,—indecision, vagueness, fear, even, seemed to be her lot, the beautiful days coming and going and not fulfilling themselves.[30]

She was also neither selfish nor strong enough to withstand what she perceived as the demands of her family. Although she had nurses and maids to look after the children, she spent much time taking care of them instead of writing, and could never resist "the little ones banging on the door." Although she led a full life, she would acknowledge later that she had lost what might have been her writer's career under a "niggle" of little things.[31]

This feeling of personal failure is often sounded in Anna's

later notes, bringing out the ironies and ambiguities of her life. Rereading a letter she had written to Jack London from St. Petersburg on 24 March 1906, where she extolled the Russian Revolution as the "incarnate beginning of a wonderful end," and where she vowed never to "have a home, never to belong to a clique, never to prevent life from playing upon [her and English], never to shield each other," she added at the end of the letter a note dated 10 August 1953: "We had a house in Greenwich, Conn. for thirty-two years, simultaneously with one in [unreadable]. We had nothing but homes, it seems. Jack London had believed that I would never be a mother, that my children would be books—I had five children, only two small published books!"[32]

Luckily, Anna was away when the news of Jack and Bessie's divorce broke in early August 1903. She had left in early July for Europe with $500 advance royalties on *The Kempton-Wace Letters* and did not return to New York and San Francisco until early November. She heard of the separation in Europe and wrote to Jack in mid- to late September:

> I am sorry for all the unhappiness, and I am strong in my faith. You never meant to do anything but the right and the good—poor, ever dear, dreamer! You will never do wrong. I cried over the news, half in gratitude for your strength and half in sorrow, perhaps all in sorrow, for all the sadness with which you are weighted.[33]

It is probable that her friend Cameron King had sent her a fairly neutral newspaper clipping and that she remained unaware that Bessie and the newspapers were blaming her for the breakup until her return to San Francisco. Since she knew nothing at that time about the affair between Jack and Charmian, she certainly must have wondered ruefully at the usefulness of her own self-sacrifice in order not to hurt Bess—and even more so when she found out about Bessie's accusing her in the divorce petition of having alienated Jack's affections. In any case, she described her return to San Francisco as sad—her mother was sick and her sister-in-law had died recently—and commented that "she had missed [happiness] so often!"[34]

When Jack decided to put distance between himself and his problems and go to Japan to cover the Russo-Japanese War, Anna also started negotiating with San Francisco newspapers to be sent to the East as a war correspondent and was planning on leaving on the same steamer, the SS *Siberia*, that was to carry Jack over on 7 January 1904. This may well have been an attempt to live on Jack's terms, develop her abilities as he had urged her to, and perhaps rekindle their relationship. But it seems that she asked for too much money, and that the *Bulletin* would not pay it. When she heard, a few months later, that Jack had ruptured a tendon in a leap on the *Siberia*, she mused in her notebook, "Sometime in life I will find him again and he me, sometime when we are both old, in the barren years when there will be nothing to gain! How ashamed we will be before each other at our shameful renunciation! Will we stop and make apologies?"[35]

Although Anna remained loyal to Jack and felt sorry for him, she found it hard to bear her notoriety as a home-wrecker resulting from Bessie's accusations. According to James Boylan, she came to believe later, and probably accurately, that she had been "a pawn in a plan initially designed by Bessie's lawyer to make a divorce impossible. The papers accusing Anna were to be held in a 'sealed' file, and when Jack returned from the Far East, he was to be told that he could have a divorce—but only at the cost of injuring Anna. But the story became public almost at once and that part of the plan, if such it was, fell apart."[36] At that time, Anna knew nothing about Charmian, although Bessie did, who had heard about Charmian on the day of Jack's departure for Japan. This would suggest that Bessie used in her complaint the woman she felt London might be most loyal to rather than the one she believed he was only having an affair with. The scandal reduced Anna's mother to a state of nervous prostration, and Anna was battered by the press for more than a month, until Bessie amended her complaint from adultery to desertion—upon which basis the divorce was granted three months later. Despite the pity she felt for Bessie, Anna deeply resented being named in the divorce petition.

When she heard that Jack's divorce had been granted, Anna confided to her closest friend:

> There hasn't been much more unpleasantness for me though what there was was hard enough to bear. It was a plain case of blackmail. . . . I am very glad he has his freedom at last. He has suffered bitterly. Further, I do not know.
>
> . . . I think we do not love each other but I may be slandering a supreme feeling in thinking so. I am too breathless from the race for happiness and do not know. After all, I have not raced very hard.
>
> I have the semitic temperament that gives up over readily and I have ever had a genius for giving up. I must be fought for gallantly to be won and I think Jack would rather wait than fight. He, too, is tired.[37]

Clearly, Anna knew nothing yet of Charmian, as Jack, determined to protect Charmian's reputation, had kept her (as well as almost everyone else) in the dark. But, upon hearing of Jack's impending marriage in the spring or summer of 1905, Anna apparently sent Charmian a bunch of lily of the valley[38]—a very graceful thing for her to do, given her own fondness for Jack, which she had clearly expressed a few short months earlier when she wrote for him a birthday poem that was still, in many ways, a love letter:

> The way was long and you were at its ending,
>   Night fell and still it stretched before me
> The Sea leaped up and mocked me for my feebleness
>   It was a bitter war and hard, my love!

Oh baffled heart when turnings grew too sinuous,
  Oh wild despair when stony trail misled!
My soul grew sick and shrieked to all the hills around
  That I must live and reach you, O my love!

Oh dearest love, this gray gulch swayed and beckoned me
  The trackless forest lured me to its rest.
The swollen river pledged me dreadful promises
  To lay me like a gift before my love!

Then the road died and fast I reached the trysting-place
  You were not there, O much besought and dear
I turned my face and took the bitter length again
  And groped my way, forgotten by my love.[39]

Anna and Charmian became good friends—a close friendship that continued and, in fact, became closer after Jack's death.
They corresponded regularly and, when Charmian was in New
York, she would visit Anna for one or two weeks, and occasionally
longer, and they would talk much about Jack. Charmian also became close to Blanche Partington, who had been in competition
with her for Jack's love after his separation from Bessie. While it
took her longer to be reconciled, Blanche also conceded defeat
graciously to Charmian (she had fought harder and not always
fairly), and brought her a bunch of roses. Charmian forgave her
rival, writing her that, loving Jack as she did, she could not dislike
a woman for having loved him too.[40]

Jack's and Anna's lives separated after his marriage to Charmian and hers to English Walling, but they did not forget each
other and remained in contact. Anna would get upset if she did
not hear from Jack for any length of time, and she still carried his
picture in her wallet.[41] Either alone or with Charmian, Jack visited her whenever he was in New York. When they saw each other
again after seven years, in February 1912, "it was as if he had

never been away. [They] stood laughing in low, hushed voices, in joy at meeting again." They talked the night away. Charmian and Jack stayed overnight, and, the next day, they lingered over a long lunch while they talked of the *Snark*. Nearly two years later, in January 1914, Jack and Anna saw each other again while he was in New York alone. Anna visited him in his "garish Broadway hotel around forty-ninth Street" with her two daughters (the oldest four years old and the youngest nearly two years old). "As [she] stood there beside him, looking out his sixteenth floor window into a court, watching the soft large flakes of snow turn to rain, [she] thought how like he was to his hero, Everhard, in *The Iron Heel*, beating with tireless wings the void, soaring toward what was ever his sun, the flaming ideal of human freedom!" She saw him several times during that particular trip of his, and she recalled vividly their last meeting:

> One afternoon in early February we walked up Fifth Avenue in clear, Spring-like weather. People turned around to look at him. They knew him for a stranger, one hailing far from these pavements, these houses spiring towards the sky. We dined at Jack's, because of the name, he said, with hardly anyone there but the waiters at that early hour. Then a ride of a few minutes to Grand Central Station. He had something the matter with his foot and I would not let him get out. We kissed each other good-bye. A Red-Cap held out his hand for my little manuscript case. I shook my head to the porter, and turned around to smile at him. But I saw he looked disappointed. I should have accepted the porter even if I did not need him. That was our last glance at each other. We never saw each other again. (393, 122)

She felt that Jack had sensed the disappointment of the porter at losing a tip and would also have preferred to see her go off free-handed.

Anna found these last meetings with Jack very stimulating, his mind agile, his nature generous and practical as ever. She appreciated him as much as, if not more than, she had in the past, and she was happy that he now insisted "that nothing in the world matter[ed] but love, therefore a woman (and a man, too) ought not to care about anything but love. (Dane Kempton gone mad!)"[42] It is therefore not surprising that she should have wondered after his death why they had spent so much time and energy arguing about love in their youth:

> Those differences—what were they but the healthy expression of our immaturity, of our aspirations toward the absolute of truth and right and justice. . . . The differences tortured us as they did precisely because in the great essentials we were at one—but this, youth could not know. . . . Was he not an ardent feminist and suffragist? Why, then, did I suspect him of thinking women the inferiors of men? Did he not finally marry with love and for love, and exemplify in his own life the need of love that men and women have in common. . . . Why, then, did we spend twenty-two months writing *The Kempton-Wace Letters*, trying to convert each other to positions which, at bottom, we must both have held?[43]

It is, of course, tempting to speculate on whether Anna and Jack would have had a successful marriage had she not turned him down. It would undoubtedly have been very different from either of his actual marriages. The weakest point in this imaginary marriage might have been sexual intimacy and perhaps unfaithfulness on Jack's part, as was the case in his marriage to Bessie and something Anna also had to put up with in her marriage to English. But Anna's kindness and generosity, her forgiving and nonjudgmental nature, would never have turned their marriage into a tug of war as was the case in Jack and Bessie's. Moreover, Jack loved Anna and admired her for her beauty, quick intelligence, and brilliant personality as he never did Bessie. He would have delighted in her elegance and good taste, and he certainly would never have been bored with her. However, Anna was quietly stubborn, and she might not have been willing to yield as easily and as opportunely as Charmian did. She probably would have stood up to him and "stuck to her guns" (a favorite phrase of hers, and an odd one for an uncompromising pacifist) in arguments, as she did with English[44]—which might well have resulted in interesting fights and deadlocks. Indeed, as Charmian once put it, "the main thing is not to get on [Jack's] track, for fear of collisions that block traffic."[45] Anna may not have been Jack's ideal woman and he may not have been her ideal man, but there is little doubt that they were both very much in love with each other at one time, and that this love never died entirely and became the basis for a deep and enduring friendship.

NOTES

1. For details of Anna's version of the relationship, see in particular Anna (Strunsky) Walling Manuscripts, Yale University Library, especially box 32, folder 392, entitled "Jack London" (95 pp.); box 32, folder 393, "Jack London" (116 pp.); and box 33, folder 401 (10 pp.). The manuscripts will be identified in the text by folder and page numbers. Some of the information in this essay was published previously in Jacqueline Tavernier-Courbin, "To Love or Not to Love: Jack London's and Anna Strunsky's *The Kempton-Wace Letters*," *SYMBIOSIS: A Journal of Anglo-American Literary Relationships* 1, no. 2 (1997): 255–74.

2. Joseph Noel, *Footloose in Arcadia* (New York: Carrick & Evans, Inc., 1940), 147.

3. Anna somewhat speeds up the chronology here, but not by much, as the proposal to Bessie Maddern and the wedding all took place within a week—on Sunday morning, Jack had no idea of even proposing; he proposed on Sunday evening; they were married the next Saturday. See Jack London to Ninetta Eames, 3 April 1900, *The Letters of Jack London*, ed. Earle Labor, Robert C. Leitz III, and I. Milo Shepard (Stanford, Calif.: Stanford University Press, 1988), 178.

4. Jack London to Charmian Kittredge, 18 June 1903, *Letters*, 367.

5. Dorothy Dix, *The Daily Picayune*, 13 August 1899.

6. Interview with Anna Walling Hamburger, daughter of Anna Strunsky Walling, New York City, 1997. I am very grateful to Mrs. Walling Hamburger for being willing to share with me her memories of her mother.

7. Jack London to Anna Strunsky, 31 July 1900, *Letters*, 198.

8. The first reference to the project appears in a letter from Jack to Anna dated 30 August 1900. She seems to be ahead of him at that point, and he wants them to get together to discuss and map out thoroughly the collection of letters to be written.

9. See Jack London to Anna Strunsky, 30 August and 15 September 1900, *Letters*, 202, 206.

10. On 27 February 1901, Anna wrote the following outline for a "dream story," twisting around the elements and the ending of Jack's proposal: "Accepted a man [?] meaning to marry him. He was hopeless of being loved and was about to marry, stolidly without love. He a poet. Before doing so proposed to his Adored —just to feel sure that the path he takes is the right one; wanted to kill all chance of hoping. She saw what he would do and lied. Said he loved, for the good of his soul."

11. Jack London to Anna Strunsky, 26 December 1900, *Letters*, 229.

12. Anna Strunsky Manuscripts, "Book of ideas," Diary #1, Yale University Library, box 23, folder 300.

13. See James Boylan, *Revolutionary Lives: Anna Strunsky and William English Walling* (Amherst: University of Massachusetts Press, 1998), 21.

14. Jack London to Anna Strunsky, 26 December 1900, *Letters*, 229.

15. Jack London to Anna Strunsky, 22 and 29 March 1902, *Letters*, 285–86.

16. Boylan, 23.

17. Interview given by Anna Strunsky two years later, quoted in Boylan, 24.

18. Emphasis added; by "dissolved," London did not mean "divorced." He merely meant that, as far as he was concerned, the marriage was over and that he wanted out. Moreover, the implication is that neither Anna nor his love for her was responsible for the failure.

19. Anna Strunsky may be a little confused here, for she writes on the same page of the manuscript that he left for England two weeks after she rejected him. However, his train was crossing the Nevada desert on 18 July 1902—that is, about a month and a half afterwards. London's letters to Anna offer little clarification.

20. Jack London to Anna Strunsky, 29 July 1902, *Letters*, 303.

21. Jack London to Anna Strunsky, 25 August 1902, *Letters*, 307.

22. Jack London to Anna Strunsky, 28 September 1902, *Letters*, 313.

23. Interview with Anna Walling Hamburger. Mrs. Hamburger believes that, by "something terrible," her mother meant suicide.

24. Interview with Anna Walling Hamburger.

25. Anna Strunsky's Diary #1, 19 February 1901, Yale University Library, box 23, folder 300, 1.

26. Anna Strunsky's Diary #3 (beginning 21 January 1905), Yale University Library, box 23, folder 301. Robert Wilson was the inspiration for the character of "the Friend" in *Violette of Père Lachaise* (New York: Frederick R. Stokes, Co., 1915).

27. Anna Strunsky's Diary #3.

28. See Anna Strunsky's Diary #1, Wednesday, 28 March 1901, 87.

29. Anna Strunsky Walling Collection, incomplete diary entry for April 1935, the Huntington Library, San Marino, Calif., box 5.

30. *Violette of Père Lachaise*, 57, 95.

31. Interview with Anna Walling Hamburger.

32. Anna Strunsky Walling Collection, the Huntington Library, box 5.

33. Anna Strunsky to Jack London, quoted in Jack London to Charmian Kittredge, 29 September 1903, after he had just received her letter, *Letters*, 392.

34. Anna Strunsky to Katherine Maryson, 5 November 1903, Yale University Library, microfilm reel #8, folder 112.

35. Anna Strunsky's notebook, 29 February 1904, quoted in *Revolutionary Lives*, 37.

36. Boylan, 40–41.

37. Anna Strunsky to Katherine Maryson, 2 September 1904, Yale University Library, microfilm reel #8, folder 112.

38. See Clarice Stasz, *American Dreamers: Charmian and Jack London* (New York: St. Martin's Press, 1988), 128.

39. "The Road." Several versions, dated from 1905 to 1915, are at Yale University Library, box 32, folder 385. See Boylan, chapter 7, note 12.

40. Stasz, 127.

41. Interview with Anna Walling Hamburger.

42. Anna Strunsky to English Walling, 30 January 1914, quoted in Boylan, 202.

43. Anna Strunsky Walling to Charmian Kittredge London, 17 January 1919, quoted in Charmian Kittredge London, *The Book of Jack London*, vol. 1 (London: Mills & Boon, Limited, 1921), 323–24.

44. Interview with Anna Walling Hamburger.

45. Charmian London to Ninetta Eames, 19 November 1908, the Huntington Library, file JL 10643.

GARY RIEDL *and*
THOMAS R. TIETZE

Fathers and Sons
in Jack London's
"The House of Pride"

AS EARLY AS 1816, American Protestant missionaries, most of them descended from the emigré Calvinists of the Eastern seaboard, had taken an interest in securing the salvation of the heathen Pacific islanders. Two Hawaiian natives, Opukahaia and Hopu, had attached themselves, like Melville's Queequeg, to service in various American merchant ships, eventually arriving in Boston. Such was their personal beauty, coupled with their deplorable lack of moral inhibition, that these two youths awakened in their Protestant companions a conviction that God had sent them to America purposefully. Their hearts melting in sympathy for the plight of all those other, yet unknown damned heathens, church leaders recognized their responsibility and began almost at once to take decisive steps to set things right. Between 1816 and 1820, their stern inspiration moved them to organize the American Board of Commissioners for Foreign Missions, which set up a school in Cornwall, Connecticut, "for the sons of various heathen tribes, where they were taught the rudiments of an academical education and the doctrines and duties of the Christian religion, to which their superstition readily gave place."[1]

It was obvious, however, that little could be achieved while staying at home, so the board sent forth a call not only to clergymen, but also to those of the laity with useful and practical skills that could be helpful to the establishment and maintenance of a religious community on the other side of the world. Their mission was urgent—nothing less than an effort to wrest the ignorant and benighted natives' souls from the equally dangerous attractions of primitive superstition and Roman Catholicism, both of which were seen as evidence of the devil's efforts to ensnare the uneducated and unwary. In 1820, the American vessel *Thaddeus*, packed with couples recruited by the board—many of them comparative strangers whose marriages had been hastily arranged by the board—set out for Hawaii.

The missionaries understandably interpreted as a sign of providential interest in their project the fact that they arrived in Hawaii virtually upon the death of Kamehameha I, the first monarch to unify all the islands under a single, autocratic, and ruthless regime. The king's son and heir had decided only days before the *Thaddeus*'s appearance to abandon the old heathen ways, going so far as to end the time-honored practice of human sacrifice and to order the lifting of terrifying taboos as well as the destruction of all (now false) idols. This religious vacuum was indeed one of the reasons the islanders allowed the missionaries to land in the first place.

The missionaries set about the selfless but quixotic enterprise of converting the islanders' cultural traditions to American middle-class religious and social values. Almost from the moment the first missionaries to the islands disembarked, they noted with hor-

ror the innocent nudity and wanton sexual practices of the natives. Hawaii had been for decades one of the most popular sites
for crews of whalers and merchant vessels to visit for what their
officers termed "refreshment," and the islanders were startled to
find white men whose views were decidedly narrower than those
of their earlier visitors. The missionaries set about instilling a
more restrained attitude toward sex, citing procreation as the
only fit reason for sexual relations.

The early missionaries also attempted to instill a work ethic as
a way to inoculate against moral backsliding. After so many years
of producing food that went largely to the caches of their mon-
archs, the Hawaiians appreciated the more relaxed lifestyle that
loomed before them. Despite the missionaries' best efforts to depict the values of backbreaking labor in the best possible light, the
natives remained skeptical. It was soon manifest that the islanders did not share the New Englanders' zeal for the rigorous life of
the farmer, and the natives, even after the Great Mahele of 1846
allowed them to own property, found themselves uninterested in
working so hard for so abstract a notion as cash. The missionaries, unlike their Vatican-backed Catholic counterparts who
arrived seven years after the Protestants, had only themselves to
rely on for financial support of the Hawaiian enterprise. Consequently, they "began . . . by having the natives bring in tradable
commodities (palm oil, arrowroot, etc.) as contributions to the
church in lieu of nonexistent coin. This institutional trade to
make the missions self-sufficient was considered laudable."[2] At
first, the attitude was that missions could engage in this type of
trade, but individuals could not. However, this view was not
binding, and many missionaries concluded that "trade by a godly
man was a godly trade, and they laid up considerable treasures on
this earth as a consequence."[3] On their part, the Hawaiians often
decided that, since the white men seemed to want their land more
urgently than they did themselves, they would sell the properties

it had taken them so many generations to acquire. And the most available market for land happened coincidentally to be the missionaries and their families. Some whites, realizing that the natives were making a mistake, bought up all the land they could, apparently sincere in the paternalistic hope that they could preserve the land until the Hawaiians became sophisticated enough to know they were being cheated. Needless to say, the land was never given back. The investment made during the two generations to follow resulted in staggering financial power; its consequent political influence certainly helped to make the descendants of the original missionaries very important. All this was familiar to Jack London and provides necessary background for understanding his 1907 Hawaiian short story, "The House of Pride."

Perhaps atypically for a story composed by the man often accused of barbaric attentiveness to violent and brutishly detailed action, during the entire narrative of "The House of Pride," the main character Percival Ford doesn't stir from a chair. He has located himself between a lanai and a Honolulu beach, from which he commands a view of a social gathering being put on by the officers and men of the United States Army.[4] Percival is a thirty-five-year-old heir to a fortune left to him by his father, Isaac Ford, a former missionary to Hawaii as well as one of those "godly traders" and land-acquirers discussed above.[5]

Because of his religiously puritanical upbringing, Percival is repulsed by what he perceives as raw sexuality in the dancing motions and revealing gowns of the officers' wives, and he turns to a conversation with local physician Dr. Kennedy. In the course of their conversation, Kennedy defends a young Hawaiian man, Joe Garland, whose energy, vivacity, and virility have deeply and consistently offended the humorless and earnest Percival over the years. To his shocked amazement, Percival learns two important bits of information: one, Joe is actually Percival's half-brother by a native woman; and two, everybody on the island has always known it. The story ends when Percival gets Joe to agree to leave the island and to promise never to return.

Despite this rather bloodless summary, much of interest happens in this carefully crafted but apparently uneventful tale. Lawrence Berkove has recently drawn attention to the psychological dynamics of this story of two brothers who could only be wholly fulfilled through unification of their opposite natures;[6] in these terms, Joe functions as a Jungian "shadow" to Percival—a shadow that demonstrates the unlived potential of a person's life. For us, this story plays intriguingly with questions about how a character either succeeds or fails in integrating his personality. According to the thinking of certain poststructuralist psychoanalysts, especially those influenced by Jacques Lacan (1901–1981), such integration is achieved through a series of stages that allow an individual to effect a synthesis between the way he sees himself subjectively and the way society and its forces try to determine the person he is to become.[7]

The narrator takes us into the mind and emotional worldview of Percival Ford, with mock sympathy explicating the character's values right from the start. As he looks at the officers dancing with their wives, Percival is repulsed by the women's "bare shoulders and naked arms"[8] and their "challenging femaleness," though he also deplores the army men for their "essential grossness of flesh" as well as their lighthearted orality, causing them to be forever "drinking and smoking and swearing their way through life" (1345). With unusual insight, Percival identifies the source of his uncomfortable association with them: "He felt, always, that they were laughing at him up their sleeves, or pitying him, or tolerating him. Then, too, they seemed, by mere contiguity, to emphasize a lack in him, to call attention to that in them which he did not possess" (1345–46).

In other words, Percival has been presented with the specter of the Other, and he wishes the Other would go away. It is at this precise moment that he can make the decisive choice in determining his relationship to the world of sensory and sensual realities. He can choose to change, to take charge of his life, to find out what he has been missing while denying himself the pleasures and challenges of human society, and, finally, to test the authenticity of his dry reluctance to live heartily in Paradise. But, instead of grasping the opportunity, he immediately undermines the possible self-liberating implications of his insight when he adds that "he thanked God that he did not possess" such grossly human characteristics. As for the men, Percival can only direct his profoundest scorn toward them: "Faugh! They were like their women!" (1346). His nausea reflects not only the inability to distinguish between men and women, but also his disgust with the earthy options he has determined to deny himself.

The narrator pulls back from his ironically friendly omniscience to characterize the physiological characteristics that play a decisively naturalistic role in shaping Percival's attitudes: "He lacked vitality. His was a negative organism. No blood with a ferment in it could have nourished and shaped that long and narrow face, those thin lips, lean cheeks, and the small, sharp eyes. The thatch of hair, dust-colored, straight and sparse, advertised the niggard soil, as did the nose, thin, delicately modeled" (1346). The passage recalls the theories of the then-influential alienist and criminologist Cesare Lombroso (1836–1909), who famously developed the theory of the so-called "criminal type," linking physiological features of the individual with resultant and predictable patterns of behavior. Lombroso's work, though controversial, was regarded widely as good, cutting-edge science at the turn of the century. Also, his work fit in with the naturalist aesthetic nicely, since it seemed to show that factors outside the individual's willing choice helped to determine personal development. As a result of his apparently physically determined fer-

vorlessness and his grimly religious upbringing, Percival rejects
the possibility of any future association with dangerous femininity. Marriage for Percival exists only as a "remote contingency."
Having no personal experience of love, "he looked upon it, not as
mythical, but as bestial" (1346).

This alienation from ordinary human life is exacerbated by
Percival's sense of racial superiority, which reminds him that, after all, "anybody could marry"—even coolies (1346). He defines
his difference from others by a self-constructed personal mythology that seems almost a parody of the Virgin Birth as well as an
unwitting denial of the primal crisis that occurs when a son first
considers his father's sexuality:

> He had come of no petty love-match. He had come of
> lofty conception of duty [London's use of ambiguity is richly
> evidenced in this clever phrase] and of devotion to a cause.
> His father had not married for love. Love was a madness that
> had never perturbed Isaac Ford. When he answered the call
> to go to the heathen with the message of life, he had had no
> thought and no desire for marriage. . . . The Board com-
> manded Isaac Ford to marry. Furthermore, it furnished him
> with a wife, another zealous soul with no thought of mar-
> riage, intent only on doing the Lord's work among the hea-
> then. They saw each other for the first time in Boston. The
> Board brought them together, arranged everything, and by
> the end of the week they were married and started on the
> long voyage around the Horn. Percival Ford was proud that
> he had come of such a union. (1346–47)

Postmodern psychoanalytic critics might find that Percival's
case lends itself to explication. Born outside ordinary human
love, and growing up with no inclination toward or anticipation
of it, Percival, in his efforts to identify himself as an individual,
has focused on his relationship with his father—or rather his re-

lationship with the idealized image of his father. This construct Lacan calls "the Name-of-the-Father." Distinct from the actual father's true personality, and also distinct from any remembered image of the father, this artificial reconstruction of the absent father consists of a list of characteristics assembled unconsciously by the son. This happens at least in part so that the son can emerge victorious from the classic psychological battle with the father that constitutes the main business of every boy's childhood. Thus, Percival's Father-idea has been built up in his infancy to represent the repressive power of the Father, including perhaps purely imaginary restrictions and fantasized laws, consistent with the needs of at least one portion of the superego. Percival's curious passivity can also be understood in an Oedipal light, for, as Robert Con Davis says, "Passivity is a particularly important conception. That is, the castration threat, the central event of the Oedipal crisis, must be resolved in an acceptance of passivity in regard to the father's authority for the crisis to be ended."[9]

Somehow, in the inculcation of anti-sexual, puritanical values, Isaac has managed, in psychoanalytic terms, to castrate his son. In this light, Percival's pride in his father may be seen as a reaction formation—the unconscious construction of a persona that reflects exactly the opposite of a subject's repressed feelings. Thus, it is typical for Percival to virtually worship his father, even though (the Name-of-the-Father) Isaac has effectively ruined his life. As the narrator tells us, Percival's feelings for his father are "a passion with him." Still more significant are the first adjectives Percival uses to describe Isaac: "erect" and "austere" (1347). Even in death, the Father maintains his potency.

The iconographical status of the Father's image is curiously privileged: we are given no details about Percival's bachelor bedroom, except that it is decorated with a portrait of Isaac Ford in his role as prime minister to the island monarch, a portrait that probably shows him decked out in the full regalia of that office. Missionaries in the islands not infrequently mixed their spiritual and political influences.[10]

Isaac is thus both idealized and fictionalized as Father in three dimensions of ever-increasing authority: First, he is the biological parent, though Percival imagines his role in the conception to be dutifully remote and without emotion. Second, he is the authorized vicegerent of a fatherly island monarch, and his portrait almost certainly shows him adorned with the sorts of plumes, medals, braids, and epaulets (characteristic of such uniforms in those days) that function as signs and symbols of authority. Third, in his function as missionary, he is the representative of, or visible substitute for, the ultimate Absent-Father-figure, God Himself. These multiple conduits for the release and expression of Isaac's power serve to intensify and magnify, in Percival's mind, that potency already associated with the Father in the unconscious of any son.

The power of this paternal fictional construct is so central to the son's image of himself that any alteration or modification of the Father-idea must be denied or disallowed; it is from this specific, subjective concept of the law-giving authority of the Name-of-the-Father that Percival derives his own power. Ironically, the very thing that has filled him with protestant disgust for sex, that has determined him to define himself by his erotic dysfunction, is the emasculating Father stereotyped in psychoanalytic mythology, the same father who has provided his son with all the financial security that ensures his identification as "one of the big men of the islands" (1345).

More important to his self-imposed alienation, however, is the sense of moral self-righteousness that makes him feel distinct from and superior to the objectified population of Hawaii. This righteous superiority also makes more congenial and comfortable the imaginative (fictional) constructs of religious, moral, and political ideas that Percival associates with his father's memory. It may be argued that the process of compromising the subjective sense of self, in order to accommodate the expectations of family or society, constitutes the ordinary person's maturation. This compromise—perhaps synthesis is less pejorative—Percival is unable to accomplish. He remains selfishly infantile throughout the story, not even demonstrating the ability to stand or walk, and (with an infant's sense of the fitness of things) commanding others to come to him.

On the other hand, Joe is emblematic of the "smoke of life,".as Kennedy explains. "You are pure New England stock," Kennedy tells Percival. "Joe Garland is half Kanaka. Your blood is thin. His is warm. Life is one thing to you, another thing to him. He laughs and sings and dances through life, genial, unselfish, child-like, everybody's friend. You go through life like a perambulating prayer-wheel, a friend of nobody but the righteous, and the righteous are those who agree with you as to what is right. . . . You live like an anchorite. Joe Garland lives like a good fellow" (1350). Joe is the open-air, vibrant, active, musical, cheerful pagan who lives without the restrictions Percival thinks are inextricably bound up with the living of a moral life.

But he is also a kind of double for the Father in two important ways. First, Joe is, as Kennedy outlines the notion, the passionate and human aspects of Isaac Ford, while Percival embodies the bloodless righteousness of the missionary Isaac also was. Second, Joe also doubles as a symbolic Father by presiding at Percival's re-birth when Joe saves his brother in the swimming pool. At school, as part of an initiation ritual, several boys forcibly tried to dunk a terrified Percival three times in the swimming pool. Joe, even in boyhood aware of his relationship to Percival, dived into the pool to rescue him before the boys could push him under for the second time (1349–50). A perverse deconstruction of baptism, the ritual would have resulted in Percival's becoming a member of the larger school community; but by Joe's act of intervention, Percival is ironically stunted socially as well as spiritually. Thus Joe stands in as another person (again, like the Father) who, in the process of doing the "right" thing, the thing demanded of him by his sense of duty, causes long-term bad effects. Had Percival gone through the full initiation ritual, he might very well have become humanized through ordinary social fellowship instead of spending his life in alienated withdrawal. Still, Joe's act was a generous one, even a self-sacrificing one, since the other boys had nearly drowned Joe in their anger at his intervention. This selfless act of courage, however, is not reflected in Percival's subsequent treatment of Joe. As the whiskey-scented voice of true moral consciousness, Kennedy accusingly recalls an incident when Percival failed to return Joe's generous boyhood act: "When Joe got into that smuggling scrape . . . and he sent word to you, asked you to pay his fine, you left him to do his six months hard labor on the reef. Don't forget, you left Joe Garland in the lurch that time" (1349). Bitterly conscious of the fun-loving and, to Percival's thinking, sinful lifestyle Joe enjoys, Percival takes Joe's behavior as a purposeful attempt to thwart the missionary effort on the islands. To Percival, Joe's life not only undermines by example his own effort to reshape the world into his image, but also mocks the accomplishments of Isaac Ford himself; it seems that Joe is erasing everything Percival tries to write.

Joe's physical characteristics also make it possible for Percival to have a highly significant psychological experience shortly after Percival learns that Joe is his brother. Kennedy tells him, in order to prove the truth of the relationship, that Percival can prove it to himself: "Turn around and look at him. You've got him in profile. Look at his nose. That's Isaac Ford's. Yours is a thin edition of it. That's right. Look. The lines are fuller, but they are all there" (1352). In the passage that follows, London manages to create a scene that dramatically reflects the key moment in infancy in which the baby perceives its reflection in a mirror—an experience, Lacan argues, that marks the beginning of the quest for self-identification:[11]

> Percival Ford looked at the Kanaka half-breed who played under the hau tree, and it seemed, as by some illumination, that he was gazing on a wraith of himself. Feature after feature flashed up an unmistakable resemblance. Or, rather, it was he who was the wraith of that other full-muscled and generously molded man. And his features, and that other man's features, were all reminiscent of Isaac Ford. (1352)

Like the infant's first glimpse of the reflected image of the self, this reenactment is a shocking realization of his new identity and his new relation to a real nonsubjective world, a moment of awareness that one's subjective understanding and perceptions have borne little resemblance to reality. Joe has become a psychoanalytic "signifier" whose presence at once signifies himself, his brother, and their father. "Lacan," writes critic Ellie Ragland-Sullivan, "defined an *ecrit* as that which stands for the materiality of the Signifier, itself a demand to interpret the human push to interpret."[12] Joe is himself a text composed in sin by an errant Father, and Percival is his reader and interpreter.

Note, too, that it is not the "real" Isaac whom Percival, now on the brink of a life-altering new awareness of his own identity, calls up in his memory to double-check against his immediate perceptions. Instead, it is a remembered montage of images of the Father, the posed or constructed, artistically rendered or photographical image of Isaac:

> Every line of Isaac Ford's face he knew. Miniatures, portraits, and photographs of his father were passing in review through his mind, and here and there, over and again, in the face before him, he caught resemblances and vague hints of like-

ness. . . . Once, the man turned, and for one flashing instant
it seemed to Percival Ford that he saw his father, dead and
gone, peering at him out of the face of Joe Garland. (1352)

Dr. Kennedy departs, and Percival, shocked and appalled by
this discovery of indisputable evidence of his father's sex life, is
left in prayerful solitude. In this mood, he is disturbed by the
sounds of the nearby party, the singing and the dancing, particularly the sensuous tones of a woman engaged in playing some
flirtatious game with some unseen man. "Arose the laugh of a
woman that was a love-cry." He notices with disgust and horror
that his "train of thought was aroused," and he blushes at the possibility of his own vulnerability to the allurement of sexuality. At
this point, "the house of pride that Percival Ford had builded"
falls in ruins.[13] Failing even to consider this as an opportunity
to try to change the shallow person he has become, Percival, at
an emotional and psychological nadir, begins instead to use "a
cunning and subtle logic" (1355) to reconstruct the image of the
Father.

He reasons that "old Isaac had been only in the process of becoming, while he, Percival Ford, had become" (1355). As he reha-
bilitates this fictional Father, he necessarily reshapes in a completely inauthentic fashion a new vision of himself. "His lean
little ego waxed to colossal proportions" (1355)—the only arousal
he will allow himself. He has succeeded almost at once in re-
building the house of pride. Here he can once again hide in arrogant, life-denying isolation, and here on the bedroom wall he can
rehang the newly restored picture of the Father. Now it will be
Isaac, the Father, who may be understood to be incompletely developed, caught by the accident of death while still involved in
the process of becoming what Percival imagines he himself has
achieved. In this disingenuous way, Percival will have convinced
himself that he has succeeded in seizing the potency of the Father.

But one thing remains to be accomplished before Percival can surrender himself to this new fiction: he must rid himself of his brother, the living image of his father's transgressions, and in doing so he will accomplish a second resolution of the Oedipal conflict. He will erase the public specter of his true identity as the son of an all-too-human Father, an identification that Joe so inconveniently and embarrassingly represents. Summoning Garland, Percival offers him a sum of money to leave Hawaii, his friends, and the only life he has known to go to San Francisco, with the promise never to return.

It is, Joe recognizes, Percival's final act of denial. The offer of money is not an attempt to atone for a lifetime of cruelty and betrayal; instead, it allows Joe to see with genuine clarity his brother Percival's selfishness. At this moment, "birth and station [are] bridged and reversed," and Percival (with unmistakable sexual symbolism) sees his brother "tower above him like a mountain, and [feels] himself dwindle and dwarf to microscopic insignificance" (1357). However, the fiction that Percival has only just rebuilt allows his "meagre" ego to regain control. It is his absurd and false belief that Joe's departure will effectively remove the evidence of the dual nature of the father. If it is true, as some psychoanalysts suggest, that our perception of ourselves is partly based upon how we imagine others perceive us, then Percival is here trying to limit the data available to those who would try to pluck out the heart of his mystery. Joe agrees to go but refuses the money, and in doing so shows his complete independence from Percival, as well as his accurate reading of the psychological and emotional limitations of his brother.

As Joe turns and walks away without saying good-bye, the final picture is of Percival sitting in real and symbolic darkness, contentedly sipping a lemonade—an act perhaps suggestive of the sour illusion of a life so relentlessly devoted to the conscious avoidance of every opportunity presented for self-enlightenment.

Long before the application of postmodern psychoanalytic theories to literary interpretation became fashionable, Jack London's "The House of Pride" reveals an uncanny understanding of the many psychological dimensions of the development of character in light of private and public perceptions, as well as an appreciation of the often twisted adaptations made by sons in order to reconcile their relationship with absent fathers.

NOTES

1. Hiram Bingham, *A Residence of Twenty-One Years in the Sandwich Islands* (1849; reprint of 3rd edition, Rutland, Vt.: Charles S. Tuttle Co., 1981), 58.

2. C. Hartley Grattan, *The Southwest Pacific to 1900* (Ann Arbor: University of Michigan Press, 1963), 201.

3. Ibid., 202.

4. Jack London conflates the Twentieth Regiment of Infantry and the Tenth Regiment of Infantry in the first paragraph of the story. According to information kindly supplied by the United States Army Museum of Hawaii, the Twentieth Regiment arrived at Fort Shafter on 23 June 1907, with part of their mission being the task of examining the possibility of creating a facility to care for American soldiers who needed to recuperate from their service during the Philippine insurrection, though this plan was never followed up. Russ Kingman's *Jack London: A Definitive Chronology* indicates that Charmian and Jack London attended a military dance on 24 June (probably held in celebration of the arrival of the Twentieth). The Tenth Regiment of Infantry had been reassigned to Alaska. They sailed on 28 June 1907. From this information, we may state with some certainty that the narrative of "The House of Pride" takes place on the evening of 24 June 1907.

5. The Ford family has not been identified as one of the prominent missionary families of the islands. London probably got Isaac's name, as Berkove (125–26 below) suggests, from the Old Testament conflicted father figure, and we suggest that the last name is inspired by London's friendship with the globe-trotting Alexander Hume Ford, with whom the Londons were spending a lot of time in Hawaii in June 1907, within two weeks of the composition of "The House of Pride." See Russ Kingman, *Jack London: A Definitive Chronology* (Middletown, Calif.: David Rejl, 1992), 78–79.

6. Lawrence Berkove, "London's Developing Concept of Masculinity," *Jack London Journal* 3 (1996): 117–26.

7. Jacques Lacan, *Ecrits* (New York: Norton, 1977), 1–7.

8. Jack London, "The House of Pride," in *The Complete Short Stories of Jack London*, ed. Earle Labor, Robert C. Leitz III, and I. Milo Shepard (Stanford, Calif.: Stanford University Press, 1993), 1345. Subsequent quotations from the story are cited parenthetically.

9. Robert Con Davis, "Critical Introduction: The Discourse of the Father," in *The Fictional Father: Lacanian Readings of the Text*, ed. Robert Con Davis (Amherst: University of Massachusetts Press, 1981), 8.

10. For example, in Tahiti, notes Grattan, "the missionaries discovered that there would be great profit to them if they could command the allegiance of whoever [*sic*] had a claim to be king. The monarchical principle in the South Sea islands was directly derived from the idea of chieftainship. As a rule to establish a king on any particular island, the missionaries had to select and back, even to civil war, the chief who appeared to have the best chance of gaining general dominance. No island group had come under the sway of a single 'king' before the arrival of the missionaries and the kings (and queens) who figure in the subsequent annals of the islands were ordinarily promoted to that eminence by the missionaries and, sometimes, other interested whites" (199).

11. Lacan, 1–7.

12. Ellie Ragland-Sullivan, "The Myth of the *Sustantifique Mouelle*: A Lacanian Perspective on Rabelais's Use of Language," *Literature and Psychology* 34 (1998): 10.

13. Edmund Spenser used the expression "The House of Pride" in *The Faerie Queene*, Book I, cantos 4 and 5. In the allegory, it stands for the vanity and worthlessness of worldly desires.

LAWRENCE I. BERKOVE

Jack London's "*Second Thoughts*"

The Short Fiction of His Late Period

NTIL RECENTLY, it was believed that, except for the final stories London wrote under the influence of Jung, the short fiction of London's later period consisted mostly of potboilers.[1] But one of the exciting discoveries resulting from recent London scholarship is the realization that, far from declining in its level of quality, the short fiction of London's later years is intellectually sophisticated and surprisingly subtle, and his work soared to new artistic heights. It may seem strange to speak of early, middle, and late periods of an author who was only forty years old when he died, but chronological categories are helpful to an appreciation of London's art even though these categories are rough and overlap. The stories of London's late period, long overlooked, hard to find, underrated,

This essay is a revised and expanded version of an article that appeared in French in *Europe* (1999).

or even forgotten—but now accessible in the definitive complete edition of the short stories[2]—are a new frontier in London studies. They are literally new to most readers because they are unfamiliar, but recent scholarship has also shown that these stories reveal different dimensions of London's mind and art and open up exciting possibilities of interpretation.

Most readers of London, for example, are familiar with his Klondike stories, primarily the early works that established his fame and are still the ones most highly regarded. These stories of adventure and heroism are intensely appealing even though some of them reflect attitudes such as racism and machismo that have been sharply critiqued in our time. If these stories may be considered works of his early period, then those that reflect his socialist inclinations represent his middle period. Indeed, London's highly regarded reputation in the former Soviet Union and eastern Europe rests heavily on works that can be interpreted as a criticism of capitalism and an endorsement, either explicit or implicit, of socialism. What I choose to call his late period may also be termed his "second thoughts" stage, for it is clear in the works of this category that London rethought many of his ideas, modified some of them, and even reversed others. While a few of these revisionary works were written as early as 1902, many of them were composed within the last decade of his life, especially after 1909, when he returned from the South Seas after abandoning his plan to sail the *Snark* around the world.

It is not sufficiently recognized that London developed rapidly, continuously, and deeply during his short life, and was at the peak of his form when he died. This phenomenon is most evident in his short fiction. In the stories, London experimented with ideas and techniques. He tested and retested his former ideas, and as he learned new information or deepened his understanding of theories that he had espoused, he worked out new combinations and permutations of his thoughts. Nothing was sacred to him except honesty, and he was both audacious and courageous as he recorded in fiction the stages of his mental conclusions. These later stories are more skillfully subtle than has been generally recognized, and the irony that frequently appears in them requires close and thoughtful readings.

An excellent example of the depth and extent of the surprises that emerge from the later stories can be found in "The Unparalleled Invasion," written in 1907 but not published until 1910. The story appears to be a future historian's account of the total extermination of the Chinese people by a bacteriological war launched by a concert of Western powers alarmed at China's expansion into adjacent countries: French Indochina, Siam, Burma, the Malay Peninsula, and Siberia. This unparalleled invasion was motivated by China's huge population surpluses that were made possible by its use of Western technology. China was driven not by the desire to create an empire but by its need for more lebensraum for its people. As China conquered country after country, it immediately colonized the newly won territories with enormous numbers of its citizens. Confident of the ability of its birthrate to overwhelm the populations of its neighbors and to quickly replace its insignificant war losses, China arrogantly ignored the appeals and warnings of Western countries. This perception turned out to be a fatal underestimation of the determination and ability of the West to stop it. China's leaders did not even imagine bacteriological warfare and had no defenses against it. Western armies on China's borders kept the Chinese from fleeing the virulent bacteriological organisms unleashed by the war—another unparalleled invasion—until China was "sanitized," cleansed of both its human and its pathological germ populations. After their victory, the Western countries repopulated—colonized—China with their own population surpluses, thus accomplishing yet another unparalleled invasion. The story ends with the resettlement undertaking that followed the "democratic American program" of heterogeneity instead of racially or nationally exclusive zones, and the participating Western nations "solemnly" pledging never to do to each other what they did to China.

"The Unparalleled Invasion" was long thought to be an expression of London's concern over the "Yellow Peril." London had, of course, been raised in California, and was therefore familiar with its notorious bias against the use of Chinese and Japanese laborers and its support for the restriction of Asian immigration. During his stint in 1904 as a war correspondent in the Russo-Japanese War, London expressed alarm at how quickly and successfully the Japanese had absorbed Western technology and tactics, at the industriousness of the Chinese, and at how prolific the Asians were. In short, if we look for evidence of racism in his environment, his life, and his works, it is there to be found. Reasoning from his biography to his fiction, therefore, generations of readers assumed "The Unparalleled Invasion" was evidence of his prejudice against Asians. But when the story's text is examined closely, we see that this interpretation cannot be valid.

The story is steeped in irony. Its narrator, a historian of the future named Walt Mervin, is woefully unaware of how deep and extensive his own prejudices are. Almost all of his references to the white, Western countries are complimentary, while his references to Asian countries are characterized by subhuman imagery: Japan is "vulpine" and its agents "swarmed" over China; Chinese people are an "over-spilling monstrous flood of life" and are further described as "hordes," a "wave," a "fearful tide," and a "glacier." His phrase the "sanitation of China" grimly prefigures Hitler's euphemism of the "Final Solution" for genocide, and he does not express shock or even regret at the annihilation of the Chinese people. He completely takes for granted all signs of Western expansionism: that Indochina is French, that the Malay Peninsula and Burma are British, and that the indigenous peoples of Siberia are ruled by Russia. He does not see that Japan and China are, in effect, copying the West. So self-centered is he that in the story's first paragraph, he blames China for having interfered with the plans of Western nations, as if those plans were somehow sacred or more important than the plans of China. Finally, he ignores even recent history when he believes the solemn pledges of Western countries not to use germ warfare on each other, despite his knowledge that France and Germany, two of the nations that united to fight the "Yellow Peril," were at war with each other just twelve years later in a renewal of their "ancient quarrel." In short, Mervin is more of a propagandist who believes his own propaganda than a historian. Once he is recognized as an unreliable narrator, the whole story changes and the surface-level values become insupportable.

The narrator's failings, once recognized, are too many and too serious to be accidental. Mervin is *not* London's spokesman; he is a target for London's irony. Between 1904 and 1907, London changed his views about Asians and quietly and unobtrusively shifted from stating prejudices in his own voice to having an unreliable narrator state them. The change is even more apparent in a story like "The Chinago" (1909)[3] and in London's uncompleted work-in-progress, *Cherry*, which was published posthumously as "Eyes of Asia" in 1924. After 1909, in fact, London no longer implied the primacy of one race. The criticism of Western imperialism and notions of ethnic or racial superiority in "The Unparalleled Invasion" is echoed in many other stories, such as "Koolau the Leper" (1909), "Mauki" (1909), and, most obviously, "The Inevitable White Man" (1910).

In "The Unparalleled Invasion," however, London was not simply reversing the target of his antipathy from Asian to Western nations. The story does not exculpate China from all blame: it *was* invading other nations and it *was* indifferent to their rights. Instead, the story criticizes the inhumanity of national and ethnic aggressiveness, whether manifested by the West or the East, especially when that aggressiveness is disguised by lofty rationalizations. Even more basically, the story is a depressing meditation on the Darwinian notion of the "survival of the fittest," for, by its standards, human beings are just animals, more intelligent than the other animals, but ultimately governed by the same pressures they experience, and naturally inclined to the same brutal responses.[4]

The story "Goliah," completed, like "The Unparalleled Invasion," in 1907 and published in England in 1908 and in the United States in 1910, not surprisingly has some significant resemblances to its companion tale. "Goliah" also has an unreliable putative author; an "editorial note" at the end identifies him as Harry Beckwith, a fifteen-year-old high school student who won a prize for its composition in the year 2254. Like Walt Mervin, Harry Beckwith is also naive and uncritical. He is blind to the unscrupulousness of the pseudonymous personage who gained political and social control of the world and established the "utopian" order into which he was born. Beckwith's historical panegyric is so slanted that the murders, deceits, and extortions that Goliah used to achieve his ends are played down or justified on the grounds that those who opposed Goliah were really enemies of the people's true good. Beckwith overlooks as inconsequential Goliah's large-scale exploitation of African and Asian laborers and captives.[5] Without realizing it, Beckwith has adopted the position that the ends justify the means. What appears, therefore, to be London's approval of benevolent dictatorship is in reality its very opposite.

If there was a constant concern in London's mind, it was respect for Darwinism. But although London *respected* Darwinism, he hardly celebrated it. London saw it as a law that linked human beings to animals and ultimately controlled and restricted their destiny. This theme appears memorably in the early story "The

Law of Life" (1901) and, even more memorably, once recognized, in one of his greatest and most brilliant stories, "The Red One" (1916). It is remarkable that this story, which bears favorable comparison to Conrad's "Heart of Darkness" and is without doubt one of the great classics of the short story genre, was not reprinted until 1972 and was not widely available until 1982. It is a masterpiece of subtlety, irony, and allusion, and only since 1996 has it been explained how profoundly and gloomily Darwinian it was.[6]

In "The Red One," an English naturalist named Bassett is collecting butterflies on Guadalcanal, a South Seas island in the Solomon archipelago. He has entered the jungle in search of the source of a magnificent sound, a heavenly sonority, when, suddenly, he is ambushed by headhunters and his assistant is decapitated. Bassett saves himself by killing some of the natives and fleeing, inadvertently, toward the interior. The jungle is a sort of hell that "stank with evil": it is full of biting insects that torment him and make him feverish, of a "monstrous parasitic dripping of decadent life-forms that rooted in death and lived on death" (2300), and of cannibal tribes that tortured their victims first with fiendish ingenuity. In a matter of days, Bassett is reduced to savagery as he fights to stay alive. His gun makes him superior in this contest to determine the survival of the fittest, and he quickly becomes ruthless and vindictive. Occasionally, that wonderful, sweet sound is repeated, and Bassett crawls toward it.

His strength sapped by illness, he collapses, ready to die, when he is discovered by Balatta, a filthy, ape-like young woman from a headhunting tribe. She saves him and carries him back to the "devil-devil" house of Ngurn, her village witch doctor. There, among smoked and shrunken heads, Bassett is slowly nursed back to partial health, learns the language, and becomes friendly with Ngurn.

Realizing that Balatta loves him, Bassett forces himself to respond to her affection in order to pressure her to lead him to

the source of the glorious sounds. Although she is barred by taboo and risks the certain penalty of a week of slow torture before death just by approaching the place, such is her love for Bassett that she violates the taboo. Bassett then at last discovers the
source: a sphere of cherry-red and iridescent metal, two hundred
feet in diameter, resting in a pit and surrounded by dead and
dying human sacrifices. When Bassett touches the sphere's surface, it instantly quivers "in rhythmic vibrations that became
whisperings and rustlings and mutterings of sound . . . so mellow
that it was maddening sweet" (2310). He speculates that it might
have come from another world and contain a message. Looking
around, he understands that the heavenly resonances that he first
heard many miles away came from its being struck by a battering
ram, which was used every time another human sacrifice was
offered to it.

The difficulty he experiences returning to the village makes
Bassett realize that he will never recover his health, and that he
has not long to live. He decides to bargain with Ngurn to take
him once more to the Red One and let him hear its full sound,
offering in exchange his head, which Ngurn covets for the wisdom it contains. Ngurn accepts the offer and Bassett, accompanied by Balatta, gets his last wish just as he yields up his life.

This brief plot summary cannot do justice to a story whose
every line is functional, and it especially cannot adequately represent the wealth of biblical and mythological allusions that add
richness and complexity to the narrative, but it does allow the
reader to glimpse the central allusion to Darwinism. The story
uses not only the Darwinian theme of the "pitiless rule of natural
selection" (2314), but also the idea that the individual is expend-
able in order to save the group. Ngurn cures the heads of his
tribe's captives in order to assimilate the wisdom in them and
advance his tribe. Killing outsiders, in other words, is ultimately
supposed to benefit his community. Bassett ironically parallels

Ngurn in his readiness to destroy the entire population of Guadalcanal in order to "extract from the Red One the message of the world from other worlds" (2314) and bring the knowledge back to his own people. But for his fatal sickness, he would have been willing to carry out this intention. He reasons, however, that Ngurn represents the best of his tribe and that by allowing himself to serve Ngurn's purposes instead of killing him with his shotgun, he might be helping that primitive society evolve into one that has a place for ethics and gentleness (2317). This high-minded reflection, however, is undercut by the fact that the reader knows what is inside Bassett's head, and it is neither wisdom nor gentleness. Indeed, the use of the word "curing" for preserving heads is ironic, for when a head is cut off and smoked, it is definitely "cured" of seeking wisdom or thinking about truth.

Bassett's relationship with Balatta also recalls the story of Adam and Eve in the garden of Eden. She is, in fact, introduced by the description of being "as innocent of garb as Eve before the fig-leaf adventure" (2301). While Guadalcanal does not seem like much of an Eden, or perhaps even suggests an inverted Eden, London treats the story of Eden as mythically and relativistically—but not literally—true, and he thus represents it anthropologically. Just as the biblical story has Adam and Eve transgress a commandment and consequently be punished by death, so does this pair also incur death by breaking a taboo; she as a female and he as a white man. Sad to say, Bassett doesn't give a moment's thought to the fact that Balatta's love for him will cause her to suffer a week's torture before being put to death. Nor is there a hopeful view of either a heavenly afterlife or some contribution to human betterment in his own death; his last vision is of being reduced to a cured head "always turning, in the devil-devil house beside the breadfruit tree" (2318).

"The Red One," written in the second year of World War I, is an intricate, powerful, fascinating story, but it is not a hopeful one. In it, evolution proceeds only so far and then a cataclysm or death drowns hope in blood and forces a return to the beginning. Ultimately, its depiction of the operation of a pitiless process of random natural selection is equivalent to confirming a recurrent pattern of human regression. The same idea is presented more straightforwardly and less deeply in the short novel *The Scarlet Plague* (1912), in which a mysterious plague wipes out all but a tiny fraction of the human race and makes it impossible to maintain civilization. Nature reclaims the land, and the few random survivors revert to primitive society and the rule of strength.

The short stories of London's late period enable readers to observe his mind seesawing back and forth as it reflects on ideas and views them from different perspectives. In novels like *The Sea-Wolf* (1904) and *Burning Daylight* (1910), London seems to be hopeful for the human race and civilization. His correspondence on *The Sea-Wolf* particularly expresses his antipathy for Wolf Larsen, the Nietzschean superman whom he intended as the villain of the novel. But in stories like "When the World Was Young" (1910) and "The Captain of the *Susan Drew*" (1912), both studies of atavistic default personalities buried in outwardly civilized modern men, London sees something valuable and admirable in this hidden atavism that is lost in the civilized veneer.[7] The arrogant masculinity of Wolf Larsen cows his crew and intimidates Maud Brewster and Humphrey Van Weyden, the two soft-handed socialites who are rescued by Larsen when shipwrecks set them adrift. Despite London's explicit opposition to Larsen and what he stands for, the character of Larsen has always impressed readers with its splendid vitality. Humphrey Van Weyden and Maud Brewster do not overcome Larsen on their own; sudden, crippling headaches break his health and ultimately kill him. Even his victim Maud is moved to utter a final compliment at his burial: "Good-by, Lucifer, proud spirit." London apparently had second thoughts about the Larsen type of man, for "The Captain of the *Susan Drew*" has a number of parallels to the novel and sympathetically revives the kind of masculinity that London had earlier denounced. In this story, driven by Stevenson's study of divided personality, *Dr. Jekyll and Mr. Hyde* (1886), London's use of atavism treats divided personality in a Darwinian way.

A blow to the head while he is being shanghaied on a sailing ship transforms the wealthy, pampered socialite Seth Gifford into a crude and pugnacious sailor. Calling himself Bill Decker, he quickly rises in his new career and becomes the captain of a smuggling ship, the *Susan Drew*. By coincidence, a ship on which his onetime family and retainers are traveling is wrecked in the Pacific Ocean. While the family group is adrift in a lifeboat, they are rescued by the *Susan Drew*. But so changed is Gifford/Decker that he does not recognize his wife and daughter, nor they him. Decker is profane and violent, rugged, independent, and hard-handed, and controls his crew by brute force. The civilized socialites despise and fear him, but obey him. After some weeks, however, another blow to the head ends the Bill Decker personality and restores that of the ineffectual Seth Gifford. He is bewildered by his surroundings and is especially distressed by his rough hands. When the daughter urges her mother to kiss him, she refuses, and the daughter's suitor confesses that "I feel as if I had witnessed a murder" (2257). The final view of Gifford at the ship's rail, moaning "Oh dear, oh dear" and "gazing seaward and unconsciously striving to fling overboard his dirt-grimed hands" (2258), is pathetic.

Obviously, "The Captain of the *Susan Drew*" is a reworking and a revision of the story of *The Sea-Wolf*. While this story may seem slight if read by itself, in the context of London's development, its significance emerges as a reconsideration of London's earlier position. Seth Gifford and Bill Decker are opposites, but whereas the effete and overly civilized Gifford can exist only in a hothouse environment made possible by his wealth and an artificial society, Decker could find a niche for himself somewhere in the lower levels of civilized society as well as on a ship on the high seas. Decker is not the hero of the story; he is too crude and violent to be admirable. But in Decker's courage, strength, and independent spirit, London recognized positive and perhaps necessary values for a man in the strife that is life that London had earlier thrown away with Wolf Larsen. He was feeling his way toward a point of balance between the two extremes, toward a civilized Wolf Larsen. He may well have found it in the character of David Grief, the hero of a group of stories written in 1911. It is productive to read the stories in the collection entitled *A Son of the Sun* (1912) as the adventures of a moral and humane Nietzschean superman.[8] If so, these stories represent another reversal of attitude by London.

London's search for types of a balanced human being led him to explore the human psyche. In addition to his Darwinian reflections, he also delved into psychology. His readings of Stevenson and Jung, especially, encouraged London to set aside the ideal of a self-sufficient hero who asserts only his individual potential, and explore that of a socialized hero who grows by assimilating, psychologically or even mystically, the capacities of others through bonds of family, culture, or humanity. Considering that he apparently first read Carl Jung in translation in 1916, the last year of his life, the fiction that he wrote as early as 1903 reveals an extraordinary adumbration of Jungian psychology. If we had not known that London read Jung in 1916, internal evidence would lead many scholars to assert confidently Jungian influence in many of the stories of London's late period. "The Red One" may also be considered as a study of a potentially wholesome human personality that is divided among the three principal characters, Bassett, Ngurn, and Balatta. Because they do not integrate with each other, they all suffer failure as deficient individuals. Bill Decker and Seth Gifford of "The Captain of the *Susan Drew*" are obviously what Jungians would call "shadows" of each other, complementary but unexpressed parts of a personality that deny or do not recognize each other. "The House of Pride" (1907) and "By the Turtles of Tasman" (1911) are a pair of related stories, both of which deal with brothers who are shadows of each other. In the first story, both brothers unhappily fail to integrate with their opposite halves. In the second, one brother benefits when he assimilates a vigorous and outgoing part of his brother that he had earlier denied.[9]

More complex proto-Jungian character portraits can be found in other stories of London's late period. In "Samuel" (1913), for example, London created an archetypal female who represents the indomitable life force. A woman names her first-born son Samuel after her deceased brother. When her son dies, although her village neighbors claim that the name is cursed, she gives that name to her next son. When he dies, to the next. And when he dies, to a fourth born to her when she is forty-seven. This son, however, is an idiot, and her husband finally kills the boy and then hangs himself in crazed guilt. When asked by an interviewer if she has any regret, her response is only that she has not another son to give the name to. While on one level the story seems to depict a woman in the grip of an obsession, on another level, considering that the name Samuel is explained in the Bible as meaning "I have asked him of the Lord" (1 Samuel 1:20), the story directs poignant attention to the mysteries of life and death.[10]

"The Night-Born" (1911) appears to deal with a man who rejects an ideal love for materialistic gain, but functions more satisfactorily as a thematically layered illustration of the figurative as well as literal sterility of an exclusively male society that degenerates into "the grotesque sordidness and rottenness of man-hate and man-meanness" (1660). Trefethan, a miner in the Northland wilderness, encounters an Indian tribe ruled by a beautiful white woman, an escapee from white civilization, whose original name was Lucy (i.e., light) but whose Indian name means "She-Who-Must-Be-Obeyed." Lucy offers Trefethan marriage and shared authority, but he lies that he is married and returns instead to white society. According to Labor and Reesman, Lucy is an "anima-figure," a feminine side of personality that represents spiritual vitality. In not committing to her, Trefethan rejects fulfillment and spends the rest of his life sinking lower in his own eyes as well as society's.[11]

"The Night-Born," however, represents just one position London took on the status of women. If the stories of his late period cast any light on this vexed issue in his oeuvre, it is that London was testing different hypotheses. On the one hand, "The Wit of Porportuk" (1906) is an exceptionally bleak and ironical view of the situation. El-Soo, a beautiful and talented young Indian woman from the Yukon, is given a cruelly limited range of choices for her life. The nuns at the mission where she received her education wish her to renounce her worldly aspirations and dedicate herself to God. She is in love with Akoon, a young hunter from her tribe, but feels obligated to pay off the debts of her free-spending father to Porportuk, an old and cold-hearted money-lender, also from her tribe. The only way she can raise the money to pay off the debt is to sell herself to the highest bidder at an auction. Akoon is too poor to bid; therefore, her only possibilities are being owned by God, some wealthy white man, or Porportuk. She runs away with Akoon, but Porportuk catches her and brings her before an Indian court of old men. When she makes it clear that she will run away again, Porportuk gives her to Akoon but first crosses one of her feet over the other and then shoots her through both ankles. The court approves of the justice of the mutilation. The nature of the wound suggests that she has become a female Christ figure, destined to pay off the debts of men.[12] On the other hand, later stories like "Wonder of Woman" (1911) and

"The Kanaka Surf" (1916), although not as powerful as "The Wit of Porportuk," depict strong, resourceful modern women, the kind that London praised in his wife as worthy of being treated not as a subordinate but as a mate.

Almost all commentators agree that London's final stories, written in a burst of inspiration in 1916 after he read Jung, are among his finest. "Like Argus of the Ancient Times" approaches myth as it narrates how seventy-year-old John Tarwater is seized by "Klondike fever," the urge to prospect for gold in the Northland, and against conventional wisdom and family pressure goes north with minimal equipment. Where other younger, stronger, better-equipped men fail, Old Tarwater somehow survives and gets through. At the point of death, he experiences a mysterious rebirth akin to immortality (2456), recovers the power of his spirit, and finally succeeds in finding gold and becoming rich. In a variation on the biblical story of the Prodigal Son, Tarwater eventually returns to his family "a true prodigal grandfather" (2459). At the story's end, he has not only regained his family's respect but has inspirited them with his hopeful example.

Related to this story is London's last tale, "The Water Baby." The hero of this story, the old Hawaiian fisherman Kohokumu, tells a young white man named John Lakana ("Lakana" was London's Hawaiian name) the story of a mythical water baby who outwitted forty sharks in order to capture a particularly desirable lobster. In contrast to Lakana's ennui, Kohokumu is active and productive. And in contrast to Lakana's lack of spirit, Kohokumu feels close to his tradition. Put another way, Kohokumu is in touch with both his consciousness and his unconsciousness. The diving he does in the way of fishing is an outward manifestation of the spiritual diving he does into the depths of his mother the sea, and into himself, and it constantly renews his vitality. The legends of his people he has memorized and assimilated give him both goals and resourcefulness. "As I grow old," he tells Lakana,

"I seek less for the truth from without me, and find more of the truth from within me" (2488). Reesman identifies this inner truth with the "ancient, unconscious, collective knowledge of the self as a way of saving oneself from the sickness of modern self-consciousness."[13]

This short overview of London's late fiction can only hint at its richness, complexity, skill, and power. But it should counter the impression of an author who was inconsistent, or who could not make up his mind, or who wrote only for profit. On the contrary, by the time he died, London had mastered the short story form with a subtle skill and depth beyond the ability of critics of the next half-century to recognize, and he was on the verge of exciting discoveries in his intense quest for meaning in life. We can regret that his career was so short, but it would make more sense to rejoice that a career so intellectually honest and searching was so productive. London compressed into his late short stories a mentally active life's reflections that cannot fail to inspire readers with insight, self-knowledge, and courage as well as unexpected delight.

NOTES

1. James I. McClintock, *White Logic: Jack London's Short Stories* (Grand Rapids, Mich.: Wolf House Books, 1975), xi, 121ff.

2. Earle Labor, Robert C. Leitz III, and I. Milo Shepard, eds., *Complete Short Stories of Jack London*, 3 vols. (Stanford, Calif.: Stanford University Press, 1993). All parenthetical page references are to this text.

3. An excellent interpretation of "The Chinago" may be found in Gary Riedl and Thomas R. Tietze, "Misinterpreting the Unreadable: Jack London's 'The Chinago' and 'The Whale Tooth,'" *Studies in Short Fiction* 34, no. 4 (1997): 507–18.

4. For a fuller discussion of the story and a more detailed explication of its text, see my article "A Parallax Correction in London's 'The Unparalleled Invasion,'" *American Literary Realism* 24, no. 2 (winter 1992): 33–38.

5. This summary is largely based on the interpretive presentation of Gail Jones at the Fourth Biennial Jack London Society Symposium.

6. See my essay "The Myth of Hope in Jack London's 'The Red One,' " in *Rereading Jack London*, ed. Leonard Cassuto and Jeanne Campbell Reesman (Stanford, Calif.: Stanford University Press, 1996), 204–15, 270–74.

7. For a fuller discussion of this story, see my essay " 'The Captain of the *Susan Drew*': The Reworking of 'The Reworking of *The Sea-Wolf*,' " *Thalia* 17, nos. 1 and 2 (1997): 61–68. See also Per Serritslev Petersen, "The Dr. Jekyll and Mr. Hyde Motif in Jack London's Fiction: Formula and Intertextuality in 'When the World Was Young,' " *Jack London Journal* 3 (1996): 1–10.

8. I am indebted for this observation to Gary Riedl and Thomas R. Tietze, whose interpretation of the David Grief stories has just been published: *A Son of the Sun: The Adventures of Captain David Grief* by Jack London, introduction and notes by Thomas R. Tietze and Gary J. Riedl (University of Oklahoma Press, 2002).

9. My discussion of both of these stories may be found in "London's Developing Conceptions of Masculinity," *Jack London Journal* 3 (1996): 117–26.

10. Earle Labor and Jeanne Campbell Reesman explicate "Samuel" in the revised edition of *Jack London* (New York: Twayne Publishers, 1994), 108–11.

11. Ibid., 111–17.

12. I have here briefly summarized the presentation of Noël Mauberret and Christian Pagnard at the Fourth Biennial Jack London Society Symposium.

13. Jeanne C. Reesman, "The Problem of Knowledge in Jack London's 'The Water Baby,' " *Western American Literature* 23, no. 3 (fall 1988): 201–15.

JOSEPH R. McELRATH JR.

Jack London's Martin Eden

The Multiple Dimensions of a Literary Masterpiece

POPULAR WORKS of literary art can maintain their special status over time if, after their initial positive impression, they continue to engage our imaginations, stir our emotions, and stimulate us intellectually. But works that are eventually credited with having risen beyond popularity to the highest level of classification, that of a masterpiece, must do something in addition. They must reward readers to such an extent that, eventually, they become the subject of discourse not only in academia but also among sophisticated readers of all stripes whose shared experiences and interests define our culture at its best. While some literary works achieve this status by virtue of the simplicity of their design, these are indeed rarities. More frequently, the text that affords a complex reading experience invites another perusal, generates discussion, and separates a work with enduring appeal from the others of its day that now seem weary, stale, flat, and unprofitable.

What makes the difference in Jack London's *Martin Eden* is the quality it shares with two other turn-of-the-century American novels. Both of these novels have also compelled seasoned readers to return to them again and again, and their power resides in their dual nature as works that both satisfy and, on another level, perplex in the way that several of Edgar Allan Poe's most distinguished tales do. That is, we are pleased upon a first reading to grasp the high humanistic significance of what transpires in the artfully constructed story. At the same time, as we conclude our reading, it seems that there was yet more to be understood than became clear during that particular interaction with the text and its author. Those who enjoy a challenge—especially those argumentative souls who revel as much as London did in a battle of wits with a worthy contender—assume that their perplexity is only temporary. They confidently anticipate the satisfaction that will come when, with further reflection or a rereading, they discover the correct interpretive response to the author's cleverly designed complications. For example, readers with a taste for resolving dialectics anticipate the pleasure of reconciling contradictions that appear to have been deliberately implanted in the text.

Kate Chopin's 1899 novel *The Awakening* provides a case in point in that, as with *Martin Eden*, its significance seems at first easily apprehended. Narrator Chopin, that is, resembles modern feminists as she develops a plot and characterizations resulting in a sympathetic portrayal of a young wife and mother of two boys who suffers keenly when, after a prolonged period of arrested development, she at last seeks to define herself and achieve maturity as an individual. Doing so is not easy. Edna Pontellier's problem is that she lives in a world where her gender and maternity have limited her to roles she must perform. Self-definition is more than difficult for her because, as a wife and mother in a traditional Roman Catholic culture, her assigned identity, constantly reinforced by those around her, virtually precludes personal reformulation of who and what she is. When she nevertheless experiments with a radically new self-definition, she finds that it is impossible to sustain a makeover, particularly because the binding obligations to her two children cannot be met if she persists. Unable to be either the traditional wife and mother or the free spirit she yearns to be, she refuses to remain conflicted and commits suicide.

What makes the novel a great one and not merely a well-wrought feminist fictional tract, though, are the two points of view exercised by the narrator—and they seem at odds with each other. On the one hand, Chopin is much more sympathetic to her heroine than Gustave Flaubert was in a similar work published over four decades earlier, *Madame Bovary.* On the other, she resembles Flaubert because she also manifests hostility toward her grievously immature and self-centered heroine, whose propensity for unintelligent decision making is sometimes dismaying. In short, the reading experience of this ambivalent novel is rich because of the tonal counterpointing. Further, when the novel ends, the experience of it does not, for Chopin invites the thoughtful reader who is sensitive to dissonance created by the narrator's use of two voices to participate in the generation of the novel's ultimate meaning. The challenge is to situate the reader somewhere between the two extremes of unqualified sympathy for and impatience with Edna as an appropriate empathetic perspective on this problematic heroine.

Frank Norris's 1901 *The Octopus*, a novel London admired, presents a similar problem. For most of this large work, Norris describes what may be considered an evil in human behavior: the exercise of the acquisitive instinct, unbridled by Judeo-Christian morality and unrestrained by extra-religious values originating in humane sentiment. A laissez-faire capitalist context appears in which the principal characters engage in economic warfare and thus wreak havoc in California's San Joaquin Valley. Suffering abounds as a group of wheat growers unsuccessfully attempts to outwit a rapacious railroad trust; and, for both sides, traditional ethical principles are at a discount when financial gain is the issue. Norris, then, channels his considerable energies into the creation of a credible and pathetic portrait of the horrendous consequences of greed. Whereupon, in the final pages, it is surprising that the last word is given to a character named Presley, whose interpretation of the events in the valley contradicts their obvious meaning for anyone who is not a thoroughgoing Social Darwinist. Presley denies the importance of the "evil" he has seen because in the long run, he reasons, the grain over which the wheat barons and the trust have squabbled is produced and distributed to the masses who require it for their survival. "Good," after all, is the issue of the debacle Presley has observed; and the "evil" suffered by a few in the valley is more than compensated for by the "good" enjoyed by the many. Is Norris being ironic at the end of his novel? Or does he share Presley's point of view that the benign outcome outweighs the malign means to that end? Is he contradicting what he seemed to have made crystal clear earlier? As with *The Awakening*, so with *The Octopus*. The experience of the novel is protracted as one closes the book and attempts to reconcile the diametrically opposed points of view with which Norris leaves the reader.

Martin Eden is properly located in this tradition of novelistic writing, along with Herman Melville's *Moby-Dick* and Stephen Crane's *The Red Badge of Courage*. London also forces second and third thoughts by writing in such a way that, upon completion of a reading of the novel, one is at least as perplexed as gratified—and is forced to identify the work as an intriguing one worthy of further attention.

During a first reading of *Martin Eden*, one finds a straightforward, logically sequenced, and ever-intelligible description of the admirable rise and pathetic fall of a young sailor with extraordinary potential. The tale concerns a rough with little education and virtually no literary experience who recreates himself as an intellectual, essayist, and short story writer. His talent is eventually recognized and rewarded by the American publishing industry and the consumer class it serves. That one of the three titles London considered was *Success* makes good sense. Here a Californian, whose socioeconomic origins are decidedly ignoble, manifests and validates the reality of the "American dream" with his self-propelled rise from rags to riches. London, of course, did the same, and in this quasi-autobiographical portrait of Martin, he illustrates how the genetically superior, sensitive individual initially malformed by a bad environment and long confined within the culture of the lower classes can, by dedicated effort, transcend the limitations associated with his past.

As his story proceeds, he meets middle-class expectations for those aspiring to enjoy upward social mobility. Better, he eventually stands head and shoulders above those who once looked down upon him and who sought to perpetuate his exclusion from their ranks. When he reaches his acme, this one-time denizen of a working-class neighborhood in the San Francisco Bay area comes close to being able to purchase a mansion on Nob Hill. The sailor who in chapter 1 had to be told how to pronounce the name of Algernon Swinburne not only transmutes into the stylish literary sensation of the day but also is recognized as a world-class social theorist and philosophical adept. The suitor once rejected as a lowly brute by his lover's upscale family even becomes a prize catch in their eyes; and thus the formally educated, well-heeled, and, of course, virginal heroine who was once "too good" for a penniless would-be writer even offers to live with him without the benefit of marriage—so grand is his socioeconomic ascent once his writings find a readership.

The remarkable rise pictured is more than the stuff of romance. What would otherwise be dismissed as a none-too-original fantasy tale resembling other, less believable novels by London becomes wholly credible through the extraordinary amount of real-world detail that London, respecting the demands for literary realism in his time, infuses into his text. Chapter by chapter he makes clear just how motivated Martin is, how hard he works to achieve his goal of self-transformation, and to what degrees he resolutely suffers as he deals with obstacle after obstacle in his chosen path. Because London does not depend upon coincidence and deus ex machina but instead provides the "solidity of specification" that Henry James viewed as essential to the generation of a vivid impression of real life, the "Success" phase of Martin's story is, indeed, a success.

The depiction of Martin's fall is as compelling as that of his rise—perhaps more so because greater psychological complexity must, and does, attend the development of his character as he fails to find a positive way to deal with an unprecedented crisis. Ironically, the attainment of his goals precipitates this crisis. Early in their relationship, Ruth Morse's love for him is conditional. He eventually meets her conditions through a self-education regimen. But he does so only to find that they cannot meet her parents' socioeconomic requirements for approval of their marriage. He then persists alone, hoping to return to Ruth and her parents with the bourgeois tokens of his worth that they require. Becoming a financially successful author is his chosen means to that end. Along the way, his burgeoning love of learning blossoms into extraordinary intellectual acumen and, unfortunately for him, results in a poisoned fruit: by the time he grasps success in all of its aspects, he has outgrown the timid and conventional-minded Ruth and learns to despise the archetypal representatives of the middle class, her family. Her shallowness and the meretriciousness of the world she inhabits stand revealed in full. When at last able to grasp the golden ring, he has already discerned that it is made of brass.

The summum bonum for which he sacrifices both physical and mental health is a chimera, and the middle-class realm that once seemed so desirable to a rude sailor is nothing more than a whited sepulchre, but these are discoveries of the kind that many individuals survive. Martin, however, does not. London makes clear in as detailed a manner as his dynamic quest for success Martin's profound disillusionment, lapse into apathy, descent into clinical depression, and—finally—his desire for the peace that annihilation seems to promise. Put another way, London's descriptions of how the too-long-hyperactive hero suffers from the plain and simple psychological experience of burnout and from a rigid idealism making impossible his adjustment to things-as-they-are—an idealism that he will not abandon except in the manner of the *idéaliste manqué* who insists upon all or nothing—are credible and pathetic. By the close of this bildungsroman, nothing measures up to the hero's standard for the way things ought to be; therefore, as does Kate Chopin's Edna Pontellier, he turns his back upon the world, drowning himself in a final exercise of his exceptionally strong-willed personality.

Literarily, then, *Martin Eden* meets every conventional expectation of a popular novel describable as emotionally engaging and true to human nature. Like the works of one of London's turn-of-the-century inspirations, then immensely popular Rudyard Kipling, it is primarily addressed to the mass readership rather than an intellectual elite. That is, London shaped its prose style, characterizations, dialogue, and plotting so that it would—and did in 1909—prove intelligible and moving both for young readers who have not yet personally experienced Martin's glory and gloom and for those more seasoned readers who have adjusted to and survived the kind of frustration that drove him to his death. It features the sine qua non of the popular novel, the love interest; and sensations abound as the hero of this grand quest tale melodramatically struggles against seemingly insuperable odds to achieve success—only to find, in the twist-ending fashioned by London, that it is not worth the price paid for it.

Elitists with a disdain for popular novels will, of course, be inclined to sniff condescendingly at London for fashioning mass-appeal art, dumbed down by a too-democratic author whose continued popularity nearly a century later must be an index of his middle- and low-brow gifts. But, if they refrain from judgment and initiate a first reading, they too will find much to delight them as they deal with an author who liked to display his own intellectual sophistication as much as they do, but who happily demonstrates as well a remarkable aptitude for appealing to multiple readerships. Professional authors err when they exclude any sector of the market for their wares, and London—who became rich by the labor of words—did not usually make that mistake. In *Martin Eden*, for example, the more sophisticated reader will find that London charges his text with a philosophical content that is, in itself, beyond the ken of the average reader not familiar with even the grossest distinctions between philosophical idealism and empiricism—which is to say that *Martin Eden* is not the typical popular novel. At the same time, though, London consistently makes the necessary adjustments so that the average reader can register more generally these enrichments of characterization and plot related to the philosophical influences at work in Martin's life. When treating such matters, London is careful to contextualize succinctly a reference to a figure such as George Berkeley or Joseph LeConte so that readers not familiar with the philosopher's point of view can infer it easily and relate it to what is transpiring in the plot. Sometimes he is less sparing and provides a full explanation of the thinker's effect on Martin. For example, why Herbert Spencer's philosophy appeals so strongly to

Martin is detailed at length in layman's language. The average reader cannot be in doubt about that once London has finished explaining why Martin is rhapsodic when he discovers Spencer's synthetic worldview. The more sophisticated will nod approvingly as London summarizes the reasons for Spencer's high standing in Anglo-American culture of the late nineteenth century.

Should the cognoscenti continue to balk and require more to satisfy their exclusive tastes, *Martin Eden* is not wanting. They will find that London does provide special fare for the few able to position the novel in the context of the relationship between the thought of Arthur Schopenhauer and Friedrich Nietzsche. The latter figure's concept of the superman (or *übermensch*) is referred to and glossed so often that there can be no mistaking that Martin measures himself by that heroic standard for dedicated resolve and endurance in the face of frustrations of his will to succeed. What is not spelled out but implied is Schopenhauer's different attitude toward the frustrations of one's desires. Martin represents both points of view as he vacillates between extremes in his attitude toward life; and he does so without being aware that, in the conclusion of the novel, he is modeling the Schopenhauerian perspective.

Both philosophers focus on human beings in the way that London's contemporary, Theodore Dreiser, consistently did: as creatures of desire naturally prone to project ideal conditions that they would like to enjoy and to exercise their wills toward the end of satisfying their wants by obtaining the objects of their desire. Schopenhauer's position, put simply, is that we inevitably fail to find satisfaction, whatever the object of desire. If we do not obtain what we long for, we are dissatisfied. Worse, if we *do* succeed in obtaining whatever it is we want, we are again dissatisfied—for it does not quite sate as we thought it would. Either way, the cycle is then repeated as we long for the addendum or new experience that seems to promise satisfaction at last. Such is our fate. The intelligent use of the will, according to Schopenhauer, is to break the painful cycle by employing volition in a new way—consciously desiring to desire nothing. No desires, no frustrations: pain is at least minimized.

Nietzsche acknowledges the condition in question. But he defines human nobility as the heroic ability to persist in the face of likely failure, motivated by the belief that the cycle of pain can someday be broken and satisfaction can be had by the strong-willed individual—the "man on horseback" referred to by Martin[1]—who refuses to concede that the status quo is unalterable. Even without London's many renderings of Martin's thoughts and statements concerning his wish to conform to Nietzsche's conception of a hero, the philosophically informed reader familiar with Nietzsche's influence in the nineteenth century and well past 1909 will immediately recognize the resemblance between the superman and the willful Titan that Martin becomes. But there is for Martin a last straw. Not experiencing the satisfaction of his desire for the ideal world that he thought he would enjoy once he qualified himself to enter it, he steps off what has come to seem to him a treadmill, and he surrenders to the Schopenhauerian alternative of resignation. For those familiar with that alternative, London is quite explicit with Martin's dialogue in chapter 45. This is not to say that Martin understands that he has realigned himself with Schopenhauer; he is quite disoriented in the scene where Ruth offers to him without conditions what he no longer wants, herself. Rather, Martin's statements function as London's commentary on his hero's departure from Nietzschean principles when he declines Ruth's offer: "It is too late. . . . I seem to have lost all values. I care for nothing" (464). When the once-primary object of his desire is again proffered, Martin unwittingly repeats the Schopenhauerian response, saying "Something has gone out of me. . . . I am empty of any desire for anything" (465).

But Martin has not actually achieved the condition of Herman Melville's Bartleby. He has not wholly escaped from the cycle of frustration. We find him instead lapsing to his previous point of view. The "Nietzsche-man" seems to revive, fantasizing about beginning a new life as a trader in the South Pacific and, with vaguely formed intentions, boarding a steamer for Tahiti. At this point London resolves the dialectic he has established with the aid of the two German thinkers' opposed points of view. As he slips through the porthole of his cabin into the Pacific and the steamer continues westward, Martin desires nothing that life may offer; at the same time, London images him exercising his indomitable will as he acts upon the desire to end his life by the difficult means of drowning himself.

Martin Eden, then, is a layered work inviting those who, by virtue of a traditional liberal education, are equipped to follow London to this level on which the novel makes a special kind of sense vis-à-vis the Western philosophical context in which London situated it. But it should again be noted that London as philosopher does not give this virtuoso performance at the expense of the work's popular appeal. If the reader does not infer Martin's relationship to the thought of Schopenhauer and Nietzsche, the novel's concluding section is not in consequence flawed. For the popular readership, Martin's dazed condition as a profoundly depressed individual, wholly fatigued by the struggle for existence as he knows it, alone provides a cogent elucidation of how even so promising a contender for greatness may become, evolutionarily, one of the unfit to survive.

While *Martin Eden* offers easy satisfactions as a popular novel, dramatically limns the role of natural selection in everyday life at the turn of the century, and pleases as a fictional contribution to philosophical discourse, it does more—as a masterpiece must—than feed the reader. As has been suggested, the masterpiece must also perplex, that is, challenge the reader and thus effect an interactive relationship between the reader and the text (and, ultimately, the author). London's novel does not disappoint in this respect. Indeed, one may conclude that in certain respects Martin's characterization is deliberately developed by London to provoke the reader. For example, how could it take so long for so otherwise bright a fellow as Martin to recognize Ruth Morse for the petty, conformist model of the unassertive, dutiful daughter she is? It is precisely because Martin is so sympathetic a character, and because one is rooting for him to triumph over exclusionary caste distinctions by virtue of demonstrated merit, that one becomes impatient with and critical of him for long failing to identify as such an unnecessary cause of suffering in his personal life. That he believes he has to measure up to the standard that Ruth represents irritates the reader as much as it does Martin's friend Brissenden when, late in the novel, he so unflatteringly takes her true measure as a woman unworthy of such devotion. Martin is not Othello. Yet Shakespeare's character may come to mind as one wonders how long it will take until Martin finally penetrates the illusion to which he is a thrall and—one hopes—makes corrective adjustments in his vision before it is too late to escape dire consequences of his misjudgment of Ruth.

That the most engaging heroes must be flawed may again have been the notion guiding London when a yet more egregious and doubly surprising development follows upon Martin's sudden ascent from obscurity to celebrity as a writer. At this late juncture in the novel, Martin's self-education regimen has made him a veritable sage. Equality with the one-time paragon of liberal education, Ruth, has long since been achieved; now her dialogue, compared to his, is that of a dunce. As a debater, Martin has crushed Judge Blount and Mr. Morse; attending to the abstruse, jargon-laden arguments of the "real dirt" intellectual community, he has understood every word. Brissenden and he are peers. Whereupon, with Martin having been elevated to near-genius status, London contradicts this characterization and again provokes the reader.

In chapter 44, we encounter the hero's memorable mantra of "Work Performed." In the next chapter, we find that Martin remains dumbfounded by the fact that everyone wants to be associated with a literary celebrity, whereas no one wanted to have anything to do with him when he was a nobody. On the face of it, this behavioral phenomenon is not particularly strange or difficult to understand in the community to which Martin has long belonged. Certainly anyone who could read and understand the turbid prose of Herbert Spencer or take the measure of Judge Blount's personality should be able to read the evidence of sycophantism immediately and not be so disoriented by the results of his analysis. Why is it, for Martin, so stunning a development that, when he is discovered and touted from coast to coast, Ruth, her parents, and many others rush in to become intimates of a man possessed of fame and fortune? How could London's precocious quester for knowledge and intellectual prodigy not have previously noticed this unfortunate characteristic of human nature, particularly as he was observing and commenting upon virtually every failing of the bourgeois personality type through scores of preceding pages? How could he have missed fawning as a well-exercised means to the end of self-aggrandizement?

One may perhaps credit his obtuseness—or unanticipated descent into stupidity—to the depression that is at this point overtaking him. To employ a Londonism, his think-machine is not working well. Another way to eliminate the apparent contradiction in character is to reason that London is alerting us that Martin's store of knowledge is largely book-derived and that he is still a very naive young man in regard to the ways of the world. After such speculations, though, Martin continues to annoy, and further consideration of what London's motivation actually was when constructing these chapters seems warranted.

When one goes on to reflect more on this matter, the result is a further enriching of the reading experience because finding a satisfying answer requires viewing the novel within another frame of reference. As one turns from the text and puzzles over London's intentions, *Martin Eden* is necessarily relocated to a biographical context. The various biographies, autobiographical writings such as *John Barleycorn*, and especially his letters disclose repeatedly that London—in his early thirties when he wrote *Martin Eden* and only forty when he died—never got beyond the get-even mentality that most of us struggle with and dispose of at some point in our lives. One sees this mentality at work earlier in *Martin Eden* when, in chapter 33, his hero is dispatched to the editorial offices of a San Francisco monthly magazine dubbed the *Transcontinental*. His errand is to collect the five dollars out of which he has been soldiered for a short story that its editors published. At the same time, London's own errand is to humiliate with true-to-life personal descriptions the editors of the *Overland Monthly* who once treated him similarly. Recognizing the thinly veiled attack, the *Pacific Monthly* published a substantially rewritten version of the chapter when it serialized the novel. When the novel was published in book form by Macmillan, however, London was still intent on drawing blood. Similarly, the "Work Performed" scenario in chapters 44 and 45 admits of another interpretation than those already considered—an act of authorial whining, reflecting London's persistent bitterness over how he, like Martin Eden, was unappreciated, even abused, by others before he achieved celebrity and then suddenly became everyone's long-lost friend. The outcome of this enquiry is not flattering to London. Then again, it was he who challenged the reader to find a rationale for Martin's peculiar reaction to the arrival of fame. And it was—to his credit—he who fashioned a *Martin Eden* that reveals itself as even more multidimensional when placed in a biographical context.

Worthy of note here is one other way in which *Martin Eden* affords a reading experience of the kind that separates it from other popular novels of its time, as well as distinguishes it in a special manner from similar masterpieces. Melville, Crane, Chopin, and Norris did not explain at length how one should interpret their major works. London, however, insisted in a series of letters on exactly how the story of Martin Eden should—indeed, *must*—be understood. In doing so, he created yet another frame of reference within which he placed a Martin Eden that most readers are unlikely to recognize. The perplexities one has experienced previously seem minor when one attempts to reconcile what *Martin Eden* appears to mean and what London said it does.

The fullest exposition of London's point of view on the novel's significance will be found in his three-page letter of 17 January 1910 sent to all of the newspapers in the San Francisco Bay area.[2] Others written from 1909 through 1914 are consistent with the points he made therein. But London was not only consistent; he was also absolutely convinced that his too-often-misinterpreted novel was designed as and could only be read correctly as a critique of individualism and, more specifically, the Nietzschean concept of the heroic individual; a demonstration of the high value of socialism; and, on a more personal level, a work differentiating the Martin Eden type who does not love his fellow man from its opposite represented by individuals such as Jack London himself.

An immediate positive consequence exists with regard to the richness of *Martin Eden* as a literary experience when it is viewed in relationship with these letters. An argumentative dialogue between the author and his as-articulate novel is created. The reader can mediate, noting the degrees to which the author and the novel are in agreement and at odds with each other, and attempting to resolve differences judged minor. One may also side with London if his interpretation of *Martin Eden* demands assent, or one may adopt an adversarial attitude toward London should his explanation of his own work prove inappropriate. Likely to profit most are those who conclude that they cannot countenance

London's *post facto* claims regarding the intentions that guided him and their realization.

They will point out, first, that it is at least debatable that Martin represents those who do not love their fellow man. True, he comes to despise the bourgeoisie as a class, loathes particular individuals such as his brother-in-law Bernard Higginbotham, and is particularly unkind to the politically conservative press represented by the cub reporter who interviews him. In short, he is very much like London himself in this respect; so this could not be what London had in mind when focusing on his alleged misanthropy. The novel, moreover, pictures numerous instances in which Martin is just as loving as London, in his letters, claimed to be. Martin will not marry Lizzie Connolly because he *does* care for her, wants her to be happy, and knows that he cannot be the man she thinks he is. While he becomes increasingly apathetic after his success, he still takes an interest in others. He bestows a large amount of money on Kreis, one of the "real dirt" philosophers who contributed to what he calls the greatest intellectual experience of his life. He more than kindly takes care of his landlady Maria and one-time laundry coworker Joe in the same manner, bankrolling both for a new start in life. He helps his sister Gertrude—to whom he has always been loving—though doing so means assisting her unspeakably undeserving husband. Martin is concerned about individuals in the lower socioeconomic order, even though he is not a socialist. Ironically, the self-proclaimed socialist Brissenden is the man who better fits London's description. This old-money gentleman, after delivering a millwork monologue on socialism as a historical inevitability destined to succeed individualism, confesses to caste-bias and disdain for the lowly: "Of course, I don't like the crowd, but what's a poor chap to do?" (389). One notes that Martin is his only friend. It seems, then, that Martin has a very good heart, at least as open as London's.

One of the more dramatic assertions in London's 17 January 1910 letter is that individualism led Martin to his death; the notion that a socialistic perspective would have saved him is also implied. In a 5 November 1912 letter, he was more explicit as he chided Philo M. Buck Jr. for his misreading of *Martin Eden*: "*Sea Wolf, Martin Eden, Burning Daylight*, were written as indictments of individualism. Martin Eden died because he was an individualist. Individualism failed him. For heaven's sake re-read the book" (*Letters*, 1096). If one now takes this advice, two questions arise during the rereading. First, how did individualism kill him? The obvious answer provided by the novel is that, if he had not become so self-reliant and then introverted, he might have turned to others for emotional support and to a physician for the professional treatment appropriate for what was then termed neurasthenia and is now known as clinical depression. That seems obvious today, given Martin's symptoms, but that was not London's take on the novel's portrait of Martin. Rather than focus on a Martin who needed to receive assistance from others, London instead emphasized the necessity for him to *do* for others. As he related to Fanny K. Hamilton on 6 December 1909, the Martin who did not love his fellow man

> was an individualist. He was unaware of the needs of others. He worked for himself, for fame, for love, for all self-satisfactions. When these illusions vanished, there was nothing to live for. Ergo, he died. But had he taken Neal Brissenden's advice and tied himself to life by embracing socialism, he would have found that there were a few million others to live & fight for, etc. etc. (*Letters*, 847)

Thus one turns to the scene in which this advice is given and quickly identifies a reason for the misunderstanding between London and the adversarial reader.

The first problem is that the scene is a much less prominent one than London imagined it was. The more significant problem, though, is that the call to socialism is not compelling. Says Brissenden, "I'd like to see you a Socialist before I am gone. It will give you a sanction for your existence. It is the one thing that will save you in the time of disappointment that is coming to you. You have health and much to live for, and you must be handcuffed to life somehow" (389). To paraphrase, life will prove worth leaving, but if you live for the sake of others you will find a reason to continue your life. The argument does not make a strong impression because, practically speaking, the panacea identified does not involve a fundamental change in Martin's personality, for he would merely be replacing his idealistic dedication of his life to Ruth with an as-selfless devotion to the masses. Further, how that would play out is not given additional attention in *Martin Eden*; and, after all, how seriously can the reader take advice of any sort from the alcoholic poet who somehow manages to be loyal to the socialist cause while wavering between a pessimistic worldview and a nihilistic one at odds with the progressive tenets of socialism? Finally, if how to have Martin "handcuffed to life" is the question and dedication to a cause is the answer, why not any cause—evangelism, temperance, female suffrage, the gold standard—that would rivet Martin to the here and now? In fact, why cannot the cause of Nietzschean individualism be, or remain, Martin's raison d'être? One of Martin's diagnoses of his condition is that he is not much of a "Nietzsche-man." London's analysis aside, is there in *Martin Eden* an insuperable impediment to concluding that Martin is correct—that he needs more of the "man on horseback" vigor rather than less?

It appears that London, living and fighting for "a few million others" by composing *Martin Eden* aboard the *Snark* during its voyage through the South Seas, did to some degree want to return to the anti-Nietzschean theme of *The Sea-Wolf*. Fine. The novel does shed light on the dangers of radical individualism, especially the condition of isolation increasingly known by Martin. But, for the reader, the "Nietzsche-man" personality so fully delineated is a chief attraction of the work, one of the major reasons to keep turning pages. Martin is undeniably and successfully fashioned as a grand heroic figure; and when he fails—or falls from the high station we assign him because of his demonstrations of merit—that is tragic rather than merely pathetic. Despite his arrogance at particular moments and whatever his other shortcomings, he does not deserve either the disease from which he suffers or the fatal outcome to which depression contributes. More to the point, his individualism does not appear to be the crime for which he was "punished" by death any more than Brissenden's death was the price paid for being a socialist.

London *could have* written the novel he later claimed he did. If his main intent was to identify individualism as an evil, he could have clarified that intent by making Martin less attractive and by introducing a socialist who is an alluring, more likeable version of the insufferable Ernest Everhard of *The Iron Heel* perhaps. Significantly, he chose not to—very likely because, despite the lip service he gave to socialism after he completed *Martin Eden*, he had strayed from the path of party-line virtue while writing it. Reading the novel, one receives the impression that London was simply mesmerized by the image of the splendid Nietzschean— so much like himself—that he was creating.

If *Martin Eden* was primarily intended to expose individualism and to reveal socialism as the apotheosis of the good, London failed miserably. His actual failure, though, is not to be seen in his work as an artist but in his pronouncements as a critic intent upon *using* his novel as a soapbox while propagandistically responding to his contemporaries' misreadings. As London rebutted the argument that Martin Eden was a socialist, he only stated the fact of the matter. When he went on to proclaim that his novel trumpeted another truth, that individualism is a malaise with fatal consequences, he simply went too far. In both *John Barleycorn* and in his letters about *Martin Eden*, London proved an inept diagnostician. It was when he wrote *Martin Eden* that he displayed genius.

D. H. Lawrence, in his 1923 *Studies in Classic American Literature*, models the behavior of the thoughtful reader in the presence of literary masterpieces of the eighteenth and nineteenth centuries. Lawrence responds to the quality of the works before him so that it is clear he has made his selections on the basis of not merely the pleasure they afford but the complex relationship between the text, the reader, and the author that they engender. Some authors and works challenge him more than others: Edgar Allan Poe merits one chapter; Hawthorne and Melville are each given two. Hawthorne especially intrigues him because of the disparity he sees between what is so conventionally said on the surfaces of his romances and the radically more daring import of the tales. It is unfortunate that he did not later expand the scope of his interest in complexly wrought works to include the early twentieth century, for *Martin Eden* comes to mind when Lawrence enunciates the following principle: "The artist usually sets out—or used to —to point a moral and adorn a tale. The tale, however, points the other way, as a rule. Two blankly opposing morals, the artist's and the tale's. Never trust the artist. Trust the tale. The proper function of the critic is to save the tale from the artist who created it."[3] Reading London's letters concerning *Martin Eden*, Lawrence would have found perfect confirmation of the truism he offers, observing in this case that London varied from the norm by attempting to "point a moral" *after* the tale was told and a quite different theme than the one he identified had been developed in the novel.

But he would also, to be sure, have found much else to engage his interest in *Martin Eden*. This novel repeatedly invites the reader to become as responsive as Lawrence when he chides

Hawthorne for his disingenuous pretense of naivete about matters familiar only to a well-traveled visitor to the dark side of human nature. Only the great works of art merit such energetically analytical and markedly personal reactions that bespeak full engagement with a text. One can be a mere spectator in the presence of the vast majority of popular novels. Works such as *Martin Eden*, on the other hand, take one beyond merely witnessing spectacle to a different order of experience, daring the reader to understand its hero whose traits are *not* rendered in simple, explicit terms for a very good reason: the fictional person focused upon is as complex as a real-life counterpart would prove to an observer, and more than a single series of observations is necessary for understanding. It is because Martin is so true to life—and not the allegorical figure to which London reduced him in his letters—that one is willing to take a second and third measure of him. Although they have their charms, one cannot say the same about the principals in *The Call of the Wild, The Sea-Wolf,* and *The Valley of the Moon.* In *Martin Eden*, London's powers were at their peak. He produced his novelistic masterpiece—no matter how poorly he remembered what he had done when commenting on it later.

NOTES

1. Jack London, *Martin Eden* (1909; reprint, New York: Penguin, 1985). All further references are cited in the text.

2. Jack London, *The Letters of Jack London*, 3 vols., ed. Earle Labor, Robert C. Leitz III, and I. Milo Shepard (Stanford, Calif.: Stanford University Press, 1988), 864–66. All further references are cited in the text.

3. D. H. Lawrence, *Studies in Classic American Literature* (1923; reprint, New York: Viking, 1961), 2.

MARÍA DeGUZMÁN
and DEBBIE LÓPEZ

Algebra of Twisted Figures

Transvaluation in *Martin Eden*

BY THE TIME Jack London wrote *Martin Eden*, he already had a vast audience; yet his semiautobiographical artist's "success" ends in the protagonist's suicide. Doubly isolated by his pledges to write great literature and to champion the woman, Ruth, who is his Romantic icon, Eden endures starvation, accusations of plagiarism, swindling publishers, and periods of purblindness in his daemonic quest. Poverty propels him into a vicious cycle, forced to choose between hocking his bicycle, his one physical mode of transportation, and his one good suit, essential to social mobility. Yet ironically, the crass casualty of his ultimate success leads to his final demise. Like Martin's rolling seaman's gait described at the outset of London's story, the novel is a narrative that heaves and plunges between seemingly diametrical aesthetic, philosophical, psychological, and sociopolitical oppositions: for instance, aestheticism/utili-

tarianism, high art/low art, art/work performed, idealism/
materialism, mysticism/positivism, culture/nature, human/
animal, fascination/repulsion, equality/inequality, freedom/en-
slavement, whiteness/blackness, and masculine/feminine. The
heaving and plunging, up and down, over and under movement
can be analogized to the "jugglery"[1] of fixed numbers and letters,
constants and variables, in the algebra problems that constitute
part of Martin's self-education. This jugglery produces new values out of old values or, to put it more precisely, revalues and
transvalues the "positives" and "negatives" on either side of an
equation such that what was assumed to be a differential relation
turns out to be one of equivalence. What was presumed to have a
particular numerical/conceptual identity contains within it a
self-canceling difference suggestive of the grammar lesson Ruth
gives Martin when she points out that two negatives yield a positive (62–63). Through various figural twists of logic, *Martin Eden*
transvalues the "difference" (4) presumed from the slash separating the elements of a binary opposition into the "likeness" (4) implied by an "equals" sign.

The ultimate algebraic ploy of the narrative is not merely to
balance two sides of an equation, but to turn positives into negatives and, moreover, constants into variables, an operation that
surpasses simple oxymoronic structures such as the name "Martin Eden," "Martin" having been a Christian martyr and Eden a
garden paradise, predating and blissfully ignorant of all martyr-
doms. The operation may be encapsulated in the question, for example, "How does Horatio Alger equal Algernon Swinburne?"
Philosophically speaking, *Martin Eden*'s narrative acts of "transvaluation" (59) in which seeming opposites not only receive their
value in terms of one another, but also, from certain perspectives,
come to be equated can be traced back from the references to
Nietzsche in the novel to the immense influence of Nietzsche's
work attempting to move beyond what the philosopher perceived

as an impending collapse of Western civilization's traditional values and modes of interpretation—hence, *Beyond Good and Evil* (1886), *On the Genealogy of Morals* (1887), and so forth.

Transvaluation in *Martin Eden* involves a vast array of factors, the most salient sociopolitical ones being class, race, and gender. We focus on the entwined variables of race and gender precisely because these have so often been treated as unsavory constants in London's work, considered racist and misogynist. This essay complicates these accusations by examining in close detail the algebra of twisted figures in passages such as "He had not dreamed he was so *black*. . . . He *twisted* his arm, rolled the biceps over with his other hand, and gazed underneath where he was least touched by the sun. It was very *white*. . . . Nor did *he* dream that in the world there were few pale spirits of *women* who could boast fairer or smoother skins than he—fairer than where he had escaped the ravages of the sun" (35; emphasis ours). The picture that leaps out in these lines—of a laboring white man who is also black and yet white to the extent that his whiteness is remindful of the fairness of high-born women—indicates that the alleged misogyny and racism feeding fantasies of degeneration at the fin de siècle and during the early twentieth century, as Bram Dijkstra has documented in *Idols of Perversity* (1986) and *Evil Sisters* (1996),[2] cannot be divorced from an obsessive narrating of the "Other."

In the case of *Martin Eden*, this narrating of the "Other" both literally and metaphorically composes the self, or rather the main protagonist Martin, with whose struggles, fortunes, and demise the novel is concerned. First published in 1908, *Martin Eden* appeared one year before works such as Rachel Crother's play *A Man's World*, about the position of women in modern times, and Gertrude Stein's *Three Lives*, a story of two servant girls and a black woman. Both these works attempt to represent the subject position of the Other, the subaltern within dominant culture —for instance, women within patriarchy, African-Americans

within Anglo-America, and so on. Analogously, *Martin Eden* portrays for a middle- and-upper-middle-class audience a working-
class man's fight to better himself and his conditions. Moreover,
the novel marks as Other this purportedly Anglo white man who
becomes the object of a blonde, blue-eyed bourgeois woman's fascination. This woman, Ruth, can never quite shake off her mother's view of Martin as "an unclean sailor" stained by the "pitch"
with which he has played, "a man from outer darkness . . . evil"
(21). Through a few "strange twists" and "quirks" (20), the narrative itself reinforces the notion not only that Martin, in the
service of the United States' expanding commercial "empery of
[the] mind" (23) and the seas, has consorted with what Anglo
culture classified as non-white (Eurasians, South Sea Islanders,
Mexicans, Hawaiians, even the Portuguese), but also that, like
Melville's Ahab in the "deadly skrimmage with the Spaniard
afore the altar in Santa,"[3] he has been branded indelibly by the
Other. "The blaze of tropic suns" (69) and "a Mexican with a
knife" (6) leave their signatures upon his skin, specifically upon
Martin's neck, "bronzed" and with a "red line" (6) running down
it. The figuration or, perhaps more to the point from the perspective of a largely Anglo readership, the disfiguration of Otherness
renders him simultaneously fascinating and repulsive to Ruth,
whose eyes and hands wander repeatedly to his neck.

Bypassing for a moment the temptation to apply Freud's theory of the anxious substitution of some anatomical feature of the
upper half of the body (most commonly the nose, mouth, or neck)
for the genitals in the lower half as a defense against both castration and the unmasking of blatant sexual desire,[4] one may concentrate exclusively on the narration of Otherness in terms of
"race" and ethnicity to conclude that, although the romance between the white, bourgeois woman and the always non-white
"noble savage" was a favorite formula of nineteenth-century
frontier potboilers, *Martin Eden* presents us with a twist on this

formulaic expression of the supposed *frisson* occasioned by difference. Martin is as white as Ruth, perhaps even whiter, judging from the passage quoted earlier about his biceps. And yet this whiteness does not preclude his repeated casting as black. Martin is "so black" (35), "a great black mass of ignorance" (110), "play[-ing] . . . with pitch" (164), and Ruth "listen[s], like any Desdemona" (228) to her Othello. The passage about Martin's biceps suggests that whiteness depends on blackness and vice versa. A twist of the flesh reveals that the blacker, the whiter. The question is whether this twist, literal and figurative, reinforces in yet another guise or erodes the binary "either/or" upon which nineteenth-century racial typology rested: either you were suitably Anglo-Teutonic "white" or you were not. The logic that governs the depiction of Martin seems to be "both/and." And yet Martin, like the dominant society to which he thinks he wants to belong, also rejects blackness in the form of a girl "with bold black eyes" (53) and his lack of so-called "culture," which he associates with "a great black mass of ignorance." Nevertheless, at the novel's conclusion, his suicide by drowning is figured more in terms of whiteness—"white glare of life" (408), "milky froth of water" (410), "white body" (410), and "a flashing, bright white light" (411)—than of blackness, a "fall[ing] into darkness" (411). However ideologically fraught, London's narrative ventures beyond the "narrow little formulas" (263), to borrow a phrase from the book, that pattern, direct, and ultimately constitute the binarism of racial categorization, especially in the late nineteenth and early twentieth centuries.

The extent to which the novel *Martin Eden* ventures beyond landlogged binaries into the Nietzschean liminal zone of transvaluation—in which binaries become, if not equivalent, then counterparts forever dependent for their "value" on one another rather than antipodes or absolute opposites—is evident if one compares the novel to the few illustrations that accompanied the first couple of chapter installments when the novel was serialized between September 1908 and September 1909 in *The Pacific Monthly*.[5] The illustrations provide a trigonometric $(20)^6$ foil of coordinates to the constants turned into variables in *Martin Eden*. The first illustration (Fig. 1) shows a big, white man respectably suited and bow-tied reading a book of Swinburne's poetry. Nothing about the figure of the man suggests that he is working class or especially short of cash. The second (Fig. 2) portrays this figure shaking hands with Ruth. The caption reads, "She shook hands, frankly, like a man . . . Never had he seen such a woman." Despite the titillating caption, nothing remarkable characterizes the woman in the illustration. She is Gibson-girl-like, although with a face that lacks the physiognomic or expressive strength usually attributed to this type. The female figure, rather than grasping the male figure's hand to shake it, is simply extending her hand in a manner faithful to social etiquette for women at the time. The third illustration (Fig. 3) depicts Martin and Ruth seated in conversation. While the text dwells on Martin's scars, his bulging biceps muscles, and his awkwardness and embarrassment in talking to Ruth, the drawing presents a scarless and composed gentleman, again respectably dressed. The female figure next to him may be gazing at the scar on his neck, but no scar and no sun-darkened skin are visible. As if to guard against the impression that this male figure has lost himself in effeminizing activities, reading Swinburne's poetry and spending time sitting around with women, the fourth illustration (Fig. 4) treats viewers to a scene of Martin asserting himself in a fistfight between men. This drawing seems to be intended as a reassertion that the novel is primarily a story about a fighter determined to succeed, not some man governed by his passion for a woman or, worse, reduced to the status of her love object, a huntress's trophy. All in all, these images whiten, heterosexualize, and masculinize the narrative of *Martin Eden* by ignoring or completely erasing all the

FIG. 1. "Swinburne! That fellow had eyes and he had certainly seen color and flashing light. But who was Swinburne?"
The Pacific Monthly 20, no. 3 (September 1908), 237

figural twists that in the novel wreak havoc with simple oppositions.

Only the drop caps (Fig. 5) that adorn the text of the serialization of *Martin Eden* match the curious aesthetic of London's novel.
In these drop caps, one finds the pictorial counterpart to the ara-
besque convolutions or sinuosity of the textual figures. The drop
caps, however, are not particular to the serialization of London's
story. They appear throughout the items in *The Pacific Monthly* and
symptomatize the vogue for Art Nouveau. *Martin Eden* itself un-
disguisedly demonstrates an awareness of this vogue in lines such
as "'Ephemera' had been featured, with gorgeous head-piece
and Beardsley-like margin decorations" (345). If Swinburne was
considered the literary archimage of effeminizing decadence,
Beardsley signified as much in the visual field. That the novel described by critics as the "rugged," "brutal," and "epic" "Confes-
sions of a Conqueror" so self-consciously takes on these figures
in its deployment of race and gender tropes goes to show how
invested it is in narrating the Other as a means of composing itself and how impossible it is to separate seemingly opposing figures that have become strangely equivalent, twisted around each
other.

Central among the oppositions questioned is the one Martin
himself draws between the novel's earthy dark ladies and the
ethereal light lady, Ruth, or—to borrow from D. G. Rossetti, with
whose works London was familiar—between Body's Beauty and
Soul's Beauty; or, to put it in other words, between the ethereal
muse one should pursue, and the detouring sensual temptress
who continually deflects this pursuit. The resulting threat is described by Hélène Cixous: somehow, man, rushing in to conquer
the "dark continent" of the female other, will ultimately find
that foreign territory inescapable. Throughout most of the novel,
Eden draws emphatic lines between Ruth, the "pale, ethereal
creature, with wide, spiritual blue eyes and a wealth of golden

hair" (4), and, on the other hand, "women of the cattle camps, and swarthy cigarette smoking women of Old Mexico . . . Japanese women, doll-like, stepping mincingly on wooden clogs . . . Eurasians, delicate featured, stamped with degeneracy . . . [and] full-bodied South-Sea-Island women, flower-crowned and brown-skinned" (5).

Eden's fall comes about largely because he finds that, awakened, his ice maiden, Ruth, is closer to a sensual vampire, or Lamia, the mythical succubus and snake-woman. Of course, John Keats gave Lamia her first full literary incarnation, and not coincidentally, London had been reading Keats's letters at the time of his correspondence with Mabel Applegarth, who has frequently been suggested as a model for the novel's Ruth. In a letter to Mabel dated 28 January 1899, he quoted with approval the poet's judgment that "one of the reasons that the English have produced the finest writers in the world is that the English world has ill-treated them during their lives and fostered them after their deaths."[7]

Ostensibly, London creates in the poet, Brissenden, a foil for the more practical Eden. Though the former is based on London's friend, the San Francisco poet George Sterling, as depicted in the novel, Brissenden bears striking resemblance to the popular image of John Keats, particularly as he had been depicted in the American media. Keats's own treatment at the hands of the press was legendary, and a prominent component of his caricature as an apostle of art for art's sake, an "artist of the beautiful," who died young of a broken heart. As Susan Wolfson has argued, the press tended to feminize Keats, in large part because of his fascination with powerful female figures such as Lamia. Throughout Keats's works, "his deepest anxieties take shape in confrontation with power in a female form or in separations from, losses of, or betrayals of women."[8] He presents the "feminine as a force against male independence," partly, as Wolfson

FIG. 2. "She shook hands, frankly, like a man . . .
Never had he seen such a woman."
The Pacific Monthly 20, no. 3 (September 1908), 239

FIG. 3. " 'But I'm goin' to make it my class' . . .
His voice was determined, his eyes flashing,
the lines of his face had grown harsh."
The Pacific Monthly 20, no. 3 (September 1908), 241

argues, thanks to his own hostile reception by critics who branded his work "effeminate" and onanistic, and because of his own antagonism toward the powerful female reading public.[9] Agreeing with this argument, Anne Mellor goes on to point out that Keats's characterization as a "Cockney" poet also implicitly feminized him by characterizing him as a lower-class writer,[10] as one of the Oxford English Dictionary's definitions for Cockney includes: "A derisive appellation for a townsman, as the type of effeminacy, in contrast to the hardier inhabitants of the country."

Like Keats, Brissenden is consumptive and leads a "posthumous existence"; like the "Poor Keats" of legend, he believes that "beauty is the only master to serve" (286). And, with grimly ironic foreshadowing, he advises Eden to "love Beauty for its own sake . . . and leave the magazines alone . . . You can read the magazines for a thousand years and you won't find the value of one line of Keats. Leave fame and coin alone, sign away a ship tomorrow, and go back to your sea" (286). Like Keats, Brissenden only wins fame after his early death, and then largely because of it. The title of his masterpiece, "Ephemera," is also suggestive given Keats's famous self-description, inscribed on his tombstone, of one "whose name was writ in water."

However, though Eden's physical constitution is much hardier than Brissenden's, the former not only admires the poet, but also shares many of his characteristics. As one of London's contemporary reviewers summarized, "Martin Eden is a child of the slums, a sailor rough and blunt, [but] with the delicate soul of a sensitive plant."[11] London repeatedly emphasizes those qualities Eden shares with, for example, "Poor Keats," so often regarded as a "sensitive plant." Like the English poet, Eden is blessed with negative capability. We learn on being introduced to him that his "gift [is that] of sympathy, understanding" (2). He is an artist of "quivering sensibilities" (4) which make him "responsive to beauty" (3) and "susceptible to music" (22). "Poetry . . . [is] his

solace" (56). And, in a metaphor perhaps borrowed from Coleridge, Eden is described as "a harp; all life that he had known and
that was his consciousness was the strings . . . He did not merely
feel. Sensation invested itself in form and color and radiance, and
what his imagination dared, it objectified in some sublimated
and magic way" (23).

London is not criticizing these Romantic qualities, which sug-
gestively fit what patriarchal society has characterized as "dark"
and "feminine." However, he does ultimately offer a warning
concerning the misapplication and/or misdirection of Imagination—that power above all prized by Romantics. "The appropriate business" of literature, according to Romantic spokesman
Wordsworth, "is to treat of things not as they *are*, but as they *appear*; not as they exist in themselves, but as they *seem* to exist to the
senses, and to the *passions*."[12] But, he goes on to acknowledge, this
same literature may prepare for "the inexperienced" a "world of
delusion."[13] Eden is an earnest but inexperienced reader of the
"text" of Ruth, the woman he perceives as his own, pure Romantic muse.

Describing the imagination, Keats compared it with "Adam's
dream—he awoke and found it truth."[14] But what if Adam
awakes to find the subject of his dream not Eve, but Lamia, the
snake-woman (as Lycius does in Keats's own poem)? Or worse
yet—what if he awakes to find Ruth? In Eden's dream state, Ruth
is Eve: "The bid of her saint's eyes [is] mystery, and wonder, un-
thinkable, and eternal life" (53). He believes to have discovered
through her "intellectual life":

> beauty, warm and wonderful as he had never dreamed it
> would be . . . Here was something to live for, to win to, to
> fight for—ay, and die for. The books were true. There were
> such women in the world. She was one of them. She lent
> wings to his imagination, and great, luminous canvases

FIG. 4. "That bunch of hoodlums was lookin' for trouble,
an' Arthur was n't botherin' 'em none. They butted in
on 'm an' then I butted in on them an' poked a few!"
The Pacific Monthly 20, no. 3 (September 1908), 242

spread themselves before him, whereon loomed vague, gigantic figures of love and romance, and of heroic deeds for a pale woman, a flower of gold. (8–9)

In contrast, his reaction to the "bold black eyes" of Lizzie Connolly is one of "spiritual nausea" (52).

Of course, the Keats figure, Brissenden, warns Eden against the "pale, shrivelled, female thing" (287), Ruth, recognizing in her the succubus beneath the saint. And as in so many of Keats's works, Martin Eden follows a male protagonist's discovery that the Eve of his imagination is instead closer to being a Lamia. Eden succeeds at escaping from what he calls "the incubus of his working-class station" (43) only to find that he has fallen victim to a succubus of the bourgeoisie.

Although Lamia first becomes a dominant figure in Keats, she would predominate in the nineteenth century, becoming an increasingly powerful presence in both literature and art. As

FIG. 5. Drop cap.
The Pacific Monthly 21, no. 2 (February 1909), 166

Bram Dijkstra argues throughout *Idols of Perversity*, by the turn of
the century, literally hundreds of snake-women would figure in
paintings and statues. In literature, she assumed her most venom-
ous incarnations. She is a particularly persistent figure in Swinburne's work, which Eden is reading at the novel's beginning and
to which he turns for consolation (and bad advice) in the conclusion. Swinburne's poetry, which Ruth finds indecent, is a veritable reservoir of pale succubae, decadent versions of Keats's Lamia.[15] Martin, on the other hand, is mesmerized by Swinburne's
work, ironically given his inability throughout most of the novel
to recognize a true-life Lamia when he sees one. In Keats's *Lamia*,
the dreamy lover, Lycius, dwells blissfully with Lamia in her sug-
gestively described "purple-lined palace of sweet sin" (Part II,
line 31). When she is revealed as a snake, he dies from disillusionment. In "Laus Veneris," which Swinburne modeled on *Lamia*,
the lover's fate is worse: he is forced to dwell perpetually with his
snake-woman, "satiated with things insatiable" (line 142). Swinburne's Tannhauser, ensnared by vampirish Venus, and Lycius
are passion's slaves. Eden escapes largely because he finds Ruth's
passion somehow unsettling. He has elevated her as an ethereal
muse, with a "penetrative virginity" (59), fancying himself as
playing Robert Browning to her frail Elizabeth Barrett. But it
would take a somnambulistic reader to miss Ruth's almost comic
obsession with Martin's massive, phallic neck, which, "sunburnt"
(179) and scarred by the blade of a Mexican's knife marks him as
alluringly Other.

His first awareness of her physical interest in him so discom-
bobulates him that he finds he can no longer even read his beloved Herbert Spencer. And this small detail becomes significant
when considering the role played by women in theories by such
social Darwinists as Spencer, John Fiske, and Otto Weininger,
all of whom are mentioned as being authors favored by Eden.[16]
An American disciple of Spencer's, Fiske pseudo-scientifically

proved that natural selection implied basic inequalities between races and social classes, and between men and women.[17] Weininger went further, arguing in *Sex and Character* that all living things are composed of varying degrees of masculine and feminine elements—the masculine being positive, productive, and moral, while the feminine was negative, unproductive, and amoral. In 1903 he actually committed suicide, Freud theorized, "out of fear of his criminal nature," in other words, out of anxiety concerning his masculinity.[18]

For these turn-of-the-century intellectuals, a woman's degree of sexual responsiveness revealed her relative location on the evolutionary ladder. To be responsive was to be primitive. Hence, Ruth's apparent ethereality attracts Martin. He envisions her as having emerged from "the primordial ferment, creeping and crawling up the vast ladder of life for a thousand thousand centuries, [emerging] on the topmost rung, having become one Ruth, pure and fair, and divine, and with power to make him know love, and to aspire toward purity, and to desire to taste divinity" (125).

Instead, he learns that "the same pressures and caresses, unaccompanied by speech, that were efficacious with the girls of the working-class, were equally efficacious with the girls above the working-class. They were all of the same flesh, after all, sisters under their skins; and he might have known as much had he remembered his Spencer" (182). The "Colonel's lady and Judy O'Grady are sisters under the skin" (182) in that they are agents of Nature, the primitive force warring against Man's self-elevation. Eden recognizes that "every portal to success in literature is guarded by [editors]" (267). But he is slow in understanding that his beloved Ruth seldom even listens as he reads his works aloud, so possessed is she by "wanton instincts [urging] her to throw wide her portals and bid the deliciously strange visitor, [Martin], to enter in" (127).

He determines that "all that [is] most fundamental in

[Ruth's] sex" is driven toward maternity, an urge which, for the theorists influencing Eden, reveals her as an impediment to his success (175). For such thinkers, brain cells were located in the semen; to deprive a man of his limited supply of semen was thus necessarily to diminish his intellect. Apart from impregnation, women craved ejaculatory emission as health-enhancing. As early birth control advocate Marie Stopes argues in *Wise Parenthood*, "women absorb from the seminal fluid of the man some substance, 'hormone,' 'vitimine,' or stimulant which affects their internal economy in such a way as to benefit and nourish their whole systems."[19] For a frail woman like Ruth, presumably, extracting Eden's vital essence would be the nutritional equivalent of consuming a powerful tonic. Weininger and others also made a connection between man's blood and his semen, thus making the vampirish female such as is suggested in Ruth especially menacing.

Eventually, Martin exits via a ship's porthole from a life in which "everything reached out to hold him down"(43), including women and especially those such as Ruth. This sailor's end would seem to rehearse a favorite trope of adventure literature "for boys" (79) and men—that of possible death or disappearance in maritime service or piracy on the high seas. Joseph Conrad's *Lord Jim* may readily come to mind as do many of Herman Melville's and Robert Louis Stevenson's tales. Common among these stories is the portrayal of a British and/or Anglo-American male subject of empire (London's phrase "empery of [the] mind" is worth remembering) seaborne toward the exoticized "Otherness" of the tropics or the so-called torrid zones. Their heroism, bravery, and paradoxically law-bounded antinomianism are defined both *against* the backdrop and *within* the context of the often gendered feminine tropics upon which they are dependent for their definition. In relation to this trope, Martin's porthole exit from the Lamia-like, but ultimately scripted as the very bourgeois

(395), materialistic femininity of Ruth to other "feminine" climes of bays and valleys "filled with tropical fruits" (355) more amenable to *his* designs—"he would make the valley and the bay his headquarters . . . build a patriarchal grass house like Tati's" (355)—can be interpreted as the apotheosis of an "imperious," presumably "masculine" determination to "ex-press" himself on his own terms, the expression of a manly will as a "cum shot." The language of the suicide passage is suggestive of this kind of sexual release:

> He arose and thrust his head out of the port-hole, looking down into the milky wash. . . . A smother of spray dashed up, wetting his face. It tasted salt on his lips and the taste was good. . . . When his feet touched the sea, he let go. He was in a milky froth of water. (409–10)

The sea foam and spray may be analogized to semen. The sea might be seen to function here as a male element mirroring Martin's own vital "essence" that he withholds from Ruth only to toss to the wind and water. This transposition of body fluids on to non-human elements is remindful of the descriptions of the Pequod crew's interactions with whale spermaceti in the "A Squeeze of the Hand" chapter from Melville's *Moby-Dick*. Ishmael, the narrator, tells his readers:

> It was our business to squeeze these lumps back into fluid. . . . After having my hands in it for only a few minutes, my fingers felt like eels, and began, as it were, to serpentine and spiralize. . . . Squeeze! squeeze! squeeze! all the morning long; I squeezed that sperm till I myself almost melted into it; I squeezed that sperm till a strange sort of insanity came over me; and I found myself unwittingly squeezing my colaborers' hands in it . . . let us squeeze ourselves universally into the very milk and sperm of kindness.[20]

Many parallels between *Martin Eden* and *Moby-Dick* are suggested by the language of this passage, not least of all the evident interest in figural twists or twisted figures. And this parallel brings us to the observation that, in fact, the sea spray and the sperm and the sea spray as sperm or semen are not any more fixedly gendered in *Martin Eden* than is sperm in *Moby-Dick*. In Melville's work, sperm is described as "sweet and unctuous," "a delicious mollifier," "like the smell of violets," and like the fluid produced in female mammary glands, "milk."[21] At the conclusion of London's novel, the ocean and Martin's own being are described in terms of milk, languor—"he seemed floating languidly in a sea of dreamy vision" (411), and lethargy, characteristics associated with women and decadents of both sexes, usually gendered feminine regardless of their biological sex. To be sure, Martin struggles "with swift vigorous propulsion of hands and feet" to impose his will upon the ocean and drown, not float, in this also feminine element. Paradoxically, however, this assertion of "masculine" will involves the incorporation or internalization of that feminine element into himself: "He breathed in the water deeply, deliberately, after the manner of a man taking an anaesthetic" (410). Thus, Martin's final sea voyage begins to read more and more like a series of twists on the conventional affirmation of an imperial subject's masculinity in the maritime adventure story for boys and men. Conventional affirmation could stretch to include a certain degree of homoeroticism so long as the masculine remained just that—masculine. Manly Martin, however, boards a ship bound for Tahiti called the *Mariposa*, which in Spanish means not only "butterfly" or "moth," but also "whore" and "effeminate homosexual."

The name "Mariposa" is significant for several reasons, all of which feed the figural twists that transvalue into one another. As the only Spanish word in the novel besides the place names "San Francisco," "San Leandro" (300, 338), the "Marquesas" (355), and "California" and, as the language of Mexico, it hearkens back to "the Mexican" who with his knife left a mark of "Otherness" on the Anglo Eden's neck. Furthermore, in as much as the word means "moth" or "butterfly" in Spanish, and for thousands of years and in many different places (Europe, Japan, the Pacific Islands, and the Americas) the butterfly has been associated with the spirits of the dead and with the passage from death to life and vice versa, "Mariposa" hints at not only Ovidian metamorphosis, but also Nietzschean transvaluation. The specific transformation within, rather than beyond, the dimension of the social pertains to the complication of received notions of what constituted a hero's proper end, a manly death.

Martin's exit via the *Mariposa*'s porthole entails a self-canceling nihilistic synthesis of opposites as a Pyrrhic defense against the social forces embodied in Ruth. From Martin's (and presumably also London's) perspective, these forces have reduced his literary creations to hack work (189), work for hire meeting the demands of what the novel represents as the weak "slave morality" (399) and tastes of a bourgeois readership. When he commits suicide by jumping this ship, he may be following in his best friend Brissenden's consumptive, self-consuming footsteps, rejecting not only the company of women, but also his feminized bourgeois readership. Martin's rejection of women and his feminized audience involves conventional gender-role complication in how it both follows and does not follow in Brissenden's footsteps. First, it can be argued that his relationship with Brissenden is explicitly patterned after Robert Louis Stevenson's somewhat rivalrous yet nevertheless romantic friendship with William Ernest Henley. Brissenden and Eden compare each other's poetry to the poetry of both these writers. At one point, Brissenden exclaims to Martin, "Success! What in hell's success if it isn't right there in your Stevenson sonnet, which outranks Henley's 'Apparition,' in that 'Love-cycle,' in those sea-poems?" (286). The bond between

Martin and Brissenden is both intellectual and deeply emotional. On these grounds, it qualifies as a romantic friendship between men akin to that common and well-accepted between women in the nineteenth century. The novel summarizes their relationship thus:

> They disagreed about love, and the magazines, and many things, but they liked each other, and on Martin's part it was no less than a profound liking. Day after day they were together. (289)

Nor is the bond between the two men devoid of physicality. Brissenden, with his "long, lean aristocratic face" (280) and "long, slender hands . . . browned by the sun," both attracts and repels Martin who considers him to be "excessively browned": "It was patent that Brissenden was no outdoor man. Then how had he been ravaged by the sun? Something morbid and significant attached to that sunburn" (280). Martin's ambivalent reaction to the sunburn provides further evidence for the continual transvaluation taking place in this novel, for Martin's own sunburn had, earlier in the novel, connoted vitality, not morbidity. But to return to the main argument, Martin's suicide in the wake of Brissenden's from a shot "through the head" (343) lends the pathos of a lonely lover's despair to this action, adding a touch of feminine feeling to a "Nietzscheman['s]" (364) disgust with Ruth, the reading public, and the magazine editors. However, the difference between Martin's suicide and Brissenden's is also significant in this algebra of twisted tropes of gender and race.

Unlike Brissenden, Martin explicitly takes into rather than ejects from himself what would have been understood as the opposite of a manly end punctuated by a bullet from a gun—the feminine element ("fierce old mother," Whitman wrote) of the sea. This move confirms Martin to be more like Edna Pontellier in Kate Chopin's *The Awakening* (1899) than like the Keatsian

Brissenden. The point here is not whether London did or did not read *The Awakening*, published less than a decade before *Martin Eden*. What is significant is the way that the ending of this London novel defies the expectations about the proper conclusion to a story of a heroic, even a failed heroic, man. Despite being such different kinds of works, they have both their protagonists choose to drown themselves when they discover that they cannot express themselves on their own terms and that society can only bear to assimilate a tamed and wing-clipped version of their artistry, whether it be Edna's sensuous, darkly erotic contemplation of the world "within and about her"[22] or Martin's burning vision of the "bigness" (10), the beauty and horror, of "real" (205) life captured in a story at once convincing and full of his hard-won knowledge. In cultural representation, drowning was the preferred method of suicide for women within and beyond the pages of a book throughout the nineteenth century, in the Romantic period and in its long wake.[23] One need only recall the ever-pervasive figure of Ophelia, who inspired many a fictional and actual performance. That Martin ends his life this way only underscores the extent to which he is feminized even while he is masculinized. At the beginning of the novel, we are told that "he could not express what he felt and to himself he likened himself to a sailor, in a strange ship, on a dark night groping about in the unfamiliar running rigging" (10). Foiled in his efforts to truly communicate by the uncomprehending "herd" (382) mentality materialism and emptiness of society, oppressed by the very thought of the starched laundry of the bourgeoisie (389), and no longer comforted by his William Morris chair (408), Martin, just like Edna for whom "there was no human being whom she wanted near her except Robert"[24] and who "casts the unpleasant, pricking garments"[25] symbolic of her pact with society from her, slips into the sea.

Both Edna's and Martin's relation to the ocean, figured in opposition to the social order, is eroticized. Undeterred by flashes of terror and overcoming their involuntary impulses to survive, they welcome its close, closing embrace that surrounds and bathes them totally and delivers each one of them to a final series of visions. The difference between these visions is not so much their contents as their perspectives, albeit typically gendered. Edna's consciousness dissolves within itself, its memories, leaving readers with the "hum of bees, and the musky odor of pinks"[26] filling the air, or lack thereof. Martin's consciousness crystallizes around the image of a "lighthouse . . . inside his brain—a flashing, bright white light" (411), and the narrative objectifies him whole, as if to immortalize him, "a white statue" (410) sinking into darkness. This highly contrastive image composed of the inseparable combination of dark and light constitutes one of the last figural twists of the novel in which whiteness depends upon and is defined by darkness and exists only through the distinction that is not, the line between them a shading of one into the other. Precisely on this disappearing line, a horizon line where the sea meets the sky, without beginning or end, the contents of Edna's and Martin's visions resemble one another despite differences. And this resemblance is, of course, a Nietzschean horizon line of transvaluation.

NOTES

1. Jack London, *Martin Eden* (New York: McKinlay, Stone, & MacKenzie, 1908), 314, 354; hereafter cited in parentheses in the text.

2. Bram Dijkstra, *Idols of Perversity: Fantasies of Feminine Evil in Fin de Siècle Culture* (New York, Oxford: Oxford University Press, 1986) and *Evil Sisters: The Threat of Female Sexuality and the Cult of Manhood* (New York: Alfred A. Knopf, 1996).

3. Herman Melville, *Moby-Dick* (New York: Nal Penguin Inc., 1961), 104.

4. See Sigmund Freud, "Fragment of an Analysis of a Case of Hysteria ('Dora')," in *Case Histories I: "Dora" and "Little Hans"* (New York: Penguin Books, 1990), 31–153.

5. *The Pacific Monthly*, Vols. 20–21 (Portland, Ore.: The Pacific Monthly Company, Sept. 1908–Feb. 1909).

6. Trigonometry is one of the many fields of knowledge that Martin wishes to command along with algebra and geometry before he decides that "there are too many special fields for any one man, in a whole lifetime, to master a tithe of them" (112).

7. Earle Labor, Robert C. Leitz III, and I. Milo Shepard, eds., *The Letters of Jack London* (Stanford, Calif.: Stanford University Press, 1988), 44.

8. Susan Wolfson, "Feminizing Keats," in *Critical Essays on John Keats*, ed. Hermoine de Almeida (Boston: G. K. Hall, 1990), 317.

9. Ibid., 318.

10. Anne K. Mellor, *Romanticism and Gender* (New York: Routledge, 1993), 172.

11. Anon. "Recent Fiction," *Current Literature* 1909, 695–96.

12. William Wordsworth, "Essay Supplementary to the Preface of 1815," in *English Romantic Writers*, ed. David Perkins (New York: Harcourt, Brace, Jovanovich College Publishers, 1967), 336.

13. Ibid., 336.

14. Keats to Benjamin Bailey, 22 November 1817, in *The Letters of John Keats, 1814–1821*, ed. Hyder Edward Rollins (Cambridge, Mass.: Harvard University Press, 1958), I, 185.

15. See Jerome Hamilton Buckley, ed., *Poetry of the Victorian Period*, 3rd edition (Glenview, Ill.: Scott, Foresman, and Company, 1965).

16. "Henidical," which Eden describes as "a favorite word of mine which nobody understands," was a term coined by Weininger (321).

17. Dijkstra, 11.

18. Ibid., 136.

19. Ibid., 190.

20. Melville, 397–98.

21. Ibid., 397–98.

22. Kate Chopin, *The Awakening* (New York: Capricorn Books, 1964), 33.

23. See Elisabeth Bronfen, *Over Her Dead Body: Death, Femininity, and the Aesthetic* (New York: Routledge, 1992), 205–24.

24. Chopin, 300.

25. Ibid., 301.

26. Ibid., 303.

SAM S. BASKETT

Jack London "In the Midst of It All"

THE REACH of my title may seem presumptuous, but my intent is to offer a broad outline of Jack London's essential identity, considering him first as an emerging, unique individual, and then in his vocation as writer, but ultimately in a wider framework. For London up to the time of his death was acquainting himself with current psychological theory, including that of William James, Sigmund Freud, Carl Jung, and others, an awareness increasingly important in his writing of the last years. My focus is on London, however, not theory. To adapt Melville's phrase concerning *Billy Budd*, I am offering "an inside narrative" of London's developing self that his writings and actions make manifest, adumbrating five inside qualities of that self, qualities in part sequential, but with overlappings and contradictions. Obviously, in this space the presentation must be provocative rather than definitive. I will begin with *Martin Eden*. All five of these characteristics figure in the novel, albeit with varying emphases. To give a sense of London's continuing development, I will then turn to *John Barleycorn*, and, finally, and very briefly, touch on two late works, "The Water Baby" and "The Red One."

In considering London's developing self—actually, his sense of self—it is well to recognize in him that quality noted by Katherine Mansfield as a universal human characteristic: "Our persistent yet mysterious belief in a self which is continuous and permanent."[1] London's confident early sense of himself as a secret and separate person of unusual capacity is evident in his impassioned, lengthy letter to Mabel Applegarth of November 1898. He storms at her that she is "positively ignorant" of the "real Jack London," "how I feel and think." And there is a reference to this hidden special self in a June 1903 letter to Charmian: he will not bother to disclose his real self to those who mistake his "roughness and unconventionality" as his essential identity.[2] Whitman also wrote of such an interior, inviolable essence in "Song of Myself": "Trippers and askers . . . / come to me days and nights and go from me again, / But they are not the Me myself. / Apart from the pulling and hauling stands what I am . . . / Both in and out of the game, and watching and wondering at it."[3]

London most fully reveals his early understanding of himself "in the midst of it all" in *Martin Eden*, perhaps a reason he considered it his best book. Charles Watson concurs, adding, "It is the central document of his life as artist."[4] Let me push this idea a bit further. After Martin's "great visioning," his "most vital thing" is professedly his "desire to write."[5] This identification remains constant from the beginning of his "splendid dream" until he has lost desire altogether (71). For Martin, writing is a function of self, self is a function of writing. And so it essentially was for his creator. In this best book, then, London presents a portrait of himself as the young artist, albeit a portrait drawn by the somewhat older artist still grappling with the "long sickness" consequent upon the self he had built, a philosophical pessimism from which what he described as "the thousand strong arms of his mind" would not permit him full recovery.

The problematic relation between character and author needs to be marked, if only to recognize that it cannot be definitively resolved. After obvious biographical differences have been noted, however, the overall congruence of character and author is unmistakable, the differences mostly inessential, sufficiently so as to authenticate, mutatis mutandis, London's ambiguous claim, "I was Martin Eden." As to his contradictory distinction between himself and Martin that Martin was an individualist, whereas he was committed to "the collective human need,"[6] London was surely enough of an individualist for any close reader to recognize in the character an extreme embodiment of a vital component of the author's self. In casting such a character the author himself quite likely was not able to sort out precisely where and to what degree he was and was not Martin. As William Faulkner once observed, it is doubtful if any writer knows what he really puts into his work, a doubt especially relevant in creating a character based so extensively on the author's self.[7]

In any event, the novel offers in Martin's unfolding consciousness numerous revealing insights into London. This is accomplished for the most part by the approving omniscient narrator's description and analysis of the character with unmistakable empathy. In addition, Martin engages in frequent reveries as he confronts "unsummoned" apparitions in self-contemplation (82). At times, the point of view is attributed to him, although it tends to modulate into the narrator's. The effect, for better or worse, is to blur the distinction between them. The character is more removed from the author, however, in six scenes in which he addresses his mirror image; but even here it is evident that the sympathetic author is fully cognizant of the various stages of the self this vibrant, engaging young genius is becoming.

These six mirror scenes, which are carefully crafted (despite the uncertain point of view), warrant closer analysis than they have yet received, but a brief summary will have to suggest their significance: 1. Martin is first "becoming conscious of himself" (31).[8] 2. He expresses his fierce determination "to make good" (97). 3. He exhibits his megalomaniacal innocence as he forecasts a future when "you may come pretty close to knowing all that may be known. Then you will write"—his confidence based on his discovery of Herbert Spencer (101). 4. He decides, despite Ruth's insistence, not to study Latin, as Latin has nothing to do with him (107). 5. He is near despair over his apparent failure as a writer (120). 6. After a flashback in which he sees himself a creature of hate in his eleven-year fight with "Cheese Face," he now envisages himself at the top of the evolutionary ladder, an achieved self, one in which, in parallel to Jay Gatsby, he is well pleased (128). As a sequence, these six scenes emphasize Martin's essential self—and, by extension, London's concern with his identity. Martin's self and his view of the "all" in which he finds himself often tend to merge; but because of the mirror scenes, his "self" is in sharper focus than it otherwise would be. These scenes assist in seeing through the veil of his ideas to the person— and thus to London himself.

What do we learn about this self as it has been built? Most obviously, it is a self committed to, even entranced by, the Spencerian-Darwinian complex of understanding. Martin's "most vital thing" is his desire to write in this perspective (250). As London said of himself, he had indeed "opened the books," particularly those of his times that seemed to explain himself in relation to the world. Such a vision, passionately expressed, is compelling enough in a turn-of-the-century novel to mark Martin's and London's distinctiveness, although by the end of the century, the vision surely seems somewhat dated and reductive.

A. S. Byatt has recently observed that "the big belief-systems of the recent past—Marxism, Freudianism—are no longer believed, even if they live on." She adds, with even more immediate applicability to Martin and London, "The exciting Darwinian seminars [in 1998] at the London School of Economics . . . are full of informed discussion but there is also a tendency to turn Darwinianism into a belief system of the kind science should surely try to resist."[9]

Although Martin and London do enthusiastically accept the Spencerian-Darwinian explanation of it "all"—both, as autodidacts, tended to embrace sweepingly radical ideas of the moment without much internal or external monitoring—I suggest that in the innermost Me myself London had recreated in Martin, beneath their individualism in the context of the ordinary universe, they also share two mythic qualities more fundamental to self than any belief system. In the differing ways of an actual person, that is to say, of the author, and of a character that he has spun out of his mind, London and Martin Eden are both profoundly innocent and profoundly radical. These conjoined qualities constitute, in fact, the characteristic "radical innocence" of the hero in American fiction as defined by Ihab Hassan's study of that title in 1961, a peculiarly American concept susceptible to redressment by a subsequent critical generation, but hardly dismissal.[10] In fact, Hassan's definitions, admittedly unorthodox, serve to redress earlier views of the American experience. And their relevance to understanding Martin in his time, and London in his, in the context of the mainstream of the American novel remains manifest.

As Hassan saw it, the innocence of the American hero "does not merely revert to those simplicities which, rightly or wrongly, have been identified with vision in America. His innocence, rather, is a property of the mythic American Self, perhaps of ev-

ery anarchic Self. It is the innocence of a self that refuses to accept
the immitigable rule of reality . . . an aboriginal Self the radical
imperatives of whose freedom cannot be stifled. There is something in the quality of that innocence to remind us [in Jung's for-
mulation] . . . of 'an absolutely undifferentiated consciousness,
corresponding to a psyche that has hardly left the animal level.'
But [this innocence] also has a divine element in it, like Dionysus,
that inner energy of being, creative and sacrificial, which D. H.
Lawrence hoped to find in the American Adam."[11]

This innocence is infused with a "radical" quality, again as
defined by Hassan. The passion and awareness of the American
hero is radical because "it is inherent in his character, and goes to
the root and foundation of it. But radical, too, because it is extreme, impulsive, anarchic, troubled with vision."[12] In his study,
Hassan does not mention Martin Eden, nor London, although
they surely find a place in the paradigm of American fiction as he
provocatively conceives it.

Consider, for example, Martin as he appears in the following
passage. Armed with the Spencerian "interpretation" of his "pictures," he is at a "higher [intellectual] pitch than ever" (99).

All the hidden things were laying their secrets bare. He was
drunken with comprehension. At night, asleep, he lived with
the gods in colossal nightmare; and awake, in the day, he
went around like a somnambulist, with absent stare, gazing
on the world he had just discovered. At table he failed to hear
the conversation about petty and ignoble things, his eager
mind seeking out and following cause and effect in everything before him. In the meat on the platter he saw the
shining sun and traced its energy back through all the
transformations to its source a hundred million miles away,
or traced its energy ahead to the moving muscles in his arms
that enabled him to cut the meat, until, with inward gaze, he

saw the same sun shining in his brain. He was entranced by illumination, and did not . . . notice the rotary motion of Bernard Higginbotham's finger, whereby he imparted the suggestion of wheels revolving in his brother-in-law's head. (99–100)

In his divine afflatus, he is enraptured by the dream of the unification of all knowledge, a dream in which the vision of "a world elsewhere" coalesces with the physicalistic ontology of "the ordinary universe," to use the terms of a later generation.[13] Such outbursts—and they are numerous—bring to mind London's own vehemently held radical and often contradictory enthusiasms, his extraordinary self-confidence, and his openness to new knowledge and encompassing theories, especially the new biology, the term also used in reference to evolution. The character, in a sense, is the author given mythic dimensions.

Character and author share another primary quality, nonmythic, or at least *less* mythic, a quality that is passionately intermingled with radical innocence. In the novel, self is also considered in its confrontation with the particulars of the American culture and society. First, let us consider Martin in this circumstance. Initially attracted to the bourgeois cultural refinements of the Morse home, he comes to see it as a "den of traitors" (264) and Ruth's father, a corporation lawyer, as the "unconscious henchman" of "the masters of society" (236). Martin is also set in wider opposition by his appraisal of social inequality and, personally, by the steady flow of rejection slips from the editors of the magazines read by such as Ruth's family. Brought to his knees as an aspiring writer, he is reduced to a "work beast" at the Shelley Hot Springs Laundry, toiling for the idle rich (141). "A black screen was drawn across the mirrors of inner vision" (141). His inner self is all but obliterated by a "grisly monster," a class society (238). He agrees with his fellow worker, "Better a hobo than a beast of toil" (146).

The London who repeatedly wrote of his early struggles, who signed himself, "Yours for the Revolution," even after he had become one of the most popular and highly paid writers of his time, surely agreed with this view of society. The difference is that Martin remains totally committed to his individualist stance, whereas London was at least a visceral socialist, as Martin surely is not.

They are alike, however, in that both are extreme, individualistic, passionate in their stances, personifications of the "opposing self," the term used by Lionel Trilling describing "the self in its standing quarrel with culture," which he saw as "the particular concern of the novel for the past two centuries."[14] Trilling is referring to the identity of the hero as shaped by a given writer, and as such Martin fits Trilling's description. So, also, does London as a *writer*. For in writing this novel with the hero patterned after himself, London is most significantly an opposing self, a novelist in the Realistic as well as the Romantic tradition.

The earlier hero, in Trilling's view, had figured as the initiate, characteristically a relatively stable ego striving to position itself in a stable world and be confirmed by it. But as the novel as a form adapted to the world Henry Adams was trying to understand, and as the hero was subjected to the greater burdens of the twentieth century, the initiate tended to merge into the rebel and then into the victim, in recoil from the world, or even, as a modern consciousness developed, in recoil against itself.

In becoming conscious of himself, Martin first desires to become an initiate into the culture represented by Ruth's family, and also by the magazine editors. However, as he grows in "indignant perception" of the culture, he seeks not only to join but also to write, for he rebels against the "coercive forces" present in "family life, in the professions, in the image of respectability, in the ideas of faith and duty, in . . . the very language itself," against the culture's "assumptions and unformed valuations . . . manners, and . . . superstitions."[15] Trilling's listing of the various aspects of the culture to which heroes of a succession of novels were in opposition could be used as a gloss for Martin's discontents, eventually even with Ruth, "prisoner" of her social milieu as she is; and thus Martin is clearly akin to the range of heroes of Western literature since the eighteenth century. But his is a distinctly American version, as I have been suggesting, exhibiting the "American neurosis of innocence," and in the characteristic spirit of radical contradiction that Richard Chase says disrupts the vital connection of self and society.[16] Without claiming too much, it is possible, even important, to see Martin Eden as a pivotal heroic self—and London as a pivotal author—between nineteenth-century American heroes and their authors, and those in the twentieth century and their authors, in this respect: in one character, Martin has been crafted to embody the initiate, the rebel, and the victim. In his art as in his life, London was as much an opposing self as his chosen "office of the author" (in James Williams's highly useful term)[17] permitted.

Thus far I have attempted to see London as a person and as a writer through the mask of the early Martin Eden in his youthful vitality, supremely confident of himself in his chosen vocation, in his interpretation of it "all." With the advent of Martin's suicidal despondency, it might seem that nothing further can be learned about London from the novel. Not so. The final chapters give indirect indication of additional fundamental aspects of London's identity. His natural radical innocence conjoins easily with a natural bent toward opposition, a stance honed by his early recognition that his place in society was the bottom. These qualities were augmented by, modified by, contravened by a third characteristic: London's "need to address the Other." The terminology is that used by Jeanne Reesman in her insightful reading of "To Build a Fire," entitled "Never Travel Alone."[18] I take this need to include *love*, in the broadest as well as the conventional personal sense, a quality in diametrical opposition to the elemental hate in the

Cheese Face episode, seen by Martin as threatening his achieved identity, as noted earlier. Thus, this third broad aspect of London's identity includes the other two important elements cited by Reesman as evident even in London's most "naturalistic" stories, "the search for spirit and the desire for community," this latter a more all-encompassing element than London's more impersonal recognition of "the collective human need."

London reveals something of himself in this connection through the depiction of the course of Martin's love for Ruth. In the letter characterizing Martin as a "consistent individualist," he also wrote that Martin "found out that love had tricked him, and that he had loved his idealization more than the woman herself."[19] The novel indirectly indicates the importance of love, properly understood, in London's makeup, specifically the love of a woman but, to repeat, in more general terms as well. As has been noted, Ruth, real or ideal, is a creature of Martin's imagination, and the reader is inescapably aware of her shortcomings in both roles. Martin's inadequate, contradictory, and potentially self-destructive concept of love—which certainly would not withstand contemporary analysis, feminist or otherwise—is dramatized with particular emphasis in a long scene in chapter 30, perhaps, it seems possible to argue, with conscious authorial intent. Throughout the scene, Martin vacillates between dependency and masterfulness with regard to Ruth and his love for her. He beseeches, "I do not ask you to have faith in me, nor in my writing. What I do ask of you is to love me and have faith in love" (248). He continues, "What I want is you; I am more hungry for you than food, or clothing, or recognition. I have a dream of laying my head on your breast and sleeping an aeon or so" (249). Then, directly following this image of almost infantile dependence, a contrasting chord is struck as Ruth is described as being overwhelmed by his "wild spirit": "The strength that had always poured out from him to her was now flowering in his impassioned

ABOVE: Anna Strunsky, ca. 1900.
LEFT: Bess Maddern, Jack
London's first wife, ca. 1900.

ABOVE: "Bert" and Jack London, ready for hop-picking, England, 1902. RIGHT: Jack London, in the East End, London, 1902. OPPOSITE: Jack London as proponent of the physical culture movement, ca. 1904.

ABOVE: Charmian and Jack London on the
bow of the partially completed *Snark*, 1906.
ABOVE RIGHT: The *Snark*, Hawaii, 1907.
BELOW RIGHT: Jack London aboard a
dinghy alongside the *Snark*, ca. 1907.

ABOVE:
Jack London at work,
Pearl Harbor, 1907.
RIGHT: Charmian
London, Hawaii, 1915.

Jack London at Waikiki, 1915.

RIGHT: Charmian London on Sonoma Boy, ca. 1915. BELOW: Jack London with his Shire stallion, Neuadd Hillside, ca. 1915. OPPOSITE: Jack London, ca. 1900–1905. London's most autobiographical character, Martin Eden, plunged to his death from a porthole.

RIGHT: Jack London, ca. 1914.
BELOW: Jack and Charmian London
at the ranch cottage, ca. 1915.

voice, his flashing eyes, and the vigor of life and intellect surging in him," as "she caught sight of the real Martin Eden, splendid and invincible." But the note of dependence again sounds as he concludes ambiguously with "triumph" in his voice, "All things may go astray in this world, but not love" (251).

Throughout this scene, Martin is supremely his vital self in his radical innocence, but also a self dependent on love, albeit from the "ethereal creature of his own creating" (365). In this love, it should be remembered that Ruth has been his first real appreciation of the Other, in fact, his only close human contact except for Brissenden, who recognizes Martin's danger and recommends socialism as a possible means of salvation. As to his regard for Ruth, however, does Martin in his impulsive, extreme, even anarchic self-centeredness truly address her as the Other?

London seems to be distancing himself intentionally from Martin in this important scene, although it is difficult to be sure, since even his most extreme utterances appear to have the author's admiring authentication. A critical attitude toward Martin is at least implicit, however. Denis Donoghue's recent explication of the topic of love in the writings of Emanuel Levinas, whom he sees as "The Philosopher of Selfless Love," may be helpful in illuminating the implications of this scene. For Levinas, widely regarded as one of the defining thinkers of our time, "ethical life starts with a prescription, . . . my saying 'You' and recognizing the preeminence of 'the Other.' In love, one resigns one's self to the possibility of not being loved in return. . . . It is only by acknowledging you that I come to be myself. . . . Until I make that commitment, I can merely, in the sordid language of individualism, insist on being my sole self." Such commitment "entails a leap of faith." The ultimate aim of Levinas's work, as seen by Donoghue, "is to displace the priority of knowledge by the priority of faith—and not faith in God per se, but in God as the ultimate manifestation of the Other."[20]

Echoes of Martin's expression of his love for Ruth, even some of the exact terminology, as well as his affirmation of the centrality of love itself in his scheme of things, are surely discernible in Levinas's perceptions; but they also can serve as a measure of how far short of selflessness Martin is in actuality. If, as London claimed, the novel is a rejection of Martin's unmitigated individualism, including his stance toward his beloved, his goddess, a finer, less selfish appreciation of love seems to have been London's ideal, even a part of his achieved self, a self thus distinguished from Martin. This London is the lover who could write Charmian in 1903, "You are more kin to me than any woman I have known," even as he was confiding in her his "dream" of a "great Man-Comrade." What he had briskly sketched in a letter to Cloudesley Johns four years earlier, he expands to five paragraphs, more than five hundred impassioned words, in the letter to Charmian.[21] This, in a love letter to the woman for whom he was turning his life inside out. She *must* understand, as Charmian, to her credit, seemingly did.[22]

If Martin, to a degree, is London's alter ego, did someone in London's life correspond to Ruth, as a woman, as a goddess, whose defection had threatened his very self? Neither Charmian nor Bessie, patently enough. Generally recognized as Ruth's prototype, Mabel Applegarth fits some of the superficial details, but no evidence proves that she was to London as Ruth to Martin, nor that the long-ago failure of their relationship to blossom had caused him great emotional distress. It was a different matter with Anna Strunsky, however, the woman who Bessie immediately assumed was the reason Jack wanted a divorce. To Anna, London had written in July 1900, "we were attuned . . . a real unity underlay everything"; despite a theoretical disagreement, "we, the real we, were undisturbed."[23] Later that year he writes of their "white beautiful friendship . . . the world cannot imagine such a thing."[24] Again, the next year, "Large temperamentally—

that is it. It is the one thing that brings us at all in touch. We have flashed through us, you and I, each a bit of the universal, and so we draw together."[25] London was distraught, almost incoherent in his letter to her at the point of her understandable withdrawal when she learned of Bessie's second pregnancy; but he immediately faced up to the fact that he would not achieve his ideal in love with the woman with whom he had coauthored an epistolary debate on that topic. The desire for such a love remains, however. "And now it is over and done with. So be it. Henceforth I shall dream romances for other people and transmute them into bread and butter."[26]

And so he did. In *John Barleycorn*, London made what may be read as a passing reference to the impact of these heart troubles, as I shall note later. In his fiction, as Charles Watson has concluded, *Burning Daylight*, *The Valley of the Moon*, and *The Little Lady of the Big House* "all testify to his belief that his only salvation lay in the love of a woman,"[27] as did, on a personal level, his relationship with Charmian. London describes none of these relationships in precisely Levinas's terminology, but his attitude is consonant enough with such an advanced, sensitive understanding of the Other to make clear that his desire for an outgoing and reciprocally sustained love was a significant and continuing component of the self he achieved. But at some point, although fully attuned to the anguish of his character, London managed to dissociate himself, at least to a degree, from Martin's vitiating sickness, insofar as it stemmed from a loss of faith in love.

An additional dimension is inside Martin's disabling and ultimately suicidal despondence, however, one not only related to his idealization of Ruth, but also an extension of it. The point with regard to London himself is only implicit in the novel, but it was to be fully developed in *John Barleycorn*. Martin cannot write or even muster the will to survive (in his radical innocence as defined) in a world on which he had expected to make his imprint (despite being in essential opposition), a world he thought he understood so well and even felt called upon to interpret. Personally, he is bereft of his sustaining faith. Philosophically, his loss of faith is a canker at the core of his being, incapacitating his will. He concludes despairingly that Nietzsche was right in his "madness": "there was no truth in anything, no truth in truth—no such thing as truth" (377). This early-twentieth-century vision of what Hemingway was to term "nada" is also at the bottom of London's "long sickness," or such is his explanation in *John Barleycorn*.

Before dismissing London's meditations in that work as alcohol-induced, it is well to consider the matrix of his explanation. This is not necessarily to affirm the validity of such ideas, filtered as they are through a "radical innocence," but merely that they were widely held in the books London had opened in his search for truth, and that he was influenced by them even at the time he was writing *Martin Eden*. According to Watson, the porthole suicide reflected the author's state of mind during his return voyage to the South Seas as he neared completion of the novel. The fourth fundamental aspect of London's identity is a profound and lasting consciousness of "blackness," from which in Melville's view no thinking mind is ever wholly free, the perception of nothingness that unites human beings as common victims—in London a state varying in intensity from time to time, and thus in fluctuating relationship with the characteristics that I have previously adumbrated.

The ideas of Hegel are useful in approaching this aspect of London's self. No evidence exists that London had read Hegel, but, as Jonathan Auerbach has remarked, Hegel "powerfully informs American literature's conceptual foundations."[28] In any event, Hegel is considered to have understood better than most of his early-nineteenth-century contemporaries what was happening to the understanding of the self. He declared in the preface to

Phenomenology of the Mind that "ours is a birth-time and a period of transition to a new era." He foresaw the emergence of a new Self apart from any "external grounding," possibly a more mature autonomous self, but one consequently in grave peril of what became designated as the Hegelian "highway of despair."[29] This transition, on an abstract level, delineates the broad outlines of the route to despondency traversed to different lengths by Martin Eden and his author. Such is Martin's predicament, "the modern temper" as defined by Joseph Wood Krutch in "Love—or the Life and Death of a Value,"[30] that, bereft of Ruth's love, he finds himself without the only "external grounding" he can envisage. Already in recoil against the world, deprived of the "divine" meaning with which he invested his love for Ruth, unable to forge a mature, autonomous self, in a state of cosmic shock, Martin turns inward in a kind of "radical disease of consciousness" explored by Dostoevsky and Kafka as well as many later writers, torturing himself until he seeks relief through suicide. London also turned inward in his "long sickness," but not so completely and irrevocably, it now seems established. Instead he chose to explore the disease of modern consciousness, even while going through his pain, thereby adding another dimension to the part of his self that he named "Martin Eden."

The question becomes that raised by Emily Dickinson, a modern consciousness ahead of her time: how to face "The Missing All": "The Missing All, prevented me / From missing minor Things, / . . . a World's / Departure from a Hinge / Or Sun's extinction . . . / I could not lift my Forehead from my work / For Curiosity."[31] Whether or not London achieved the determined serenity implied in Dickinson's lines, he continued at his "work," using his time with the élan of the self he continued to attempt to build. And in some of his most lasting writing, he continued to explore himself, *the self* in the midst of it all, even "the missing all." Charmian reported that six days before her husband died he had said "something like the following": "Man—the brain of man, the effort that man had put into man's supreme task—organizing! That is the work of man . . . to take something second-rate and chaotic and to put himself into it until it becomes orderly and first rate and fine."[32]

In understanding the darker aspect of London, *John Barleycorn* is of prime importance. Considerable debate has arisen over the extent to which the first-person narration is trustworthy autobiography. Keeping in mind Picasso's belief that art is other than nature, I think that, with certain caveats, it is. In an early essay, "Jack London on the Oakland Waterfront," I maintained otherwise, in part because of what seemed obvious, self-aggrandizing, even immature exaggeration, in the early chapters, of his superhumanly successful efforts in whatever activity he entered into, including Dionysian drinking bouts.[33] I now see this account of his youth in a different light, as an expression of his inherent radical innocence coming to the surface as he wrote of his initial encounters with his world, a quality similar to that portrayed in the early Martin Eden.

As for the later, darker chapters, even perceptive critics appreciative of London's work have tended to discount London's revelations of himself, of *the* self for that matter, their considerations shaped by taking the subtitle, "Alcoholic Memoirs," as covering the entire autobiography with equal relevance. John Sutherland, for example, in his perceptive introduction to this "classic of American autobiography" for the Oxford University Press World Classic Series, writes that it is as "a meditation on pessimism or alcohol induced melancholy that it is most unequivocally successful." Seemingly, philosophic pessimism, London's at least, is a function of alcohol, an implication that somewhat detracts from Sutherland's laudatory conclusion: "The later chapters are among the 'most thoughtful things he ever wrote.' *John Barleycorn* is not merely 'a confession of alcoholism,' but a much more 'complex' and 'rewarding text.' "[34]

It is by now fully evident that London was mistaken in thinking of alcohol as a stimulant rather than the depressant it actually is. But considerable external evidence demonstrates that the pessimistic bent of London's mind existed well before any sustained period of excessive drinking. To turn again to Reesman's insightful essay, even as she refers to "the White Logic brought on by alcoholism," she equates it with the "White Silence" of which London wrote in 1898, at the time of his first confident, youthful acquisition of his perspective, when alcohol was less an issue.

London insists as much in the retrospective narrative of *John Barleycorn*. Writing of the time of his growing success, he notes, "[When] I descended into my slough of despond, I never dreamed of turning to John Barleycorn for a helping hand."[35] Although the chronology as given is somewhat vague, contradictory, and even misleading, it seems likely that London's "long sickness of pessimism" began as early as 1902, following, if not concurrent with, the breaking off of his burgeoning relationship with Anna Strunsky. In any event, after a long interval "when I was convalescing came the love of woman to complete the cure" (157). Thus, his despondency has to have begun before his rapturous involvement with Charmian in summer 1903.[36] A number of interesting issues are raised by London's account, but the point to be stressed is that his pessimism, personal or intellectual as the case may be,[37] at this time had nothing to do with alcohol.

It might seem to be a different situation by 1913, but again there is external evidence to be considered. On the five-month, alcohol-free voyage of the *Dirigo* around Cape Horn in 1912, when the idea of *John Barleycorn* began to occupy London, he read and carefully annotated William James's *The Varieties of Religious Experience*, making notes especially on the margins of the chapters

"The Sick Soul" and "The Divided Self." On one page he wrote, "The White Logic that enables us to see through all the vital lies whereby we live." The phrase "Vital Lies," which recurs in *John Barleycorn*, is from Violet Paget's *Vital Lies*, her title taken from Ibsen's term in *The Wild Duck*. London also read her book on the *Dirigo*. On another page of *Varieties*, he wrote, "See Saltus's Philosophy of Disenchantment for the whole list of disenchanted thinkers."[38]

Also, internal evidence in *John Barleycorn* shows that London's pessimism, at least in his own mind, was not based on the consumption of alcohol. This is not to say that London did not drink a great deal, even at the time of writing the book, following the *Dirigo* voyage. And one must consider London's frequent linking of *John Barleycorn* and pessimism. Often, however, he takes a contradictory tack. His is a "cosmic sadness that has always been the heritage of man," a sadness countered only by not opening the wrong books, or not taking them too seriously—a self-censorship contrary to London's very being. And, at times, there is the reference to the White Logic as of "the truer order of truth" (188), that of the universe—the view of man as "a sole speck of life journeying across the ghostly wastes of a dead world," presented in "The White Silence" so many years before. That is to say, a world without "external grounding" in Hegel's terminology, a journey that is indeed on the "highway of despair" unless the self can achieve the imperiled possibility of becoming more mature and autonomous. That it is still a difficult journey is the thrust of Don DeLillo's 1998 novel of building a self, *Underworld*.

Time and time again, as I have indicated, London misleadingly attributes his state of mind, his now pessimistic understanding, to alcohol. In the most quoted passage in the book: "John Barleycorn sends his White Logic, the urgent messenger of truth beyond truth, the antithesis of life, cruel and bleak as interstellar space, pulseless and frozen as absolute zero, dazzling with the fact of irrefragable logic and unforgettable fact" (188). In this power-ful passage, London deftly uses "John Barleycorn" and "White Logic" interchangeably—as if the White Logic, which is nothing other than the perception of ultimate truth as postulated by Mel-ville's "power of blackness," would never pertain without John Barleycorn, an implication entirely at odds with the "no uncom-mon experience" of "cosmic sadness" London refers to earlier in the book. Surely the conclusion is possible that, if London had never mentioned John Barleycorn in relation to his examination of the self, we would see this aspect of his identity as much the same, but we would see it more clearly. That is to say, if London had never taken a drink, his vision, for better or worse, would, as that of Melville's, have included "blackness."

Why, then, does London term this book his "Alcoholic Mem-oirs" and refer so many times to alcohol as a causal agent? I sug-gest that he saw his experience with alcohol, considerable to say the least, as indeed providing a theme running throughout his life which, if recounted, for a complex of reasons would have attrac-tive commercial possibilities. Moreover, throughout *Martin Eden*, drunkenness had served London as a metaphor, first, of Martin's initial and delirious response to Ruth; then, inspired by his "splendid dream" of becoming a writer (71), he is in an almost Di-onysian frenzy; and he is "drunken with comprehension" over his "knowledge" gleaned from Spencer (100). Once the theme of al-cohol was incorporated in *John Barleycorn*, artistic unity required that he weave together that theme with his meditation on himself, on *the* self. One recalls Martin's description of his esthetic: "be-neath the swing and go of the story . . . was always the great, uni-versal motif" (292). On the surface in *John Barleycorn* London gives a "swing and go," scandalous, and thus attractive for many readers unlikely to purchase a work meditating pessimistically about the human situation.

To disentangle these themes and to see London's "sickness"

for what it was, it is also necessary to disentangle his metaphors, to separate "John Barleycorn" from the "White Logic," which, as noted previously, like the "White Silence" is a view of the world as quite possibly without human meaning. Only then can we appreciate the depth of London's vision of "darkness" and the authentic attempt he makes to come to terms with that vision. Wright Morris's understanding of the "modern temper" is to the point. It is to be remembered, of course, that Morris, like Hassan, Trilling, Krutch, and Chase, from all of whom I have drawn insights, was writing around or before mid-century; but it should also be remembered that they were far closer to London's time and its intellectual ambiance than are we. Morris wrote:

> If the modern temper, as distinct from the romantic lies in the admission that men are mortal, this admission determines the nature of the raw material with which the artist must work. An element of despair, a destructive element, is one of the signs by which we shall know him—the other is the constructive use to which this element is put.[39]

London, of course, was just on the verge of the "modern temper," but his 1915 letter to Joseph Conrad extolling the merits of *Victory*—one serious, world-famous writer to another—is additional evidence that he knew the stakes required: immersing oneself in "the destructive element."[40]

A final stage of London's building of a self remains to be considered. In the last months of his life, he discovered Jung and his theory of the unconscious and once again was inflamed by a new vision. It is unnecessary to recapitulate the work of Earle Labor pointing to the importance of this new world for London. Here, as in the entire scope of London studies, Labor remains unexpendable. Also notable with reference to Jung, as in other areas as well, is the contribution of James McClintock. The insights of these and other scholars are further illuminating, however, in pointing to a fifth fundamental characteristic of London, of which the interest in Jung is one manifestation: a lifelong readiness for radical exploration, as reflected in such last fictions as "The Water Baby" and, quite possibly, "The Red One."

Jung seems a direct and significant influence on "The Water Baby," although the ambiguous ending of the narrator, John Lakana, who thus bears London's Hawaiian name, suggests that London is not to be fully and finally defined in terms of the Jungian "belief system," as he is not by any of the others he investigated. Unlike Martin Eden, London kept his options open, regardless of contradictions. As Reesman points out, the tentative ending of "The Water Baby" (Lakana/London's last word is "But—") "only furthers the story's insistence on an open, hermeneutic knowledge."[41]

According to Lawrence Berkove, "The Red One" exhibits a similar openness on London's part. At the time of writing, London's mind "was churning with such powerful stimuli, Freudian as well as Jungian theory, mythology, Darwin, reflections on the implications for civilization of World War I, skepticism, and mysticism."[42] Thus, in this final surge of creative energy resulting from his reading of and about Jung, a deeply ingrained quality of the radically exploring self is still evident. It is an all-encompassing quality interlaced as it is with his "radical innocence," his "opposing self," his desire of "ideal love," and his awareness of the "power of blackness."

London's self was such that throughout his life he engaged in exploration. In bending to his work, which he saw as "man's supreme task" as writer, even in the absence of "external grounding," he became the "real Jack London," a self he was committed to be early and late. Niels Bohr, recognized by the world for his discoveries in theoretical physics, once observed that a deep truth is a true statement whose opposite is also true. Seeing that there is no ultimate human truth and yet that there must be, London was always an explorer; and believing himself "peculiarly constituted to write," he fulfilled his visionary vocation, searching for deep truth in the midst of the contradictions he found in it all.

NOTES

1. Lorna Sage, "I, too, write a little," review of *The Katherine Mansfield Notebooks*, ed. Margaret Scott (New Zealand: Lincoln University Press, 1997), in *London Review of Books*, 18 June 1998, 9.

2. Earle Labor, Robert C. Leitz III, and I. Milo Shepard, eds., *The Letters of Jack London*, 3 vols. (Stanford, Calif.: Stanford University Press, 1988), 23, 26, 366.

3. Walt Whitman, "Song of Myself," *Leaves of Grass*, in *Walt Whitman: Complete Poetry and Collected Prose* (New York: The Library of America, 1982), 191.

4. Charles N. Watson Jr., *The Novels of Jack London: A Reappraisal* (Madison: University of Wisconsin Press, 1983), 164.

5. Jack London, *Martin Eden* (New York: Rinehart and Company, 1956), 83, 250, 119. All subsequent citations appear in the text.

6. Cited by Earle Labor and Jeanne Campbell Reesman, *Jack London: Revised Edition* (New York: Twayne Publishers, 1994), 81.

7. "I write about people. Maybe all sorts of symbols and images get in—I don't know. When a good carpenter builds something, he puts the nails in where they belong. Maybe they make a fancy pattern when he's through, but that's not why he put them in that way." *Lion in the Garden: Interviews with William Faulkner, 1926–1962*, ed. James B. Meriweather and Michael Millgate (Lincoln: University of Nebraska Press, 1968), 61.

8. Gordon Mills has also marked the significance of this first mirror scene in "The Transformation of Material in Mimetic Fiction," *Modern Fiction Studies* 22, no. 1 (spring 1976): 16–17.

9. A. S. Byatt, "Review," *The Guardian*, 29 August 1998, 16.

10. Ihab Hassan, *Radical Innocence: Studies in the Contemporary American Novel* (Princeton, N.J.: Princeton University Press, 1961), 6–7.

11. Ibid.

12. Ibid., 6.

13. Cf. Richard Poirier, *A World Elsewhere* (New York: Oxford University Press, 1966), and Denis Donoghue, *The Ordinary Universe: Soundings in Modern Literature* (London: Faber & Faber, 1968).

14. Lionel Trilling, *Freud and the Crisis of Our Culture* (Boston: Beacon Press, 1955), 58.

15. Lionel Trilling, *The Opposing Self* (Oxford: Oxford University Press, 1980), preface, passim.

16. Richard Chase, *The Democratic Vista* (Westport, Conn.: Greenwood Press, 1973), 30.

17. James Williams, "Commitment and Practice: The Authorship of Jack London," in *Rereading Jack London*, ed. Leonard Cassuto and Jeanne Campbell Reesman (Stanford, Calif.: Stanford University Press, 1996), 10.

18. Jeanne Campbell Reesman, " 'Never Travel Alone': Naturalism, Jack London, and the White Silence," *American Literary Realism* 29, no. 2 (1997): 39–40.

19. London to the *San Francisco Bulletin*, 17 January 1910, *Letters*, 2:865.

20. Denis Donoghue, "The Philosopher of Selfless Love," *New York Review of Books*, 21 March 1998, 38–40.

21. *Letters*, 63, 370–71.

22. London's short story "The Heathen" is a fictional depiction of a perfect Man-Comrade.

23. *Letters*, 98.

24. Ibid., 229.

25. Ibid., 244.

26. Ibid., 313.

27. Watson, 239.

28. Jonathan Auerbach, " 'Congested Mails': Buck and Jack's 'Call,' " in *Rereading Jack London*, 236 note 16.

29. Hegel, Georg Wilhelm Friedrich, *Phenomenology of the Mind*, tr. J. B. Baillie, (New York: Macmillan Co., 1910), preface, paragraph 8, and passim.

30. Joseph Wood Krutch, *The Modern Temper* (New York: Harcourt, Brace and Company, 1939), passim, especially 106–14.

31. Emily Dickinson, "The Missing All," in *The Poems of Emily Dickinson*, ed. R. W. Franklin (Cambridge, Mass.: The Belknap Press of Harvard University Press, 1998), 2:897.

32. Quoted by Watson, 203–4.

33. Sam S. Baskett, "Jack London on the Oakland Waterfront," *American Literature* 27 (May 1955): 363–71.

34. John Sutherland, introduction to *John Barleycorn: Alcoholic Memoirs*, by Jack London, Oxford World Classic Series (Oxford: Oxford University Press, 1989), passim. Except as indicated, Sutherland offers an illuminating analysis.

35. *Barleycorn*, 155. Subsequent citations appear in the text.

36. London's narrative suggests that a considerable amount of time had passed before his "cure." In fact, it is possible to argue that it was never fully effected, that his sensitivity to the "power of blackness" remains evident as late as "The Red One." To return to what is given as a chronological sequence, as an antidote to his "sickness" (155) he had thrown himself "with fiercer zeal into the fight for Socialism" (156–57). But this surely occurs in 1905 (in 1904 he was away for many months covering the Russo-Japanese War) in his campaign for mayor of Oakland and, later in the year, in his "revolutionary" lectures as president of the Intercollegiate Socialist Society—and the pessimistic predictions in *The Iron Heel* came later yet. Moreover, "love" was only able to "lull my pessimism asleep" (157) for a time, and then only by his decision to read less "eagerly" and not to take the "big things too seriously" (157).

37. It seems evident to me that by the time he wrote the later chapters of *John Barleycorn*, London was entirely concerned with his wider worldview, not personal disappointment. Earlier, for a period but not to such a suicidal degree, his anguish, like Martin's, may have been much more personal. His early reading of "positive science," his perspective on the "white silence," had resulted not in despair but in exhilaration both as an intellectual and as a writer. In *John Barleycorn*, he recalls that at the beginning of his "sickness" he "had life troubles and heart troubles which are neither here nor there" (155). In the following sentence, however, he somewhat ambiguously qualifies this assertion: "But *combined with them* were intellectual troubles which are indeed germane" (155; italics added). That, however, was a decade and more before, and he goes on convincingly to make the case for "this long sickness of pessimism": "Mine was no uncommon experience. I had read too much positive science and lived too much positive life. In the eagerness of youth I had made the ancient mistake of pursuing Truth too relentlessly" (155).

38. See David Mike Hamilton, *The Tools of My Trade* (Seattle: University of Washington Press, 1986), 171.

39. Wright Morris, "The Territory Ahead," in *The Living Novel*, 146, quoted in Ihab Hassan, *Radical Innocence*, 6.

40. *Letters*, 1467–68.

41. Jeanne Campbell Reesman, "The Problem of Knowledge in Jack London's 'The Water Baby,'" *Western American Literature* 23, no. 3 (1988): 205.

42. Lawrence Berkove, "The Myth of Hope," in *Rereading Jack London*, 206.

BERT BENDER

Jack London and *"the Sex Problem"*

Surely, I have studied the sex problem
even in its "most curious ways."

—Jack London

J ACK LONDON SAID more than once that he had "studied the sex problem" and had "for many years specialized on sex."[1] But his work in this area remains unrecognized, in part because he is still dogged with the mistaken identity as a specialist in adventure stories of the far north. Even readers who take him seriously seem unclear as to why he or other writers of his generation *would* have developed a special interest in sex. And this is a failure of American literary history, in general: to have ignored or trivialized the reasons why people like Havelock Ellis would have thought, as he remarked in 1897, that "sex [is] the central problem of life."[2] The problem had arisen, not only for Ellis and other psychologists, but for London and virtually every other realist or naturalist after Darwin's revolutionary analysis of sex in *The Descent of Man and Selection in Relation to Sex* (1871). Writers like Howells, Henry James, and Edith Wharton knew very well that no effort to explore the reality of courtship, marriage, and love could ignore the theory of sexual selection.[3] London was certainly attuned to these writers' work in presenting the nature of love. Moreover, from his extensive and more technical readings, he knew that virtually every serious study of sexuality after *The Descent of Man* was founded on Darwin's work, including, for example, Max Nordau's "The Natural History of Love" (1896), Ernst Haeckel's *The Riddle of the Universe at the Close of the Nineteenth Century* (1900), Havelock Ellis's *Sexual Selection in Man* (1905), and Freud's *Three Essays on the Theory of Sexuality* (1905).

For very good reasons, then, London demonstrated in his extensive studies that he agreed wholeheartedly with Ellis's remark that sex, "with the racial questions that rest on it [but] that are seldom noted by critics as being related to it . . . stands before the coming generations as the chief problem for solution" (1: xxx). In London's view the solution to the sex problem involved the many psychological and social issues that Ellis addressed throughout the *Studies*, especially in *Sex in Relation to Society* (1910). But underlying London's approach to the sex problem is his constant awareness that sex is the key part in the larger cluster of evolutionary questions suggested in the titles of Huxley's *Man's Place in Nature* or Ernst Haeckel's *The Riddle of the Universe*. As there can be no evolution without reproduction, sex could be seen as the primary engine of evolution as defined by Darwin's "one general law leading to the advancement of all organic beings": "*multiply*, vary, let the strongest live and the weakest die."[4] For this reason, and because the race question was much more heated in the United States than in England at that time, London always considered the evolution of race as a more prominent feature of the sex problem than did Ellis. Indeed, the race question was no less a bugaboo for London than it was for most American realists or naturalists. Beyond this, however, London eventually approached the sex problem as part of his "agrarian vision" and his larger view of the evolutionary drive to "multiply": he imagined that selective breeding (Darwin's "artificial selection") and efficient farming could help alleviate the growing problems of worldwide hunger and the "veritable rape of the land" in North America.[5]

This essay will offer an extended reading of the culminating work in London's long study of sex, *The Little Lady of the Big House* (1916), while developing the point that no study of gender, sex, courtship, or love in his fiction can get very far without considering the principles of Darwin's theory of sexual selection.[6] This is the essential element in each of London's novels of sexual love, beginning with *A Daughter of the Snows* (1902), whose heroine "believed in natural selection and in sexual selection."[7] By the time London published *The Little Lady of the Big House*, a revolution in the study of sex occurred that is reflected in the many works he had accumulated for his library. But, knowing that the sexual revolution had begun with Darwin, he developed an extensive analysis of sexual selection in the lives of his three characters, while explicitly addressing and routing the most attractive challenge to Darwin's theory of evolution at that time, Bergson's *Creative Evolution* (1907, trans. 1911). He also presented his lovers within the larger biological reality, including the pressing issue of how to feed the world's exploding population, and for this reason described the hero's devotion to intensive farming through selective breeding (Darwin's "artificial selection"), his interest in the work of Luther Burbank, and his efforts to apply the latest developments in Mendelian genetics. Moreover, in one of the first American novels to engage Freudian theory in a serious way, London explored the biological foundations of Freud's theory of sexuality. Indeed, I am claiming that Jack London's career-long studies in the nature of sex deserve to be recognized as the most comprehensive and accomplished in all of American fiction. This is not to deny that most of his books are flawed and have justly failed to command the readership or display the aesthetic appeal of many other fictional presentations of sexual love, such as Henry James's *The Portrait of a Lady*, Kate Chopin's *The Awakening*, or Fitzgerald's *The Great Gatsby.* Still, especially for what he achieved in his own masterpiece on sex, *The Little Lady of the Big House*, London stands in the front rank of American writers on sexual love.

Studying the descent of man and the evolution of sexual difference itself, Darwin concluded, on the basis of the embryo's having both "true male and female glands," and of each sex's possession of rudimentary organs "which properly belong to the opposite sex," that "some extremely remote progenitor of the whole vertebrate kingdom appears to have been hermaphrodite or androgynous."[8] This aspect of Darwinian thought alone is too little known in literary history for the way it contributed to London's and other writers' explorations of androgyny, and for the way it revolutionized the analysis of homosexuality.[9] But Darwin went on to develop the theory of sexual selection to account for the evolution of the "secondary sexual characters" that define physical, psychological, and behavioral differences between the sexes: the male's greater sexual eagerness and size, for example, his more pronounced prehensile power (for grasping the female), his antlers (for battling other males), or his ornamental colors or appendages (in order to impress the female)—as compared with the female's instinct to mother, her smaller size (because she need not engage in sexual battle, as do males, and because she conserves her energy for mothering), and, *crucially in the courtship drama*, her capacity to judge and then select the superior male according to his strength or beauty.

Like natural selection, sexual selection is deceptively simple. It accounts for what we refer to today as the struggle for reproductive success, but both kinds of selection give rise to innumerable complexities, as in the variety of adaptive strategies that range from a snake's special tooth for feeding on eggs, to the mimetic adaptations of butterflies, the origins of music and dance as means of attracting mates, or the peacock's ornamental plumes. It is impossible here to suggest how the many implications of sexual selection were developed in different ways by novelists like Howells, James, George Eliot, or Kate Chopin, except to note that, beyond establishing the point that sex itself was subject to scientific analysis, it involved a general critique of love, new approaches to the so-called woman question, and revolutionary material for the psychological novel.[10] This was true for London as well, but it helps to note also that as he developed his studies of sex between 1902 and 1916, while keeping abreast of emerging developments in evolutionary theory, especially as it involved psychology and the new field of sexology, he kept his focus on the two essential features of sexual selection pertaining to males and females. That is, he continued to express (1) his sense that the main problem to be overcome was the male's elemental violence—his sexual jealousy and brutality, and his hope that individual males could somehow contribute to solving this problem through self-awareness and the resolve to be otherwise; and (2) his wavering belief that the agency of female choice might lead to a gentler kind of love between men and women, if not the full-blown altruism envisioned by some enthusiasts of evolutionary progress like Joseph Le Conte and, through him, Frank Norris.

In each of his novels on courtship and love, London touched on many issues that are worthy of closer analysis than can be afforded them here. But to suggest how his study of sex developed throughout his career, it will help to trace—in a very abbreviated way—a number of central issues that he addressed over the years before he began work on *The Little Lady of the Big House.* He began in *A Daughter of the Snows* by exploring the "elective affinity, sexual affinity, or whatever the intangible essence known as love is," especially the "subconscious processes" of selection that lead to the heroine's choice of mates, who, as an expression of London's optimism, would be a gentler male with a moral sense (90, 88). In the following year he coauthored *The Kempton-Wace Letters* (with Anna Strunsky), a novel that deserves far more attention as the clearest and most comprehensive exposition of the scientific critique of romantic love in American fiction from around the turn of the century. Taking the scientific part in an epistolary debate on love, London's character (Herbert Wace) voices what is very likely the most eloquent tribute to Darwin in American fiction, speculating on Darwin's "intellectual joy" in having produced "the conclusion of his 'Origin of Species': he must have experienced a nobler and more exquisite pleasure than did ever Solomon with his thousand concubines and wives." Wace goes on to explain the main features of sexual selection before declaring his intention to overcome the "erotic phenomenon" called "sexual madness" by relying on his intellect, his hopes for "domestic selection" in agriculture as one way for society to harness the evolutionary force, and on his determination to restrain his own passion for sexual possession: he will not "put the slightest hurt upon the least of human creatures."[11] Developing the same theme the following year in *The Sea-Wolf*, then, London arranged for Maud Brewster to appear midway in that novel as the crucial female part of a sexual triangle. But in arranging for Maud to select against the male with mere brutal strength and beauty (Wolf Larsen), and for the gentler male with what Darwin considered to be the highest evolutionary development, the moral sense (Humphrey Van Weyden), London went to ridiculous extremes to entrust the possibility for evolutionary progress to the agency of female choice. Wolf is cut off from his opportunity to enjoy reproductive success, but Maud and Hump sail on toward new horizons.

By the time he published *Martin Eden* (1909), London had restrained his enthusiasm for evolutionary love, emphasizing that one of the greatest sources of Martin's disillusionment is the education in biology that leaves him with no appetite for either sexual love or life. He can finally only laugh when he realizes that women are "appraising him, selecting him."[12] But by this time London had also furthered his explorations in the new field of sexology, drawing on Havelock Ellis's analysis of "the primitive sense of touch" (in *Sexual Selection in Man*) as he described Martin's lovemaking with Ruth.[13] Martin "divined" he had been "following the right course" in wooing Ruth the "old, primitive way," through "the touch of his hand" that "made its way directly to her by instinct" (217). In *The Valley of the Moon* (1913), then, a new development in London's study of sex is apparent in his attention to what had emerged as a major aspect of the sex problem, as analyzed by Ellis and Freud—female hysteria. Working in this novel to imagine a couple whose marriage could provide the foundation for his agrarian vision, London began by creating a heroine who could survive repeated bouts with the hysteria that seems almost rampant in Oakland, among women in Saxon Brown's workplace and in her own family. Partly because of her own natural instincts, partly because of her eventual mate's natural way with animals and women, and partly through what she learns about primitive sexuality from a dark-skinned woman named Mercedes, Saxon can accept her sexuality without the fear and hysteria that had come to be considered the chief element in the neurosis of civilized life. Then, free from that threat to her health and well-being, Saxon selects a strong but gentle male (Billy) who is fit to accompany her in the pursuit of her agrarian vision. They are a fertile couple returned to the land in an economy based on efficient, small-scale agriculture, including the kind of "domestic selection" that London had touched on in *The Kempton-Wace Letters* and later put into practice on the Beauty Ranch. The novel ends with an image of the expectant couple on their land, looking through the trees toward a doe with her fawn. As always in

London's fictional explorations of sex, there is an obvious auto-biographical element here, reflecting the Londons' prospects for the child whom Charmian miscarried three months after London had finished the novel. This loss contributed to but does not account for the decidedly darker view of sexual love that London produced in *The Little Lady of the Big House.*

By 14 March 1913 London had made extensive notes for what would be his masterpiece on the sex problem. "It is all sex, from start to finish," he wrote to Roland Phillips, and features a triangle of "cultured, modern" people who are "at the same time profoundly primitive." Believing "almost . . . that it is what I have been working toward all my writing life," he emphasized that it would have "all the guts of sex" and that "it will not be believed that I could write it—it is so utterly fresh."[14] Then, "after mulling it over for a year," he had his title, *The Little Lady of the Big House,* and boasted to Phillips that his story of the triangle would be "in a setting that never before in the history of all the literature of all the world was ever put in print" (*Letters* 1322, 1328). All these remarks are true, but two are especially noteworthy in this vastly undervalued exploration of sex. First, as for the "fresh" and almost unbelievable performance, readers familiar with London's career who give the novel more than cursory attention will agree, I think, that it was indeed a groundbreaking effort for him; and this is due not only to the way his "modern" characters dance to the "noise of ragtime music and slangtime song," but to the new psychological intensity he had begun to achieve as Darwinian psychology of the unconscious led to the murkier depths that many readers today mistakenly think only Freud explored.[15] Throughout the novel, but with increasing intensity in its final chapters, London found new ways to probe his characters' psyches as each unwittingly expressed or sought to conceal his or her conflicted motives and emotions. At the same time, almost anticipating Ernest Hemingway's art of the "iceberg," he found innovative ways to evoke the underlying structural realities of his story. Second, as for the "setting" that he claimed was absolutely new in world literature, his point is not only a proud reference to the lovely surrounds of his "Beauty Ranch," but also to the fact that the fictional ranch, especially, is a veritable laboratory for applied research into the nature of sex. As London wrote to a reader who had objected to the Darwinian themes in *Martin Eden*, "I breed too many horses, cows, pigs, sheep and goats, on my ranch here, to accept for a moment your baseless assertion that evolution is wrong and is not" (*Letters* 1203); or, as his hero (Dick Forrest) remarks in the novel, prefacing a discussion of the evolution of race and sex, "I am talking, not as a mere scholastic, but as a practical breeder with whom the application of Mendelian methods is an every-day commonplace" (257).

The psychological and biological elements are intertwined in London's analysis of sex, as they were in a variety of other ways in the most recent treatises on sex that he had studied: in Havelock Ellis's *Studies in the Psychology of Sex*, for example, Otto Weininger's *Sex and Character*, or August Forel's *The Sexual Question*. And London's particularly Darwinian emphasis in presenting the biological and psychological elements is evident not only in the extensive references to artificial selection (in the selective breeding on the ranch) and to sexual selection (in the triangular drama), but also in his frequent reiteration of Darwin's theme of "entanglement"—as in Dick Forrest's remark that, because "sex and soul are all interwoven and tangled together," it is impossible to "know yourself . . . your soul, your personality" when in "elated moods" of "love." In such states, he argues, one thrills, vibrates, and dances "a mad orgy of the senses [without] knowing a step of the dance or the meaning of the orgy" (262–63). Few of London's readers recognize his Darwinian emphasis in the novel's many images of entanglement,[16] and even fewer seem prepared to recognize that his concept of the sex-entangled soul or personality reflects the sense of many early Freudians that the *unconscious* might well be all that we can identify as "personality" or "soul." This idea is further suggested in Paula Forrest's remark to the second man in the triangle (Evan Graham) about how she has learned to deal with her insomnia by applying knowledge gained from swimming in the ocean; that "by not fighting the undertow . . . I . . . come quicker to unconsciousness from out the entangling currents. I invite my soul to live over again . . . the things that keep me from unconsciousness" (152–53).

As London wrote these passages in 1914, deepening his own career-long explorations of sex and the unconscious after having taken in a good deal of the new psychology (as in Ellis, Richard von Krafft-Ebing, Albert Moll, August Forel, and Freud), he was anticipating the "Freudian" idea that he underscored in a volume he could not have owned for some months later, Edwin B. Holt's *The Freudian Wish and Its Place in Ethics* (1915). As Holt speculated on "the *necessary implications* of [Freud's] discoveries, in the field of normal psychology," he asserted that "Freud's is actually the first psychology *with* a soul" (though certainly not anything that one might think of as a "ghost-soul"), for "if the unit of mind and character is a 'wish,' " and the wish is "something which the body as a piece of mechanism can *do*," then perhaps "the wishes *are* the soul."[17] London's and Holt's speculations on the unconscious "soul" will undoubtedly strike many contemporary theorists as naive or quaint, but they are representative of much of the early literary and cultural "groping"in these new "darknesses" that would continue in "Freudian" novels well into the 1930s, as in Conrad Aiken's *Great Circle* (1933); moreover, as I will explain below, in London's own "gropings" in 1914, he was intent on affirming the evolutionary reality of the subconscious in specifically Darwinian terms—as part of his explicit attack on "the glittering veils of Bergsonian metaphysics" in *Creative Evolution*.[18]

One further passage that London underscored in Holt is worth noting as a prelude to the reading of *The Little Lady of the Big*

House: it resembles the most astonishing recent studies in the biology of sex that London brings into his novel at the outset. In his chapter on "The Physiology of Wishes," Holt comments extensively on Darwin's discussion of a root-tip's remarkable sensitivity, suggesting that this organic purposiveness is like a "wish." He concludes his discussion with these sentences that London marked:

> It is significant that Darwin concludes [*The Power of Movement in Plants*] with these words: "It is hardly an exaggeration to say that the tip of the radicle thus endowed, and having the power of directing the movements of the adjoining parts, acts like the brain of one of the lower animals; the brain being seated within the anterior end of the body; receiving impressions from the sense-organs, and directing the several movements."[19]

Certainly, no sexual element is in this part of Holt's remarks on physiology, but London had become interested in this kind of thing in the studies of the sexual touch that he had found in Havelock Ellis's *Sexual Selection in Man*, and that he had incorporated in *The Valley of the Moon*: the idea that "the skin is . . . 'the primeval and most reliable source of our knowledge of the external world or the archaeological field of psychology.' "[20] But it appears that in *The Little Lady of the Big House* London examined more closely the ground on which Ellis had based his *Analysis of the Sexual Impulse*, which he began by noting that "the term 'sexual instinct' may be said to cover the whole of the neuropsychic phenomena of reproduction which man shares with the lower animals."[21] Partly on the basis of a discussion of recent remarkable laboratory studies in the sexuality of frogs, then (a point London picks up in the opening pages of his novel), Ellis remarks that the sexual impulse

> is no longer a question of the formation of semen in the male, of the function of menstruation in the female. It has become

largely a question of physiological chemistry. The chief parts in the drama of sex, alike in its psychic as on its physical sides, are thus supposed to be played by two mysterious protagonists, the hormones, or internal secretions, of the testes and of the ovary. Even the part played by the brain is now often regarded as chemical, the brain being considered to be a great chemical laboratory.

Moreover, Ellis notes, "there is a tendency . . . to extend the sexual sphere" to include secretions from all sorts of glands, "the thymus, the adrenals," and so forth, so that "it is possible that internal secretions from all these glands may combine to fill in the complete picture of sexuality as we know it in men and women."[22]

The research on frogs that contributed to Ellis's insights includes passages like the following:

> Spallanzani had shown how the male frog during coitus will undergo the most horrible mutilations, even decapitation, and yet resolutely continue the act of intercourse, which lasts from four to ten days, sitting on the back of the female and firmly clasping her with his forelegs. Goltz confirmed Spallanzani's observations and threw new light on the mechanism of the sexual instinct and the sexual act in the frog. By removing various parts of the female frog Goltz found that every part of the female was attractive to the male at pairing time, and that he was not imposed on when parts of a male were substituted.

Ellis's discussion of such experiments goes on at some length, largely in his effort to show that the sexual impulse is different from "the impulse to evacuate an excretion," although that seems to be the case with the frogs; and to argue that among human beings "the impulse of contrection" ("the 'instinct to approach, touch, and kiss another person'") plays a more important role in sexual love.[23]

London introduces the subject of frogs on page four of his novel, noting that Dick Forrest "reached for a book entitled 'The Commercial Breeding of Frogs'" as he "prepared to eat" his breakfast. As "he ate he watched the hunting of [some] meat-eating yellow-jackets" preying upon "a number of house-flies" that clung to the screen of his porch; then he marked his place in "Commercial Breeding of Frogs" and continued with other tasks in the management of his ranch. With this scene and many references in these opening pages to Dick's successes in the breeding of livestock (for example, he smiles "with pleasure" in hearing the "throaty bawl" of a prize bull), London insinuates the Darwinian point that the nutritive and reproductive "instincts *and no others* [are] the primary basis of all animal behavior."[24] With such gestures in his opening pages, London begins to suggest the massive subsurface structure of his novel, and by the time he returns to the subject of frogs in chapter 22, the novel's underlying principles have clearly shaped the plot. The triangular affair is by now rather fully developed and Dick has begun to sense that his wife and good friend are romantically engaged. This is the scene in which Dick comments on how "sex and soul are . . . tangled together," a remark that develops from the houseguests' discussion of Mendel, the evolution of race and sex, the nature of woman, and the nature of the soul or personality. Suggesting London's interest in Freud's *The Interpretation of Dreams*, Dick asks a guest, "what is your own personality when you sleep or dream? . . . When you are in love?" Then, pursuing his point that the soul or personality "is a vague and groping thing," he adds: "Possibly the bullfrog, inflating himself on the edge of a pond and uttering hoarse croaks through the darkness to a warty mate, possesses also, at that moment, a vague and groping personality" (262–63).[25]

The point of all these speculations is to shed light on the nature of sexual attraction as it leads to Paula's selection of the second male, Graham. Paula, whom one guest regards as "the soul of beauty" (340), has numerous musical encounters with Graham, and he once thinks that her odd behavior is so much "artist-dreaming . . . a listening to the echo of the just-played music in her soul" (206). In such moments, and in the repeated scenes of music and dance, London develops the then-well-known Darwinian principle that music and dance are crucial elements in courtship. Dick is certainly aware that Graham is "a beautiful dancer," but in detailing Paula's ardent awareness of "the closeness and tenderness of contact in the dancing," London builds toward Dick's final sense that Paula's "very flesh has decided" that she prefers Graham as a lover (347, 370). In this way, London suggests that the sexual impulse in her flesh is somehow like that of the frogs Havelock Ellis remarks upon; or that in the contact of their dance or their passionate kiss, "these minimal touch excitations represent the very oldest stratum of psychic life in the soul," as Ellis remarks in his analysis of the sexual touch.[26]

Now, my purpose in the foregoing remarks on *The Little Lady of the Big House* is not to suggest that London was influenced by either Darwin or Ellis in the simplistic sense that he merely reiterated their ideas. Rather, he saw himself as a fellow explorer of the sexual terrain who was working in his own field, fiction with a new psychological intensity, and who was drawing on his own Mendelian studies and experience in selective breeding.[27] There is little question that he found many useful ideas in Ellis, for example, but neither is there any question that London's essential views on the sex problem differed significantly from Ellis's. London was far more willing to explore the human being's animal nature than was Ellis, who, while basing his whole study on Darwin's principles of evolution, insisted that "far from being animal-like, the human impulses of sex are among the least animal-like acquisitions of man."[28] And an even more important difference between London's and Ellis's views on sex is evident in London's emphasis on sexual reproduction: the way his characters Paula and Dick Forrest reflect Jack and Charmian London's disappointed hopes for children; and his intention to illuminate his characters' sexual nature by setting the novel at the ranch, where the breeding of stock is the central concern. By contrast, while Ellis certainly acknowledges that "the sexual impulse is very often associated with a strong desire for offspring," he insists that "it [the reproductive instinct] is not the sexual impulse, though intimately associated with it, and though it explains it."[29] London interweaves this theme throughout the novel, from the moment in chapter 2 when a ranch employee watches as Dick "diminished down the road" after lecturing him on how to raise his daughter; he thinks to himself, "but where's the kid of your own, Mr. Forrest?" (23). Toward the end of the novel, realizing that Paula is drawn toward the other man, Dick wanders alone through her "secret patio," where he sees the fountain in which "she kept her selected and more gorgeous blooms of [gold]fish." Noticing the fountain's rollicking "life-sized babies wrought from pink marble," and finishing a "cigarette and retaining it dead in his hand," Dick thinks, "that was what she needed . . . children" (331–32). "Diminished" and "dead" in these scenes insinuate London's evolutionary perspective, his unrelenting belief that the theory of sexual selection is the necessary foundation for any study of sexual love. Moreover, such seemingly insignificant verbal touches prepare for his conclusion, when Paula tells Dick as she is dying that she is "sorry there were no babies," and when London describes how she "*nestled* her head" on a pillow and "drew her body up in *nestling* curves" (392; emphasis added).

As these materials suggest, London's views on the evolutionary issues are clearly antagonistic to the recent and much more popular views put forth in *Creative Evolution,* where Bergson's few references to Darwin (and none at all to *The Descent of Man*) give the impression that there is no theory of sexual selection. The novel's several references to Bergson conclude with one character's assertion that Bergson "is a charlatan" whose popularity derives from his having "touched . . . up" or "rosied . . . over" the more disagreeable realities that Darwin had theorized (342–43). But beyond noting this important element in London's critique of sexual love (his adamant resistance to "the eclipse of Darwinism" during his time),[30] I want to focus on three broad, related questions that he explored in this last lengthy treatise on sex. Rising from the key problem of sexual difference that had originally led Darwin to formulate his theory of sexual selection, they are London's presentation of (1) Paula Forrest's and (2) Dick Forrest's natures as participants in "the sexual struggle" (as Darwin called it); and (3) his analysis of his three characters' psychological realities. Drawing not only on *The Descent of Man*, but also on Darwin's *The Expression of the Emotions in Man and Animals* and the Freudian theory that he had managed to take in by 1914, London wrote one of the first and most impressive "Freudian" novels in American literature.

The questions surrounding the evolution of sexual difference were of far greater interest in public discourse during London's career than readers currently tend to realize. Havelock Ellis had published *Man and Woman* in 1894, and the proliferation of further biological and psychological explorations of these issues is traceable in many of the texts London owned and marked, as well as in Ellis's continuing work on *Studies in the Psychology of Sex*. In fact, London's and Ellis's parallel interests in questions of sexual difference are evident in the August 1915 issue of *Cosmopolitan*, where Ellis's article, "Masculinism and Feminism," appears next to that month's installment of *The Little Lady of the Big House*. Although this juxtaposition of London and Ellis might seem fortuitous, it is certainly not incongruous, for both writers were self-consciously advocating forms of feminism. Referring to certain "rhetorical feminists" in his prefatory remarks, Ellis reminds his readers that "the champions of feminism have nearly as often been men as women."[31] And as a growing number of women have noted in recent years, Jack London's "feminist values" are central in "a major portion of [his] later work."[32] It is not sufficiently recognized, however, that the fundamental feminist issue London embodied in his story of Paula Forrest is her freedom to exhibit and affirm her natural—that is, her animal—sexuality.

Paula's sexual freedom was certainly the most controversial aspect of the novel and was brought into focus for public view (and outrage) in one of Howard Chandler Christy's illustrations for *Cosmopolitan*'s June installment. The illustration, of Paula clad in a swimming suit and riding the stallion Mountain Lad bareback in a large cement water "tank" at the ranch, provoked a number of complaints from readers.[33] But the illustration renders Paula's sexual animalism quite harmlessly, leaving out London's most shocking image of the modern woman's bold entry into the Darwinian arena of tangled sexuality:

> As she pressed her cheek against the great arching neck, her golden-brown hair, wet from being under, flowing and tangled, seemed tangled in the black mane of the stallion. But it was her face that smote Graham [the second man] most of all. It was a boy's face; it was a woman's face; it was serious and at the same time amused, expressing the pleasure it found woven with the peril. It was a white woman's face— and modern. (104)

Depicted in this way, Paula is a modern American woman at a historical point approximately midway between Edna Pontellier (in Kate Chopin's *The Awakening*) and Brett Ashley (in Hemingway's *The Sun Also Rises*): Edna, who, like "some beautiful, sleek, animal waking up in the sun," selected two lovers outside her marriage, and Brett, the much more defiantly androgynous and sexually aggressive woman of the jazz age who selected any number of lovers.[34]

The essential similarity in these three modern women is their selection of sexual partners mainly for the male's beauty (in Edna's case, Robert; and in Brett's, Romero). Paula, "the soul of beauty," selects Evan Graham partly because he is a "beautiful dancer" and because of the physical features that London highlights in the juxtaposed portraits of the two men when Graham arrives on the scene (340, 347). Graham is slightly taller than Dick, but it is his "grace of body and carriage," his "more . . . fulsome" and "redder" lips, and so forth, that catch Paula's eye. London hints that, while both these attractive males have "mouths . . . [that] carried the impression of girlish sweetness," Graham, as his first name (Evan) suggests, is more intriguingly androgynous than Dick, who "seemed a more efficient and formidable organism" and "dangerous" (99–100). But "organism" in this context reiterates London's point—in context of the ranch's work in selective breeding and the houseguests' several philosophical discussions of evolution and love—that Paula's power to select is related to the Darwinian analysis of sexual difference. In repeated references to her "selected" goldfish, we know that she decided "to segregate [one 'gorgeous' male] for the special breeding tank in the fountain of her own secret patio"; moreover, in charge of the horses on the ranch, she can "breed them and mold them to [her] heart's desire," and Dick remarks that *she* "is the genius" at selection (330, 90, 148, 150). Whereas he can "muddle and mull over the Mendelian Law until [he is] dizzy," she "just knows it in some witch-like, intuitional way" (150). By the end of chapter 13, then, acting on her instinctive sense, including her eye for erotic beauty, Paula selects Graham as her lover. At a swimming party in the water tank where Paula had ridden the stallion, London gives us this sequence of events:

Paula swims underwater, Graham is praised as "a real fish man" for his own prowess as a swimmer, Paula and Graham discuss the "undertow" of "unconsciousness," and London closes the chapter as the guests begin a game of tag: Paula "tagged Graham," cried "You're IT!" and "plunged into the tank." But as this relationship develops from its initial playfulness toward the darker ending when Paula kills herself, London again presents his view of the evolutionary reality in contrast to another popular interpretation of sexual love—George Bernard Shaw's comic yet serious argument for "Creative Evolution" in *Man and Superman*—by displacing Darwin's image of the sexually aggressive male with the image of woman as the sexual hunter. When one of the houseguests' discussions considers questions of love, "Madonna-worship," and "woman," one guest asks, "why is woman, in the game of love, always . . . the huntress?" provoking another to respond, "that is just some of your Shaw nonsense" (265).

Still, in a later scene of introspection, as Paula looks at herself in a mirror, she cries out, "Oh, you huntress!" and admits "that Shaw . . . might be right" (311). But London pushes this idea further than Shaw does, causing Paula to realize that she is "proud" of her own sexual allure; she relishes her power in "living, thrilling," "and having "two such men at heel" (310–11). More than what Shaw referred to as "husband-hunting," London dramatizes Paula's sexual desire for two men at once and confronts the modernists' dilemma over the conflict between promiscuity (or "free love" or polyandry) and civilized marriage.[35] London emphasizes Paula's "pleasure" in riding the stallion and in selecting the breeding stock; he further notes that Dick takes "pleasure in his wife's pleasure" in selecting stock and that his enlightened, modern couple Dick and Paula "have one magic formula: *Damn the expense when fun is selling*"—and this emphasis carries the Shavian point of the husband-hunting woman toward the deeper waters that Freud explored in *Civilization and Its Discontents* (1930).

Paula can't make Graham appreciate "how tangled" the situation is for her; and when Dick and Paula finally discuss it, she confesses her alarming self-discovery: "Shaw and the rest must be right. Women are hunting animals. You are both big game. I can't help it. . . . I want you. I want Evan" (367). Moreover, in confessing her desire for both men, Paula insists, "I am straight"; that is, London suggests that although Paula is "excited [and] feverish" in her desire, she is "not nervous" or neurotic (368, 310).

In this way London brings her natural sexual desire into the open, leaving the males to admit their own occasional sexual interest in other women but confessing, as Dick does with "a slight twinkle in his eyes," that "while you [Paula] may be polyandrously inclined, we stupid male men cannot reconcile ourselves to such a situation" (368). But it would be a mistake to conclude that London wishes to celebrate the kind of popular Freudianism that had already begun to emerge in the erroneous view that Freud encouraged promiscuity. London was aware of Freud's unhappiness over such "'Wild' Psychoanalysis," and included his own critique of it in *The Little Lady of the Big House*.[36] Early in the novel Dick tells Paula that from the commotion among the wild canaries on her patio, he thinks "some free lover is trying to break up their monogamic heaven with modern love-theories" (84); and the subject comes up more seriously in one of the houseguests' discussions when a guest asks Dick about the "boasted monogamic marriage institution of Western civilization" (271). Dick responds by explaining that, while he isn't exactly "for" free love, he can "only answer with a hackneyed truism": "There can be no love that is not free." He advocates a "complicated free love" that is not "merely [a] license of promiscuity" but a belief in both "legal marriage" and "divorce," because "man, living in society, is a most complicated animal" (271–72).

Still, Dick's philosophical outlook is no solution to the novel's triangular conflict. For that, London turns to Paula, in a way that some readers might object to, for she shoots herself. But his was no more problematic a conclusion than Kate Chopin's decision to have Edna Pontellier drown herself in *The Awakening*. Moreover, London's conclusion bestows upon Paula the full humanity that another prominent sexual theorist had denied women. Indeed, London's presentation of Paula (as well as other women in his last works) is a pointed refutation of Otto Weininger's *Sex & Character* (1906), which Jack and Charmian read and made marginal notes in together. Whereas Weininger maintained that "woman . . . is soulless," that "the Phallus . . . is her supreme lord and welcome master," and that her "unfaithfulness is an exciting game, in which the thought of morality plays no part,"[37] London arranges for Paula to agonize over the hurt she causes Dick and to end their discussion about her polyandrous tendencies by remarking (ostensibly in reference to an excursion planned for the next day), "We'll all go hunting" (372). At the end, Dick had planned to kill himself, but he hears the shot and realizes, "*She beat me to it*" (382). Her greatest act of dignity, courage, and complicated humanity is to make it clear, as she dies dressed in her hunting outfit, that she still loves both the men who have come to comfort her.

As the pivotal figure in the novel's triangle, Paula reflects the emphasis on female sexuality in many early-twentieth-century studies of "the sex problem," as in such works known to London as Weininger's *Sex & Character*, E. Heinrich Kisch's *The Sexual Life of Woman*, Ellis's *Studies* in general, and Freud's "The Case of Miss Lucy R" or "The Case of Miss Elisabeth v. R" in the volume *Selected Papers on Hysteria*. But, as a self-reflective explorer in what one authority in London's library termed the "sex enlightenment [that] runs rampant at present,"[38] London was unrelenting in his study of the male, and his portrait of Dick Forrest develops his career-long effort to restrain the male's essential "secondary sexual character" according to Darwin's analysis—his prehen-

sile power to possess the female. Dick is much more aware of his
sexual nature than was Billy Roberts in *The Valley of the Moon*,
whose gentle hands appeal to Saxon, but who still retains the
identity of a successful competitor in his skill as a boxer, and Dick
has freed himself from the sexual violence or "Red Wrath" that
caused the character Darrell Standing to die for love in *The Star
Rover* (1915). Convicted for murdering "Professor Haskell in the
laboratory at the University of California," Standing awaits his
execution and explains that he "died of love" because Haskell
"was a man. I was a man. And there was a woman beautiful."[39]
While London gives us glimpses of how, "unconsciously, Graham's hand went farther about [Paula's] shoulder," of Paula
"prisoning his eager hand in hers," and of Paula thrusting "Evan's hand away," his theme in presenting the male's essential
power in Dick is that Dick has steadfastly committed himself to a
"code" whereby "he won't compete" with Graham (319, 313).
The "most horrible spiritual suffering [he] can imagine would be
to kiss a woman who endured [his] kiss"; he cannot imagine
"holding the woman one loves a moment longer than she loves to
be held" (270). He is repulsed at the thought of laying "rough
hands on love"; and, acting on his belief that "past love . . . gives
no hold over the present," he will "not lift a hand to hold" Paula.
"My hands are tied," he tells her, "I can't put an arm to hold you"
(270, 319, 349, 370).

Dick (as a reflection of London himself) is a further development of Herbert Wace, who had also sought to rise above the sexual violence inherent in the male's "prehensile organs" (*Kempton-
Wace Letters* 171). But London's study of the sex problem between
1903 and 1915 led him to be much more self-critically introspec-
tive in *The Little Lady of the Big House* than is generally recognized.
The novel's central irony is that, despite his highly efficient management of sexual energy on the ranch (through selective breeding of his stock or the control he has over his workers' lives), Dick

cannot control the sexual entanglements in his own household. This theme runs throughout the novel, from the opening words, "He awoke in the dark," to his confession to Paula toward the end that, as a result of the affair and the discovery of his unexpected jealousy, he had come to laugh "all the books and all biology in the face" (363). Although he had sensed their growing intimacy, the shock of seeing Paula's "flash of quick passion" as she kissed Graham brought him "flat [to] the pavement" with a sense of "violent suffocation"; and he began to realize that "all I have learned of books and theory goes glimmering" (351, 366). That is, this "efficiency-expert" in selective breeding of prize livestock, who prides himself in the ranch house that "defied earthquakes" and where "every fence was hog-tight and bull-proof" (13, 16); he who celebrates "fecundity!" and tiresomely but ironically repeats his performance of the stallion's song, chanting "with mane tossing and foot-pawing," "Hear me! I am Eros! I stamp upon the hills" (228, 275); he who admits that experiments might work "out splendidly on paper, with decently wide margins for human nature" and still not avoid "the doubt and the danger [of] human nature" (287)—even Dick, with his considerable knowledge of the sexual tangle, will be struck down in witnessing his wife's sexual passion for another man and in feeling the sexual jealousy and possessiveness that he had denied. Whereas the novel opens with Dick having awakened in the dark to "smile with pleasure" in hearing "the distant, throaty bawl of [his prize bull] King Polo," London ends his last two chapters with Dick's life in ruins as he listens "to all the whinnying and nickering and bawling of sex" on his ranch, including "the trumpeting of Mountain Lad and the silver whinny of the Fotherington Princess" (377, 392).

In his first novel on the sex problem London was well aware of the "subconscious processes" of sexual selection (*Daughter of the Snows* 88). He was certainly not the first American novelist to probe what Howells had called "those fastnesses of [the male's] nature which psychology has not yet explored."[40] But between 1902 and late 1914, when he completed *The Little Lady of the Big House*, Sigmund Freud and others had deepened and complicated the exploration of the unconscious. London was of course intensely interested in these developments and was attempting to keep abreast of them as a contributing worker in his own field.[41] But while Freud's debt to Darwin was becoming somewhat less visible during these years (when he became a "crypto-biologist" even as his "psychoanalytic theories became *more* biological"[42]), London's growing interest in psychoanalysis clearly reinforced the biological—that is, Darwinian—issues he had begun to address in 1902. His characters are now more than ever exposed to the reproductive instincts that earlier characters had managed rather successfully in their civilized lives, through scientific self-knowledge or sublimation. However, London's latest characters are not troubled by the hysteria or neurosis that would result, as Freud was emphasizing during these years, from the repression of the sexual instincts. Even in *The Valley of the Moon*, where hysteria had victimized the more sexually repressed women, it proved to be a relatively minor obstacle in London's effort to free Saxon Brown's natural sexuality. Because the houseguests talk quite openly of promiscuity and free love in the much more modern and intensely psychological *The Little Lady of the Big House*, the threat of hysteria or neurosis seems beside the point. Working perhaps with Freud's observation that "in the normal vita sexualis no neurosis is possible," London writes that "the young people ragged and tangoed incessantly" and that, in general, "the free and easy life of the Big House went on in its frictionless way" (230, 210–11).[43]

The problem for these modern characters is in acknowledging, acting upon, and coming to terms with the instinctive forces that reside in Paula's "secret patio" and that Dick has hidden from himself by his scientific study of sex, as London suggests in references to Dick's "book-concealed" stairway or the "concealed lighting" in his bedroom (330, 177, 2). Of course these forces prevail, causing Paula to confront and affirm her naturally aggressive sexual desire and Dick to reconsider "the bawling of sex" that now rings in his ears beyond his conscious control. Clearly, London's ultimate psychological purpose here is to expose the underlying chaotic energy of the sexual life, but it is less clear that in doing so he develops two somewhat different Freudian points: that Dick Forrest's conscious, scientific study and application of Darwinian and Mendelian principles do not prepare him for what London calls "the undertow" of sexual disruption in his own life, and that each of the three players is engaged in reading the emotions expressed by the others and in concealing his or her own.[44]

The Dick Forrest who at the beginning of the novel is "the center of a system which he himself had built and of which he was secretly very proud," including a house that "defied earthquakes," is nonetheless subject to the unconscious forces that leave him "with his love-world crashing around him" (35, 13, 375). Developing this (largely self-analytical) critique, London arranges for a guest to remark on how Dick is more "cocksure" in his evolutionary theory than Bergson (343), and he interweaves the language of Darwinian selection and the Freudian unconscious in a number of scenes, as when tracing Dick's thoughts after he had advised his sister-in-law on her own sex life: "turning off lights as he went, [he] penetrated the library, and while selecting half a dozen volumes on mechanics and physics, smiled as if pleased with himself" at the advice he had offered. "But, halfway up the book-concealed spiral staircase that led to his work room," he is suddenly stopped in his tracks and forced "to lean his shoulder against the wall." A remark she had made produced "an echoing in his consciousness" that made him think of Paula's possible interest in Graham (177).

In an even more significantly Freudian scene of Dick's conscious mind attempting to conceal from itself a disturbing underlying thought, London describes Dick's visit late in the novel to Paula's "secret patio." Here in the "fountain pools [where] she kept her selected and more gorgeous blooms of fish," Dick "glanced into the bathroom with its sunken Roman bath." London notes that Dick's response to this obvious suggestion of Paula's "sunken" sexual pleasure is that, "for the life of him he was unable to avoid seeing a tiny drip and making a mental note for the ranch plumber" (332). Further, when Dick notices the "pink marble" "human babies" that "rollicked and frolicked" in the fountain, thinking "that was what she needed . . . children," London suggests that, while Dick's sense of the fecund origins of sexual desire is true, it nevertheless shields him from the darker truth of Paula's sexual desire. As London's earlier references to the breeding of frogs suggests that the sexual motive is indeed alive in Paula's "flesh," here he extends that idea to include Freud's highly disturbing analysis of "the constitutional sexual predisposition of the child," which Freud regarded as being so "irregularly multifarious" that "it deserves to be called 'polymorphous perverse.'" Insights like this (from page 191 of the text London owned, *Selected Papers on Hysteria*, and from other passages he later marked in *Three Contributions to the Theory of Sex*) are reflected in London's description of the "alive warm human babies" in Paula's fountain, one of whom "reached arms covetously toward the goldfish," while another "on his back laughed at the sky [and yet] another stood with dimpled legs apart stretching himself" (331).

But the "Freudian" point that proved most useful to London in this novel is the one with which he was probably already familiar, from Darwin's *The Expression of the Emotions in Man and Animals*, the text that Freud had also found so helpful in preparing his *Studies on Hysteria* in 1895.[45] In *Darwin's Influence on Freud*, Lucille B.

Ritvo shows that "Freud [was] obviously well acquainted with [the] principles" Darwin had set forth and explains that he "extended the study of the expressions of the emotions to include hysterical symptoms and verbal expressions" (179, 191). Ritvo notes, for example, that certain "striking motor phenomena exhibited" by one of his patients "reminded Freud 'forcibly of one of the principles laid down by Darwin to explain the expression of the emotions—the principle of the overflow of excitation . . . which accounts, for instance, for dogs wagging their tails.' "[46]

Throughout *The Little Lady of the Big House*, but with increased intensity in the last half, as the triangular drama develops, London focuses his energy on tracing (1) the characters' inadvertent expressions of their own emotions, and their heightened interest in reading the emotions expressed by the other players, and (2) their consequent interest in concealing their emotions from the others. As these characters express, read, and conceal their emotions, then, they reveal something of the behavior of Freud's "patients" (in a passage that London marked) who, when "aware of the sexual origin of their obsessions . . . often conceal them"—except, as I have suggested, that London insists that his characters are normal rather than hysterical or neurotic.[47] Thus, as London's characters play out the psychological drama, seeking to realize their normal but conflicting sexual motives, they reveal his more pressing interest in the *foundations* of Freud's theory of the emotions—Darwin's point that "expression" is a "branch of natural history" and that "under a keen sense of shame" especially, "there is a strong desire for concealment."[48]

At an early point in the drama of expression between Paula and Graham, London positions Paula "at the piano," obviously drawing on the power of music in courtship that Darwin analyzed in both *The Descent of Man* and *The Expression of the Emotions*.[49] London writes:

As [Graham] approached he caught the quick expression
of pleasure in her eyes at the sight of him, which as quickly
vanished. She made a slight movement as if to rise, which did
not escape his notice any more than did her quiet mastery of
the impulse that left her seated.

She was immediately herself as he had always seen her.
(211)

It is worth noting that while London's reference to Paula's "pleasure" gives the scene a Freudian touch, it nevertheless remains
within the realm of Darwin's analysis of the emotions expressed
by lovers—that "with the lower animals we see the same principle of pleasure derived from contact in association with love."[50]
And as the triangular drama develops, London gives us such
scenes as the following, which serves as a prelude to Dick's remark—in the houseguests' discussion of evolution and woman—
that "sex and soul are all interwoven and tangled together" (263).
In the early stages of this discussion, London focuses on his three
players:

To look at Dick's face it would have been unguessed that he
was aught but a carefree, happy arguer. Nor did Graham,
nor did Paula, Dick's dozen years' wife, dream that his casual
careless glances were missing no movement of a hand, no
change of position on a chair, no shade of expression on their
faces.

What's up? was Dick's secret interrogation. Paula's not
herself. She's positively nervous, and all the discussion is
responsible. And Graham's off color. His brain isn't working
up to mark. He's thinking about something else, rather than
about what he is saying. What is that something else?

And the devil of speech behind which Dick hid his secret
thoughts impelled him to urge the talk wider and wilder.
(260)

Throughout the last half of the novel, then, London heightens his drama of the expression and concealment of emotions, mostly from Dick's point of view. Once, for example, he searches Paula's face and eyes for "the effect of the impact" of his own seemingly innocent remarks and finds "Graham's face . . . expressionless insofar as there was no apparent change of the expression of interest that had been there" (267). In later scenes, London notes that "Dick knew her too long in all the expressions of her moods not to realize the significance of her singing" as she moves through the house; and that he "had not failed to observe the flutter of alarm that shadowed her eyes so swiftly, and that so swiftly was gone" (285, 290). In a final example of such scenes, one of London's most memorable, he dramatizes how Dick's self-confidence in concealing his own emotions is shaken in a moment of accidental introspection. Walking through Paula's studio, he finds that "a portrait of himself confronted him." Paula had been painting it from a photograph, and London again suggests his interest in Darwin's discussion of emotions by bringing out one of the emotions that Darwin had noted in particular, Dick's "start" in noticing a difference between Paula's painting and the photograph:

> With a start he looked more closely. Was that expression of the eyes, of the whole face, his? He glanced at the photograph. It was not there. He walked over to one of the mirrors, relaxed his face, and led his thoughts to Paula and Graham. Slowly the expression came into his eyes and face. Not content, he returned to the easel and verified it. Paula knew. Paula knew he knew. She had learned it from him, stolen it from him some time when it was unwittingly on his face, and carried it in her memory to the canvas. (333)

Indeed, it is fair to say that in this highly self-reflective novel, London had discovered a new, deeper subject matter that would have enriched his fiction had he lived further into the Freudian era to produce it—the sense, as Dick remarks to himself at this point, that "it would seem that all our faces are beginning to say new things" (334). London did live to produce two memorable brief explorations of this new territory in 1916, "The Red One" and "The Kanaka Surf," and he "mapped out a new novel [*The Eternal Enemy*] that is on sex, and on sex with such a vengeance that I fear The Cosmopolitan will have to prune some of the sex out of it" (*Letters* 1553).[51] But the question to be addressed here, in closing, is what possible *solutions* to the "sex problem" does London offer in *The Little Lady of the Big House*, for this is the constant goal in his career-long exploration of sex, as in his experimental farming. In this way, too, London resembles Dick Forrest, who remarks early in the novel that he would undertake "post-graduate courses in the College of Agriculture" because "I want to do something. . . . something constructive" (73).

To begin, London's most important general point in the novel is that, in those years when Darwinism was being eclipsed by any number of "anti-Darwinian evolutionary theories," only a Darwinian view of life—and emphatically not a Bergsonian one—will enable us to understand that there *is* a sex problem and that it is rooted in the entangled reality that Darwin had presented in his theories of natural selection and sexual selection.[52] Darwin's analysis of the expression of the emotions, Freud's development and transformation of this insight in his psychoanalysis, and work in the new field of sexology, most notably in Havelock Ellis's *Studies in the Psychology of Sex*: all these converged to underscore and deepen the Darwinian view that London had always championed, as in his tribute to Darwin's achievement "at the conclusion of his 'Origin of Species'" (*Kempton-Wace* 177). As I have suggested throughout this piece, London's orientation kept him aware of this development in the theory of sexuality: that, as Frank Sulloway writes, "within the nascent sexology movement —itself largely inspired by Darwinism—virtually every important aspect of Freud's own theory of psychosexual development can be found." In London's masterpiece on the sex problem, discussions of selective breeding and Mendelian genetics are interwoven throughout the novel's extensive dramatic representations of (1) the theory of sexual selection at work, (2) the expression and concealment of emotions, (3) the "undertow" of the subconscious, and (4) the conscious mind concealing the unconscious. Composing this landmark novel, London saw more clearly than any other American novelist of his generation that, "in proper historical perspective, Freud's theory of mind is the embodiment of a scientific age imbued with the rising tide of Darwinism."[53]

As for London's *solutions* to the sex problem, his implicit first principle is certainly to welcome continued scientific, psychoanalytical, and fictional exploration in the field, in the face of growing hostility among readers who were offended by Ellis, Freud, or, for example, D. H. Lawrence. Beyond this he suggests, rather tentatively, a number of more specific possibilities that can be singled out as threads in his larger tapestry of sex. First, to trace a line of thought that seems to run from Darwin through Freud's later writings (well beyond London's career), London maintains, as did Freud, that "the evolution of civilization [is] primarily at the expense of free sexual expression."[54] That is, in *The Little Lády of the Big House* he suggests that, while the sexual impulse is undeniably chaotic and entangled by nature, to the point of being "polymorphously perverse," both the male and female are obliged to practice self-restraint, through a "code" like Dick's refusal to "lay rough hands on love," or even Paula's, as she finally "solved" "the triangle" (270, 320). Dick enforces this system of values in managing his personnel on the ranch—when he fired a man who was having an affair with another man's wife: "Smith had a perfect right to love the woman, and to be loved by her if it came to that," but "he had no right to hurt the group of individuals in which he lives" (319). A second suggested solution to the sex problem as manifested in the relationship between Paula and Dick is rather more in line with Havelock Ellis's views on the "art" of love or the kind of advice that the character Mercedes gives Saxon Roberts in *The Valley of the Moon*. Saxon already knows that "the pre-nuptial problem of selecting a husband" leads to "the post-nuptial problem of retaining a husband's love," and Mercedes helps her solve this problem by teaching her how to work with her "pretties" or "dainties" to keep her husband's sexual "appetite knife-edged and never satisfied" (145, 142–43). In *The Little Lady of the Big House*, however, London extends this obligation to the male as well, showing repeatedly that Dick is too preoccupied with his work to pay adequate attention to Paula. Once, for example, London writes that, "having tasted the pleasure of knowing [Paula] to be awake, Dick, as usual, forgot her in his own affairs" (82).

But more importantly, London interweaves the suggestion of a final, visionary solution that best characterizes his unique, career-long approach to the sex problem in its larger evolutionary context. Always interested in ethnology and the evolution of race, London had begun in recent years to develop a critique of American civilization (or what he called "the Great White Way") by suggesting that it could renew itself by incorporating the wisdom of the "old Chinese," for example, or "other old and . . . dark-eyed foreign breed[s]," as in the methods of "intensive cultivation" that his hero and heroine learn in *The Valley of the Moon* (331).[55] One aspect of this dark-skinned or primitive wisdom in *The Valley of the Moon* is the knowledge of sexual love that Saxon acquires from Mercedes. London's imagining this sort of earth-wisdom is an important, early expression of sexual primitivism that arose in the first years of Freudian fiction, wherein the over-civilized or neurotic whites are freed from their sexual inhibitions by exposure to the supposedly less inhibited lifestyles of "primitive" folk, such as the black people in Sherwood Anderson's *Dark*

Laughter. London's own efforts to court the subconscious or the "primitive" mind were sparked during these years when, in 1911, the Yahi Indian Ishi, "the last wild man in North America," walked into the "civilized" world of Northern California. As Charles L. Crow has recently noted, London "sensed an identity with Ishi," but the sexual possibilities of this encounter in London's imagination are clear only in relation to the larger questions in the evolution of sex and civilization that London was exploring.[56] London certainly did not see Ishi in the image of the promiscuous black people that Sherwood Anderson would help to popularize. Rather, in reading of Ishi's tribe in Stephen Powers's *Tribes of California*, London focused on the character of Red Cloud, whose "Acorn Song" he brings into *The Little Lady of the Big House* repeatedly, and subsequently, of course, in *The Acorn-Planter: A California Forest Play* (1916).[57] In *The Little Lady of the Big House* the song appears first toward the end of a section that traces the young Dick's education, representing the culminating wisdom that leads to his present agricultural project. London presents the song exactly as inscribed in *Tribes of California*:

> The acorns come down from heaven!
> I plant the short acorns in the valley!
> I plant the long acorns in the valley!
> I sprout, I, the black-oak acorn, sprout, I sprout! (78)

But as the novel develops, this song of the fecund world competes with another that Dick now prefers to perform, the song of the stallion Mountain Lad, which begins, "Hear me! I am Eros! I stamp upon the hills!" London emphasizes that these two songs of fecundity define a deep conflict between Paula and Dick. When we see Dick first performing it for Paula, London notes that "for a flash of an instant . . . Paula knew resentment of her husband's admiration for the splendid beast," and she immediately asks that he sing "The Song of the Acorn" (85–86). This kind of scene becomes tiresome in the novel, even though Dick's performances for the houseguests are carried off with a saving degree of comic self-consciousness. But London's serious purpose is to suggest that Dick's "mutinous" performances of the stallion's song represent an aspect of his overbearing scientific mind that is related to the sexual violence of the Darwinian male. While Dick is repelled at the idea of forceful love, of "holding" Paula or causing her to "endure" his kiss, London suggests again and again that, in his intensely scientific approach to agriculture and life, Dick unknowingly wields the "secondary sexual character" evolved for sexual combat that Darwin had described in male birds, the spurs. We first see Dick's spurs on the stairway that is hidden behind his "book-freighted" shelves: "he descended with care that his spurs might not catch" (11). Among many later examples of London's work in developing this pattern of imagery, we see Dick "stamping with jingling spurs through the Big House in quest of its Little Lady" (97). And the connection between the two songs and the idea of the male's spurs is evident in such moments as this one, late in the novel, when, at one of the parties, Paula requests, "now, Red Cloud, the Song of the Acorn. . . . Put down your glass, and be good, and plant acorns"; but Dick "stood up, shaking his head mutinously, as if tossing a mane, and stamping ponderously in simulation of Mountain Lad" (274–75).

With this pattern of imagery in the novel (echoing his earlier suggestion about Saxon's being like a "squaw" in *Valley of the Moon*), London suggests that in the agricultural origins of North American civilization, as figured in the "Song of the Acorn," a gentler kind of masculinity existed that could guide his modern Californians toward an enduring solution to the sex problem. The conflict between the "Song of the Acorn" and Mountain Lad's song of "Eros!" is resolved on Paula's deathbed, when she asks Dick, whom she calls "Red Cloud," to sing "the song of Aikut, and of the Dew-Woman" (389). In the passages from *Tribes of*

California that London marked, noting, for example, "Ishi's tribe" and "Nishinam Adam & Eve" (in reference to lines about "Ai-kut . . . the first man"), London might have seen Powers's remark that "the California Indians anticipated Darwin by some centuries in the development theory, only substituting the coyote for the monkey."[58] If he did, London would have smiled at Powers's romantic claim for the Indians and his simplistic representation of Darwinian theory, but London was certainly reading the California Indians with an awareness that ethnology, sexology, and psychoanalysis were linked in "a scientific age imbued with the rising tide of Darwinism."[59]

More specifically, it seems, London was self-consciously projecting his own version of a feminist effort to solve the "sex problem" that was known to some Europeans as "the American Cult of Woman." As Ellis noted in his *Cosmopolitan* article on "Masculinism and Feminism," one German writer was especially "appalled by what he sees in the United States. To him it is 'the American danger,' and he thinks it may be traced partly to the influence of the matriarchal system of the American Indians on the early European invaders."[60] But, right up to the end of *The Little Lady of the Big House* London dramatized his own sense of how our culture might realize his feminist vision. It would require that we recognize both the male's and female's nature as hunters in the general "bawl" of sex. Also it requires a faith equal to London's own lifelong belief in Darwin's essential principle in the theory of sexual selection, the female's power to select and thereby exert a degree of control over the evolutionary future. As in his memorable tribute to Darwin's conclusion to the *Origin of Species* (in *The Kempton-Wace Letters*), London's career-long study of the sex problem shares Darwin's sense at the end of *The Descent of Man* that he knew "no fact in natural history more wonderful than that the female Argus pheasant should be able to appreciate the exquisite shading of the ball-and-socket ornaments and the elegant patterns of the wing-feathers of the male."[61] Even as World War I had begun to produce the sense of desolation that would emerge as the Waste Land or F. Scott Fitzgerald's sense that it had been "the last love battle,"[62] London found reason to affirm Paula's sense of beauty, hoping perhaps that, as "the male Argus Pheasant [had] acquired his beauty gradually, through the females having preferred [the more beautiful males] during many generations," even the human community might find a better way.[63] One cannot mistake London's concluding image in *The Little Lady of the Big House* as more than a muted hope. It is far less promising than Saxon Brown's agrarian "vision" in *The Valley of the Moon* or that novel's concluding image of the "doe and a spotted fawn" glimpsed through "a tiny open space between the trees." But Jack London closed his darkest and most highly complicated exploration of the "bawl" of sex with "the silver whinny of the Fotherington Princess."

NOTES

1. London to Edward Carpenter, 2 March 1914, quoted in David Mike Hamilton, *"The Tools of My Trade": The Annotated Books in Jack London's Library* (Seattle: University of Washington Press, 1985), 83; London to Maurice Magnus, 23 October 1911, in *The Letters of Jack London*, 3 vols., ed. Earle Labor, Robert C. Leitz III, and I. Milo Shepard (Stanford, Calif.: Stanford University Press, 1988), 1042.

2. Havelock Ellis, *Studies in the Psychology of Sex*, 2 vols. (New York: Random House, 1936) 1:xxx. This quote is from Ellis's 1897 preface. In subsequent references to these volumes, I cite first the volume and then the particular "book" in the volume, followed by the page number. Note that this is a different method from that which the set itself uses in its confusing "cumulative indexes" at the end of volume 2.

3. For an analysis of this development in American literature, see my *The Descent of Love: Darwin and the Theory of Sexual Selection in American Fiction, 1871–1926* (Philadelphia: University of Pennsylvania Press, 1996).

4. Emphasis added; Charles Darwin, *On the Origin of Species by Means of Natural*

Selection, Or the Preservation of Favoured Races in the Struggle for Life (1859); *A Facsimile of the First Edition* (Cambridge, Mass.: Harvard University Press, 1966), 208.

5. "Agrarian vision" is Earle Labor's term in "From 'All Gold Canyon' to *The Acorn-Planter*: Jack London's Agrarian Vision," *Western American Literature* 11 (summer 1976): 83–101. This is certainly a major contribution to Jack London studies, but Labor does not deal with the sex problem. The quotation about the "rape of the land" is from a line spoken by a stand-in for London, a character named Hastings, in *The Valley of the Moon* (New York: Grosset & Dunlap, 1913), 434. Further references cited in text.

6. It is worth noting that in taking this approach to London, I strongly disagree with a number of recent critics who imply that whatever London himself might have thought and studied about sex is irrelevant. To one theorist, for example, "the philosophical import" or "conceptual content" of dramatized conversations in London's novels is "far less interesting than . . . the heated passions motivating the exchange of ideas" (Jonathan Auerbach, *Male Call: Becoming Jack London* [Durham, N.C.: Duke University Press, 1996], 222).

7. Jack London, *A Daughter of the Snows* (New York: Grosset & Dunlap, 1902), 86.

8. Charles Darwin, *The Descent of Man* (London: J. Murray, 1871), 1:207.

9. Jonathan Auerbach's analysis of London's homoeroticism, for example, suffers from his apparent ignorance of or disregard for this development in the study of sex, which in many ways tended to normalize bisexuality. For an excellent discussion of this subject, see Frank J. Sulloway, *Freud, Biologist of the Mind: Beyond the Psychoanalytic Legend* (New York: Basic Books, 1979), especially chapter 8, "Freud and the Sexologists."

10. For a brief overview of these issues and how they figured in American fiction at around the turn of the century, see *The Descent of Love*, 9–30.

11. Jack London and Anna Strunsky, *The Kempton-Wace Letters* (New York: Macmillan, 1903; reprint, New York: Haskell House, n.d.), 66, 68, 177, 241–42. Further references cited in text.

12. *Martin Eden* (New York: Macmillan, 1909; reprint, New York: Penguin, 1985), 455. Further references cited in text.

13. Ellis, 1:3:3, 6.

14. *Letters*, 1135. Further references cited in text.

15. Jack London, *The Little Lady of the Big House* (New York: Macmillan, 1916), 118–19. Further references cited in text.

16. For a brief overview of the way many writers reiterated Darwin's famous image of the "entangled bank" (in the concluding paragraph of the *Origin of Species*,

to which London had paid tribute in *The Kempton-Wace Letters*), see *The Descent of Love*, 17–18, and other passages indexed under "entangled life."

17. Edwin B. Holt, *The Freudian Wish and Its Place in Ethics* (New York: Henry Holt Co., 1916), 48–49.

18. The remarks on "gropings" and "darknesses," and on Bergson are London's in *The Little Lady of the Big House* (263, 244–45); for a discussion of Aiken's *Great Circle* in this light, including a character's complaint "What the hell's the difference between the soul and the subconscious and the unconscious and the will?," see Frederick J. Hoffman, *Freudianism and the Literary Mind* (Baton Rouge: Louisiana State University Press, 1945), 281–82.

19. Holt, 62–63.

20. Ellis, 1:3:5.

21. Ibid., 1:2:1.

22. Ibid., 1:2:16.

23. Ibid., 1:2:4; 1:2:21.

24. Sulloway, 252.

25. Also in this passage on the "fog and mist . . . [and] mystery" of personality, Dick notes that "there are seeming men with the personalities of women [and that] there are plural personalities"—perhaps indicating his (or London's) interest in the subject then much discussed in both evolutionary and Freudian theory of the human embryo's hermaphroditic nature, as I suggest in note 9 above.

26. Ellis, 1:3:12.

27. This point, which I cannot emphasize too strongly, is further suggested in an exchange between London and Upton Sinclair on the related subject of physical culture. London wrote to Sinclair on 17 July 1910, "Yes, I've been reading your 'Physical Culture' articles. But I have theories of my own. I'll expound 'em to you some day" (*Letters*, 909).

28. Ellis, 2:3:130.

29. *Studies* 1:2:20; one of Ellis's reasons for making this distinction is to free his subject from criticisms of "those who are unconsciously dominated by a superstitious repugnance of sex" and want to restrict sexual relationships to the reproductive purpose and thereby "veil the facts of sexual life."

30. In *The Eclipse of Darwinism: Anti-Darwinian Evolution Theories in the Decades Around 1900* (Baltimore: Johns Hopkins University Press, 1983), Peter J. Bowler discusses Bergson's part in the eclipse.

31. Havelock Ellis, "Masculinism and Feminism," *Cosmopolitan*, August 1915, 316.

32. Jeanne Campbell Reesman, "London's New Woman in a New World: Saxon Brown Roberts's Journey Into the Valley of the Moon," *American Literary Realism* 24 (winter 1991): 41. Imagining that her readers might respond, "WHAT?! Jack London a *feminist?!*," Reesman writes against "typecasting [of London] as a writer of boys' books and machismo survival epics." See also Reesman's remarks that "although Clarice Stasz and Tavernier-Courbin, among others, have explored London's views on women as remarkably ahead of his time, the subject has generally been ignored" ("Irony and Feminism in *The Little Lady of the Big House*," *Thalia* 12 [1992]: 34).

33. *Letters,* 1471, 1526. See also London's letter to the editor of *Atlantic Monthly,* complaining of a columnist's (Wilson Follett, though London didn't know his name) remarks not about the serial illustrations but the novel's "erotomania," "ingrowing concupiscence," and "perverted gusto" (*Letters,* 1594; *Atlantic Monthly,* October 1916, 495).

34. This passage is from chapter 23 of *The Awakening*; discussions of Edna and Brett are indexed in Bender, *The Descent of Love.*

35. For Shaw's retrospective view of his choice to leave the subject of "clandestine adultery" to others because it is "the dullest of all subjects," and his decision to treat other aspects of sexuality such as "husband-hunting" as part of "the conception of Creative Evolution," see his "My Own Part in the Matter," in *Back to Methuselah: A Metabiological Pentateuch* (New York: Brentano's, 1921), xcviii. The difference between London's and Shaw's approach to these matters is suggested in Barbara Bellow Watson's remark that "in all [of Shaw's] plays, even though they are problem plays, sex is never a problem" (*A Shavian Guide to Intelligent Women* [London: Chatto & Windus, 1964], 133).

36. London owned and made marginal notes in a copy of Freud's *Selected Papers on Hysteria and Other Psychoneuroses* (New York: The Journal of Nervous and Mental Disease Publishing Company, 1912), chapter 12 of which is "Concerning 'Wild' Psychoanalysis"; there Freud complains of the physician's "popular sense" of what the "'sexual life' means—namely, that under sexual demands nothing else is understood except the need for coitus or its analogy, the process causing the orgasm or the ejaculation of the sexual product" (202).

37. Otto Weininger, *Sex & Character* (New York: G. P. Putnam's Sons, 1906), 213, 299, 221. London was not the only writer of his generation to study Weininger. Discussions of Gertrude Stein's odd enthusiasm for Weininger in her plans for *The Making of Americans* are indexed in Linda Wagner-Martin, *"Favored Strangers": Gertrude Stein and Her Family* (New Brunswick: Rutgers University Press, 1995),

and Brenda Wineapple, *Sister Brother: Gertrude and Leo Stein* (New York: Putnam, 1996).

38. Bernard S. Talmey, *Love: A Treatise on the Science of Sex-Attraction for the Use of Physicians and Students of Medical Jurisprudence* (New York: Practitioners', 1916), 11.

39. Jack London, *The Star Rover* (New York: Macmillan, 1915), 290.

40. William Dean Howells, *A Modern Instance* (Boston: J. Osgood & Co., 1882), 40.

41. Many of London's books on sex are listed in Hamilton's "*The Tools of My Trade,*" but this excellent volume does not include many volumes on sex that London owned, such as Albert Moll, *The Sexual Life of the Child* (New York: Macmillan, 1912), which the Huntington Library card catalog shows that London owned, or, more importantly, any volumes by Havelock Ellis. In addition to London's reference to Freud in "The Kanaka Surf" (1916), several other references are indexed in *Letters*.

42. Sulloway, 391; in his chapter 12, especially ("Freud as Crypto-Biologist: The Politics of Scientific Independence"), Sulloway explains this development in Freud's career. The idea that Freud's theories became *more* biological throughout his career seems reflected in Lucille B. Ritvo's study of Darwin and Freud as well, where her "Appendix A" ("Freud's References to Darwin") records an increasing number of references to Darwin after 1912 (*Darwin's Influence on Freud: A Tale of Two Sciences* [New Haven: Yale University Press, 1990]).

43. Freud, *Selected Papers on Hysteria*, 188.

44. As noted earlier, in her conversation with Graham in chapter 13, Paula talks of "the entangling currents" of thought that she can escape by not "fighting" the "undertow" of her "unconsciousness" (152–53). A similar passage occurs in "The Kanaka Surf," when the man and woman are actually swimming in the ocean and the man advises her to "make yourself slack—slack in your mind"; this story opens with the narrator's reference to Freud's point that "where sex is involved," people "are prone sincerely to substitute one thing for another," and so forth (Jack London, *The Complete Short Stories*, 3 vols., ed. Earle Labor, Robert C. Leitz III, and I. Milo Shepard [Stanford, Calif.: Stanford University Press, 1993], 2417, 2396).

45. I know of no references by London to *The Expression of the Emotions*, but according to the card catalog of his library at the Huntington Library, he owned the 18-volume Appleton set of Darwin's works; and in Hamilton's "Appendix" to "*The Tools of My Trade,*" London's library, as catalogued by Beatrice Barrington Ragnor, contained "9 books" by Darwin in case 31, and 5 in case 32. A good deal of Freud's *Studies on Hysteria* is reflected in the existing, marked volume in London's library

at the Huntington, *Selected Papers on Hysteria and Other Psychoneuroses.* Darwin's influential work was of interest to many psychologists during these years, including William James, for example, whose index to *The Principles of Psychology* shows several references to *The Expression of Emotions.* I know only (from Hamilton) that London owned *The Varieties of Religious Experience* and *The Will to Believe.*

46. Ritvo, 184.

47. Freud, *Selected Papers on Hysteria,* 127.

48. Charles Darwin, *The Expression of the Emotions in Man and Animals* (Chicago: University of Chicago Press, 1965), 12, 320.

49. Darwin, *Descent,* 2:333–37; *Expression,* 217.

50. Darwin, *Expression,* 213.

51. This letter to Edgar G. Sisson, dated 12 June 1916, was written from Hawaii, where, less than a month before, London had finished "The Red One." As one critic has noted, "The Kanaka Surf," in which London refers to Freud, is in some ways a "miniature" of *The Little Lady of the Big House* (Howard Lachtman, "Man and Superwoman in Jack London's 'The Kanaka Surf,'" *Western American Literature* 7 [summer 1972]: 101–10). But in the rather voluminous commentary on "The Red One," it has not been remarked that the story's main character, a naturalist named Bassett, bears a resemblance to Dick Forrest—in the way his scientific expertise regarding "the cosmic variety of sex" and his certainty about "the psychological simplicities" of the people he meets at Guadalcanal fail to prepare him for his own encounter with "the grotesque, female hideousness" of an "unthinkably disgusting bushwoman" (*Complete Stories,* 2307). London resolves this scientist's confrontation with the unconscious by beheading him.

52. For an excellent study of these developments in evolutionary thought, see Bowler.

53. Sulloway, 276, 497.

54. Ibid., 391.

55. London's remark on the Great White Way is in a letter to George P. Brett dated 30 May 1911 (*Letters,* 1008).

56. Charles L. Crow, "Ishi and Jack London's Primitives," in *Rereading Jack London,* ed. Leonard Cassuto and Jeanne Campbell Reesman (Stanford, Calif.: Stanford University Press, 1996), 47, 53.

57. Stephen Powers, *Tribes of California* (Washington, D.C.: Government Printing Office, 1977), 308.

58. Ibid., 339.

59. Sulloway, 497.

60. Ellis, "Masculinism and Feminism," 317.

61. Darwin, *Descent*, 2:400–401.

62. F. Scott Fitzgerald, *Tender is the Night* (New York: Scribner's, 1962), 68; as Dick Diver surveys a battlefield on the western front, he remarks, "Why this was a love battle—there was a century of middle-class love spent here. This was the last love battle."

63. Darwin, *Descent*, 2:401.

DONNA M. CAMPBELL

"The (American) Muse's Tragedy"

Jack London,
Edith Wharton, and
The Little Lady of the Big House

WHEN CONSIDERING probable influences on the work of Western writer Jack London, the name of expatriate writer Edith Wharton is scarcely among the first to come to mind. Her background of wealth and social privilege, like her sophisticated Old New York milieu, contrasts sharply with his early poverty, socialist beliefs, and West Coast bohemianism. Yet the biographical similarities are somewhat surprising. Each was largely self-educated through voracious and comprehensive reading, not only in contemporary literature but also in philosophy, biology, psychology, and other disciplines; and both were profoundly influenced by Haeckel, Spencer, and Darwin. Both authors also won popular and critical acclaim early, earning a comfortable income from a disciplined, practical approach to their daily production of texts, only to see their later works denigrated as their critical reputations declined.

In their writings, both authors addressed subjects as varied as Taylorism and mechanization, the writing of fiction, and house construction and decoration. For example, Wharton's first book was *The Decoration of Houses* (1897), and she, like London, was asked by Herbert Stone, the publisher of *House Beautiful*, to contribute to a series on "My Castle in Spain" in which London's essay "The House Beautiful" appeared in 1907.[1] Further, during the first decade of the twentieth century, they published in the same periodicals, their stories often appearing in *The Atlantic Monthly*, the *Century*, *Ainselee's*, *Collier's*, and *The Youth's Companion* within a few weeks of each other. London's "Pluck and Pertinacity," for instance, appeared in *The Youth's Companion* on 4 January 1900, sixteen days before Wharton's "April Showers" was published in the same magazine. To see the beginning of Jack London's professional authorship in light of Wharton's, then, is appropriate even if there were no further connection.

A further connection, however, does emerge in London's hitherto unexamined response to Wharton, especially as he expresses it in a discussion of her stories, particularly "The Muse's Tragedy," in four letters written between February 1899 and February 1900 to his then-new correspondent Cloudesley Johns. In addition, some of London's "society" fiction of the period, especially a short story written in May 1899, "Their Alcove," suggests his experimentation with the Wharton style, as does an unpublished sketch of the same period. Like Henry James in *The Aspern Papers* and Wharton in "The Muse's Tragedy," London examines the complex relationships between art, ownership, commerce, and writing as he explores the ways in which female autonomy and sexuality are compromised when woman becomes objectified as muse. Reading London in light of his response to Wharton thus helps to illuminate a neglected aspect of London's development as a writer.

The Aspern Papers involves the fictional retelling of an incident in which, as James records it in his notebook entry for 12 January 1887, the aged "Miss Claremont, Byron's *ci-divant* mistress (the mother of Allegra)," and her niece are approached by a Captain Silsbee, who hopes to gain their hoard of Shelley's and Byron's letters. After the older woman's death, "he approached the younger one—the old maid of 50—on the subject of his desires. Her answer was—'I will give you all the letters if you marry me!' "[2] In *The Aspern Papers*, James recasts the Byron figure as an American poet, Jeffrey Aspern, but otherwise preserves the essential features of the original: Juliana Bordereau, the Claire Clairmont figure; her niece Tita (as she is called in the 1888 version), the "old maid of 50"; and the young writer whose concealment of his name suggests only the first of his deceptive stratagems. Upon hearing from the garrulous Mrs. Prest that Miss Bordereau is rumored to have preserved letters from Jeffrey Aspern, her long-dead lover, the narrator persuades the two women to rent rooms to him. Using their neglected garden against them, he lays siege to the Misses Bordereau with flowers and flattery: "I would batter the old woman with lilies—I would bombard their citadel with roses."[3] He seems to win their trust until, upon refusing Miss Tita's implicit proposal, he learns that she has destroyed the letters.

"The Muse's Tragedy" first appeared in the January 1899 issue of *Scribner's Magazine* and was included later that year with seven other stories in Wharton's first collection of short fiction, *The Greater Inclination*. Like *The Aspern Papers*, it is initially told from the perspective of the male writer. Through the intercession of the talkative and aptly named Mrs. Memorall, Wharton's version of Mrs. Prest, Lewis Danyers, a young American living in Italy, meets the widowed Mrs. Anerton. The notorious former mistress of the late poet Vincent Rendle, Mary Anerton acknowledges her position as the Silvia of Rendle's famous *Sonnets to Silvia*, and she at first charms Danyers solely as Rendle's acknowledged muse. She then begins to serve as Danyers's inspiration as well, encouraging his writing and suggesting that he turn his prize-winning college essay on Rendle into a book. During a month in Venice with her, however, his literary passion becomes a personal one, a change suggested in the story's architectural symbolism when the characters move from the formal marble palace and rigid structures of the Villa d'Este to the open balcony of an apartment overlooking a Venetian lagoon. After initially agreeing to write the book on Rendle, he falls deeply in love with Mrs. Anerton, and his jealousy of Rendle's memory causes him to postpone its completion. Before they can meet again in Venice to begin work on the book, however, Danyers receives a letter from Mrs. Anerton in which she confesses the truth:

> *You are not going to marry me.* We have had our month together in Venice . . . and I am to stay here, attitudinizing among my memories like a sort of female Tithonus. The dreariness of this enforced immortality! . . .
>
> You thought it was because Vincent Rendle had loved me that there was so little hope for you. . . . It is because Vincent Rendle *didn't love me* that there is no hope for you. I never had what I wanted, and never, never, never will I stoop to wanting anything else.[4] (73)

She adds that, infatuated with "a cosmic Philosophy" and admiring her intellect, Rendle had always seen her as an idealized Woman-as-Muse, never caring for the real woman behind the mask. Knowing early on that her inevitable fate is to be remembered as Rendle's mistress, Mrs. Anerton secures this reputation through various strategies. When publishing Rendle's love letters, for example, she adds deceptive rows of asterisks to suggest, falsely, the removal of intimate details from the originals. Despite her well-calculated use of him, she asks Danyers for forgiveness:

> My poor friend, do you begin to see? I had to find out what some other man thought of me. . . . From the hour of our first meeting to the day of his death I had never looked at any other man. . . . I knew the extent of my powers no more than a baby. Was it too late to find out? Should I never know *why*? (77)

"The Muse's Tragedy" concludes not with Mrs. Anerton's suicide, but with a far worse fate, as, alone again, she contemplates "for the first time, all that I have missed" (78).

The connections between James's and Wharton's meditations on the female muse exist at several levels. In its treatment of a middle-aged woman who experiences love, a love made possible only through its immediate renunciation, "The Muse's Tragedy" anticipates some of Wharton's later work, notably *The Reef* (1912), the most Jamesian of her novels. In fact, despite Wharton's later protests that she did not want to be seen as "an echo of Mr. James," critics of *The Greater Inclination* had already noted the Wharton-James connection in their reviews in *The Critic*, *The Academy*, *The Bookman*, and *The Literary World*.[5] In discussing *The Aspern Papers* and "The Muse's Tragedy," Millicent Bell finds a more specific connection between the two works, arguing that in both, "romance triangulates the relation of poet, critic, and inamorata," a triangulation that more recent critics of James have seen as masking the essential bond between the two male characters.[6] Each work examines the paradoxical nature of the exposure and concealment that occurs when private writing becomes public property that nonetheless masquerades as its essential private self. Each work is filled with masks and evasions, from Juliana Bordereau's green eye-shade and Mary Anerton's verbal elusiveness to the young men's calculated displacement of real desire (for the poets and their fragmented remains, represented by the letters) with its unconvincing counterfeit, their initially feigned (and, for Danyers, later genuine) desire for the living "remains," the aging mistresses. Further, in both situations, the young male writers believe that they control the situation, only to be outwitted by these female keepers of the flame. Also, as the loss of the never-glimpsed letters in *The Aspern Papers* suggests the fictive and elusive nature of written representations of private feeling, Mrs. Anerton's inserted asterisks comment ironically on the possibility of believing in such representations at all, even as they mock the reader's capacity for self-delusion.

In her use of the materials, however, Wharton subtly reworks James's treatment, a pattern particularly noticeable in each author's use of classical allusion. As Jeanne Campbell Reesman has shown, in *The Aspern Papers*, the narrator's involuntary exclamation of "Orpheus and the Maenads!" when he first hears Aspern's story both symbolically suggests the poet's fate and presages the dismemberment of the letters.[7] In her revisionist use of classical allusion in this plot, however, Wharton emphasizes not the formalistic connections between Eros and Thanatos but the rhetorically cogent and emotionally compelling links between Eros and Pathos. The key to the tragedy of the story's ending and of the title lies in Mary Anerton's recognition of her fate as a "female Tithonus." The allusion here recalls both Tennyson's poem and the Greek myth wherein Eos, the goddess of the Dawn, falls in love with the handsome youth Tithonus and asks that he be granted eternal life, fatally forgetting to request that he also be granted eternal youth. Facing a long stretch of empty years, Mrs. Anerton must live with the memories of her affair with Danyers and the time when, as she tells him, she was able "to get away from literature" (78). If literature preserves and extends life, as it does in these works, it necessarily also imprisons, and Wharton calls into question the value of a life thus caught in stasis. Like Jeffrey Aspern's poetry, Rendle's writing causes this stasis through its fabrication of romance. Its falsity is sealed through Mrs. Anerton's silent collaboration, as she is imprisoned in her public pose through the self-imposed medium of the asterisks she inserts into Rendle's text. Significantly, only when she tells the truth and writes her own letter, a counterpoint to her deceptive practices with Rendle's letters, does Mary Anerton break free. Through the techniques of letters, allusion, and a revisionary perspective on the muse's situation, Wharton rescues Juliana and Tita Bordereau from their position as the threatening Maenads of James's work and finds within their situation another possibility, that of the forlorn "female Tithonus" who evokes compassion rather than fear.

London seems to have read "The Muse's Tragedy" within a month or two of its publication; his habitually voracious reading during this period also included Rudyard Kipling, Robert Louis Stevenson, Mary Hallock Foote, Richard LeGallienne, Helen Hunt Jackson, Edwin Markham, Frank Norris, Ambrose Bierce, and Ella Wheeler Wilcox. This story was apparently brought to his notice by Cloudesley Johns some time between London's first letter to Johns on 10 February and the end of March 1899.[8] In a previously unidentified reference to Wharton's story, London writes to Johns on 30 March 1899:

> I liked the story you sent. No sentimental gush, no hysteria, but the innate pathos of it! Who could not feel for Mrs. Anerton? Our magazines are so goody-goody, that I wonder they would print a thing as risque [*sic*] and as good as that. This undue care not to bring the blush to the virgin cheek of the American young girl, is disgusting. And yet she is permitted to read the daily papers! Ever read Paul Bourget's comparison of the American and French young women?[9]

Of particular interest is London's placement of Wharton and her lifelong friend and literary advisor Paul Bourget on the side of the angels in his fight against censorship and magazine editors. London returns to this story in his letter to Johns of 17 April 1899 and again on 22 April, misquoting the title of the story both times: "I see Edith Wharton, writer of 'The Tragedy of the Muse,' is just bringing out a volume of short stories in which that piece figures—Scribner's, I think, are the publishers. How the short story is growing in importance in modern literature!" (*Letters* 69). Several months later, on 16 February 1900, London again wrote to Johns: "You remember Edith Wharton's 'Tragedy of the Muse'? It is the first of a collection of eight stories under the title of *The Greater Inclination*. And they are all as good. Have just finished it" (*Letters* 157). London would not have had the chance to read many of these stories earlier, for except for the much-admired story "The Pelican," which had appeared in the November 1898 *Scribner's*, and "The Muse's Tragedy," all the rest appeared for the first time in *The Greater Inclination*. (Ironically, in discussing "The Muse's Tragedy" when London habitually misstates Wharton's title as "The Tragedy of the Muse," the title recalls James's novel *The Tragic Muse* [1890], which in turn derives from the Joshua Reynolds portrait *Sarah Siddons as the Tragic Muse* [1784].)

A further connection to this Wharton story more indirectly pervades London's letters and outlasts his fascination with it during the spring of 1899. In "The Muse's Tragedy," Mrs. Anerton recalls as one of Rendle's many endearing "tricks" "his way of always calling me *you—dear you*, every letter began" (74). London's letter to Johns of 17 April 1899 addresses this relatively minor point, which apparently made a great impression on him:

> Remember 'Tragedy of the Muse'? also letter with super-scription of "dear you"? A very interesting woman who writes me regularly, began to use that phrase on me. And I

was struck by it, and appropriated it. She also had read the aforementioned tale and drawn it from that source. (*Letters* 64–65)

Although London does not identify the woman who, like Vincent Rendle in Wharton's story, begins letters with the superscription "dear you," a notation in pencil on the manuscript of the letter identifies the woman as Ernestine Coughran.[10] The endearment clearly remained a favorite with him, most obviously in his correspondence with Anna Strunsky. He first met Strunsky in March 1899 during the period of his probable correspondence with Ernestine Coughran, and he begins using this method of address with Strunsky in his letter of 22 January 1901, more than two years after he had first encountered it in Wharton's story.[11] His use of this superscription continues in an unpublished letter from August 1901,[12] and, in the letters included in Earle Labor, Robert C. Leitz, and I. Milo Shepard's published edition of London's correspondence, London uses this endearment or its variant—"dear, dear you"—to Strunsky some twenty-seven more times along with other greetings until his break with Strunsky in September 1902.

Further evidence of London's interest in Wharton exists in his reading and in his unpublished papers. Although London does not again discuss Wharton in his published letters, two key passages from Charmian London's 1905 diary suggest other connections. During the turmoil of that summer, a notation for 15 July reads, "Probably this day [Jack] saw 'Dear You,' & [I] had the blues pretty badly," suggesting that London had shared with Charmian his use of this form of address for another woman, perhaps Anna Strunsky, whom Charmian suspected him of meeting that day. A different mood prevails on 31 October, a few weeks prior to their wedding, when Charmian wrote, "Read aloud to him from 'House of Mirth' by Edith Wharton & So happy together."[13] A still stronger piece of evidence appears in London's unpublished story notes. That London at one point toyed with the idea of writing consciously in the Wharton style is shown unequivocally by this fragment dated prior to 1901 titled "Study: a la Edith Wharton":

> Writer undertakes to be taskmaster to striking woman.
> Open with letters perhaps.
> Unfold, the thread gradually tending to her being only a woman after all. Shrinking, c[l]inging, etc.
> At first seemed a complete divorce of intellectual and emotive centers. Her impersonality, sound logic, inexorable analysis.[14]

The fragment is as interesting for what it says about London's conception of Wharton and her characters as for its potential as a story idea. Unlike many of London's female characters, such as Ruth Morse of *Martin Eden,* this "striking woman" is genuinely intellectual and ruled by reason ("sound logic, inexorable analysis"). Although other women in London's life may have inspired the fragment—Anna Strunsky is an obvious candidate—the formidable intellect of this character in fact suggests Wharton herself, especially in light of London's praise of "The Muse's Tragedy": "No sentimental gush, no hysteria" (*Letters* 60). Perhaps most significant, however, is how the fragment revises and reverses some features of Wharton's story. London presents the writer as taskmaster rather than as supplicant, unlike the young male writers of *The Aspern Papers* and "The Muse's Tragedy," and the woman or muse figure as "shrinking, clinging" under the writer's control. After establishing this dominance through, significantly, an exchange of letters, the woman becomes "only a woman after all"—a restoration of the biological balance of power that Mrs. Anerton has upset through controlling her relationship with Danyers. London's story fragment thus addresses the taming of the American muse as she reintegrates intellect and emotion, assuming her proper role as an emotional complement to the male writer rather than as a competitor for intellectual preeminence.

Given, then, London's level of interest in Wharton's writing from 1899 to 1900, it is possible to reread some of his short stories from the spring of 1899 with an eye toward what he may have admired and perhaps emulated from Wharton's early collection *The Greater Inclination*. During this seminal period, London was completing and submitting not only some of his classic Northland stories, such as "The Son of the Wolf" (27 February 1899), but also such "stories of manners" or society stories as "The Unmasking of a Cad" (27 May 1899), "The Grilling of Loren Ellery" (25 July 1899), "The Proper 'Girlie' " (3 October 1899), and, the most stylistically suggestive of these, "Their Alcove" (25 May 1899), which he apparently completed and submitted for publication only one day after submitting his classic "An Odyssey of the North" on 24 May.[15] Few would rank these slight "society" efforts for *Smart Set* and other popular periodicals with London's serious stories written at the same time, for London's treatment of society themes is often facetious rather than ironic; their arch tone, consciously snappy dialogue, and swift and relentless pace toward an O. Henry denouement mark their commercial status. Like much of his fiction during this era, however, they address the fictional nature of identity, and these fables of identity frequently feature cultured protagonists who, like their Northland counterparts, risk exposure as impostors.

One of these stories, "Their Alcove," achieves something of the seriousness in tone and approach that distinguishes London's Northland tales. "Their Alcove," which appeared in the September 1899 issue of the *Woman's Home Companion*, opens as its unnamed male protagonist reflects on his recently ended relationship while he burns a stack of his sweetheart's love letters. In describing this gesture, London both establishes the character's education and gently satirizes his lofty literary pretensions, for in the character's mind this is not a simple act of pique after a lovers' quarrel but a sacrifice on the altar of Hymen with himself "officiating as high priest."[16] Like Tita Bordereau, he hopes to free himself from the past by reducing to ashes the evidence of a lost love. Congratulating himself on a lack of sentimentality, he walks to the "Grotto," a restaurant he and his lover had frequented, where he contemplates his future:

> He remembered a thousand and one little incidents—trivial events, so unimportant at the time, but now fair mile-stones to look back upon. It began to dawn upon him how large a place she had filled in his life. For the time he had lived his days in her, and now—tomorrow? The future loomed before him like a blank wall. (260)

The image of the wall immediately recalls the protagonist's destruction of the relationship's mementos, but in a more symbolically significant way it suggests London's thematic use of architecture in the story. From the small half-room that gives the story its title to the crowded enclosures that circumscribe the lovers' movements, the story's spaces dominate its action, and the blank wall here parallels the eternity of days in Mrs. Anerton's future as a "female Tithonus." The story's second major pattern, that of books, letters, and reading, merges with the first when the protagonist walks to the library where a "short, thick" volume in the second-floor alcove had served as the lovers' private post office for exchanging love letters. Recalling that he had left a letter in the book that morning, he ascends to the alcove—"their alcove"—in time to see her retrieve and kiss the letter, at which point "he cried her name softly and sprang toward her" (264). The lovers remain for a short while, and, when they leave, they remove the book that has served them as a post office during their courtship: a volume of Mechan's (not Bacon's) *Mirror of Alchemy*. In preferring the book-filled walls of the alcove to the blank wall—the eternity of Tithonus—the narrator now allows memory to take the place of the burned letters, but ironically he looks to books, to the second-hand memories of the past, to corroborate his own recollections.

Despite its brevity and its trick ending, the "skit or storiette" (*Letters* 180), as London called it, merits attention for its departure from the other society sketches in its point of view, theme of writing, and use of allusion. "Their Alcove" is told from a quietly reflective, limited third-person point of view that echoes Wharton's technique in her early fiction, and its humor owes more to gentle irony than to the facetiousness that mars some of his other society fiction. London heightens the irony of the character's self-deluding reflections subtly through the theme of time in this story, showing the protagonist moving unconsciously within the chronological rhythms of his former relationship even as he celebrates being free and "not sentimental." Further, in both stories the written word and the act of writing at once express and suppress truth in complex patterns. In Wharton's story, Rendle's poetry rests on an artfully revealed pretense of feeling that governs Mrs. Anerton's life even as it conceals the true absence of his feeling for her. Mrs. Anerton, in turn, recapitulates Rendle's action through her own fictionalizing of the experience—creating an illusion of feeling where none existed. The subject matter, too, briefly evokes another favorite theme of Wharton's: the primacy of letters and texts, of the written word's independent life and its power to set in motion the revelation of truths against which human beings may be rendered helpless.

In London's story, the written word also repeatedly succeeds in revealing to the protagonist the feelings that his unspoken rationalizations had concealed; indeed, this point is reinforced through the kind of literary allusion and architectural symbolism favored in Wharton's works. As the protagonist surveys the al-

cove, he recalls reading "Alastor" with his beloved, an allusion to
Shelley's *Alastor; or, the Spirit of Solitude.* This indirect reference to
Shelley also recalls the fictionalized American Romantic poets
Jeffrey Aspern and Vincent Rendle. According to Thomas Love
Peacock, who gave the poem its title, the Greek name suggests an
evil genius and treats "the spirit of solitude as a spirit of evil." In
a passage that glosses London's depiction of the protagonist's di-
lemma, Shelley describes his own protagonist:

> It represents a youth of uncorrupted feelings and adventur-
> ous genius led forth by an imagination inflamed and purified
> through familiarity with all that is excellent and majestic to
> the contemplation of the universe. . . . But the period arrives
> when these objects cease to suffice. His mind is at length sud-
> denly awakened and thirsts for intercourse with an intelli-
> gence similar to itself. He images to himself the Being whom
> he loves. . . . He seeks in vain for a prototype of his concep-
> tion. Blasted by his disappointment, he descends to an
> untimely grave.[17]

After warning the reader through allusion of the protagonist's
misguided embrace of the solitary life, London reinforces the
point through his use of setting. Surrounded by the written words
of others in the library itself, enclosed in the cozy, inviolate sanc-
tuary of the book-lined alcove, the protagonist must logically
progress to the next step, the magical transformation implied in
the title *The Mirror of Alchemy.*

If "Their Alcove" evokes Whartonian themes, *The Little Lady
of the Big House* (1916), written some fourteen years and a lifetime of reading after London's initial encounter with Wharton's
work, suggests another alternative reading of "The Muse's Tragedy." As in Wharton's story, architecture becomes a significant
motif. Moreover, the triangle in *The Little Lady of the Big House* involves a man whose systematic approach to his work excludes the

woman who loves him; a woman who, although past her first youth, nonetheless retains an intellectual and sexual attractiveness through which she exercises power; and a sensitive, literary-minded outsider whose first allegiance to the woman's work-absorbed partner cannot mask his attraction to the woman herself. Although it is doubtful that London consciously recalled "The Muse's Tragedy" when planning his novel—as Clarice Stasz, Robert Forrey, and others have shown, its origins are clearly autobiographical—London's famous descriptions of the proposed novel do suggest Wharton's story.[18] Based on what London called "the old, eternal triangle" (*Letters* 1322), it would be, he wrote to Roland Phillips on 14 March 1913, "all sex, from start to finish—in which no sexual adventure is actually achieved" and feature three characters who are "cultured, modern, and at the same time profoundly primitive" (*Letters* 1135). Earlier critics such as Forrey and Edwin Erbentraut focused on the biographical and sexual dynamics in the work, but recent criticism has followed a different direction, analyzing instead how the work employs sophisticated cultural signifiers. For example, Bert Bender suggests how London explores Darwinian principles of sexual selection through pitting the unconscious biological choices of his characters against their civilized attitudes.[19] Other significant perspectives include those of gender and material culture: Reesman reads the work as a feminist piece, London's self-satire at the expense of the book's grandiose but barren agricultural ideal, while Andrew Furer instead explores the implications of the New Woman type that Paula represents. In analyzing the book's depiction of material culture, Tony Williams demonstrates that London provides rather a critique than a celebration of the culture of consumption, a perception that Susan Gatti confirms in examining London's skeptical look at the Arts and Crafts movement's embrace of medievalism.[20]

Set against the agrarian Eden optimistically invoked in *The*

Valley of the Moon (1913), *The Little Lady of the Big House* tells the story of the eternal triangle between the "little lady," Paula Desten Forrest; her husband, the successful rancher Dick Forrest; and his good friend and fellow London-twin, the writer Evan Graham. Their days are occupied with systematized and systematically described activities: work, practical jokes, games, artistic pursuits, and physical culture. What Paula and Dick lack is children, an absence that Forrey reads as resulting from Dick's sexual indifference to Paula. Much has been written about this central irony in the novel: that Dick Forrest, the prophet of animal breeding who chants "I am Eros" and whose very name promises fertility, has given Paula no children save the symbolically inert pink marble cherubs that decorate the fertile, goldfish-filled fountain pool of her inner courtyard. London consistently draws on such Freudian imagery throughout the work; it is, as critics have frequently commented, a novel filled with images of both sterility and fecundity. Caught between Dick and Evan, the constraints of domesticity and the expression of sexuality, Paula commits suicide rather than choose.[21]

One effect of the sometimes obvious symbolism is to reveal that the novel tells Paula's story, despite the emphasis on Dick and his minutely described routine in the early chapters, and that, like Wharton's stories of marriage, this one focuses on the issue of control. Like the similar opening chapters of Sinclair Lewis's *Babbitt*, which likewise focus on ritualized routine in a life about to go awry, or F. Scott Fitzgerald's *Tender is the Night*, which opens with Dick Diver creating patterns in the sand,[22] an action that represents his futile attempts to order a shifting universe, *The Little Lady of the Big House* insists on Dick's managerial and organizational skills only to reveal all that he cannot control: the temper of his horse, the behavior of his ranch hands, his childlessness, and his wife's affections. Two of the novel's most extensive descriptive scenes, when juxtaposed, symbolically illustrate this point: Dick's demonstration of his automatic plowing device and Paula's dive astride her stallion, Mountain Lad. The plowing device consists of a "stout steel pole, at least twenty feet in height and guyed very low"[23] to which a tractor is affixed by a wire cable in the middle of a ten-acre field. At the press of a button, the tractor begins to plow the field in a huge spiral pattern, drawing ever closer to the pole and, as Dick triumphantly states, leaving the farmer relaxing on the porch with "his newspaper" (188). London undercuts Dick's pride in this Rube Goldberg miracle of technology in several ways, however. Dick does not, for example, describe the labor that may presumably be required to retrace the spiral pattern in moving the tractor away from the pole at the center so that the planted ground is not disturbed. A few pages later, London reinforces the futility of mechanization through the spectacle of a broken tractor stuck in the middle of the field, a situation in which the saving of one man's labor ironically becomes the expenditure of two as "the mechanics busied themselves with it in the midst of the partly plowed field" (191). Finally, the contraption itself recalls nothing so much as a giant mechanized maypole, a symbol of fertility around which machines lumber rather than dance while human beings sit inert, trusting the cold steel's contact to nurture the land while ignoring their own connection to it. Like the mechanical breakdown that stops the tractor's plowing of the fertile field, the scene suggests both cause and result of the breakdown at the heart of the Forrests' marriage.

By contrast, Paula's plunge into the pool astride Mountain Lad connects her with movement and sexuality: when Evan Graham first sees her, "her slim round arms were twined in yards of half-drowned stallion-mane, while her white round knees slipped on the sleek, wet, satin pads of the great horse's straining shoulder muscles" (103). Here, as elsewhere, the earth imagery that

links Dick to his lands contrasts with the water imagery associated with Paula. Her raising of goldfish, her cherub-surrounded
fountain-pool, her skill at swimming and diving, and even the
flowing shapelessness of the *holoku* she wears reinforce this vision
of her nature. The term Evan Graham uses several times to characterize his attraction to her reflects this idea: "He marveled at
the proteanness of her, at visions of those nimble fingers guiding
and checking The Fop [her horse], swimming and paddling in
submarine crypts, and, falling in swanlike flight through forty
feet of air, locking just above the water to make the diver's head-
protecting arch of arm" (168). Even a Proteus, however, can be
compressed into formulaic shapes by the proper master, and, just
as Dick regulates the flooding of the Harvest mine to serve his
own purposes, so too does he police Paula's performances in the
water, from her riding of Mountain Lad to her compliance with
the most cruel of his repeated practical jokes, when at his signal
Paula goes to a secret grotto in the pool to fool visitors into thinking she has stayed underwater too long and drowned.

As becomes increasingly clear, one major subject of this novel
is the exploitation of sex, love, work, and art as a means to power.
The relentless competition exemplified by the parlor games, intellectual discussions, and boxing and swimming contests testifies
to this, as do the acts of pointless dominance such as Dick's showy
horsemanship and his renaming the Asian servants to suit his
whims. Dick and Paula try various combinations of these tactics
in their struggle for meaning, yet all prove illusory in the end. For
example, in her daily pursuits, Paula, like Dick and Evan, is an
artist, a talented musician and painter whose true genius, as Evan
tells her aunt, Mrs. Tully, is "to be herself" (221). The extrav-
agance of this compliment, however, repeated with variations
in a multitude of admiring asides, masks the dual nature of
the confinement it imposes. According to Clarice Stasz, Paula is

a "trapped princess incarnate"; more prosaically, as Jonathan Auerbach acerbically but truthfully puts it, Paula is " 'the hostess with the mostest' for an entourage of hangers-on and guests."[24] The limitations of this social role deny her autonomy in work as well. Her successful breeding experiments amount only to "feminine intuition" writ large, according to Dick. In addition, during this decade the discourses of scientific management and professionalism that Frederick Taylor and others would popularize began to dominate two "natural" occupations: agriculture and housekeeping. London simultaneously celebrates and satirizes the scientific basis of farming, yet the branch of domestic science that was becoming professionalized as "home economics" should logically be equally present in the novel. By downplaying this parallel, London not only eliminates a potential subject for satire but also deprives Paula of an occupation beyond "being herself." In portraying Paula as a talented woman who has no meaningful work to occupy her, London does not so much look back at the turn-of-the-century "New Woman" as ahead to the restless American heroines of the twenties, such as Sinclair Lewis's Carol Kennicott (*Main Street*, 1920) and Fran Dodsworth (*Dodsworth*, 1929), and F. Scott Fitzgerald's Gloria Patch (*The Beautiful and Damned*, 1922). Like Mrs. Anerton and Paula Forrest, they are all in some sense muses for the male characters, and they all attempt unsuccessfully, even disastrously, to professionalize their occupation as cultural objects.

Further, as an artist whose medium is her protean self, Paula suffers the fate of all pieces of art: becoming an icon whose worth resides solely in the minds of its beholders. The marble cherubs thus not only symbolize the children that Paula cannot have; they also represent a kind of art that she cannot create—representative, symbolic, and permanent. For Dick, Evan, and the others, she is finally, as the book makes clear, not an artist, but a muse, and the only power she can wield is the power of the muse. As Mrs. Anerton tells Danyers before dismissing him from her life, "I knew the extent of my powers no more than a baby. Was it too late to find out?" Similarly, Paula explains to Dick when he confronts her about her abortive affair with Graham, "You see, I am a woman. I have never sown any wild oats. . . . You are both big game. I can't help it. It is a challenge to me. And I find I am a puzzle to myself" (366). That the exercise of this power involves the emotions of another human being, Evan Graham, seems to concern neither Dick nor Paula Forrest, nor does London insert any condemnation of them on this account. His sympathy lies in a different direction, as it had in 1899. "The innate pathos of it!" he wrote. "Who could not feel for Mrs. Anerton?" And, he might well have asked, who could not feel for Paula Forrest? In discussing this intensely autobiographical book, some critics have charged that London concluded with Paula's suicide because he harbored a cruel wish-fulfillment fantasy of killing his wife, Charmian. Yet in engineering Paula's suicide, London is not cruel, but kind, for to do so eliminates the specter of being a "female Tithonus" that was Mary Anerton's fate.

To say that London consciously recalled "The Muse's Tragedy" or indeed other stories from *The Greater Inclination* when writing this last novel would be to overstate the case. References to other Wharton works do not appear in London's letters in the intervening years, and Wharton did not hold the place in his literary affections that Browning, Spencer, Kipling, Conrad, or even Ouida were to do at various points in his life. In addition, London's comments on the subject and construction of the book show that he believed it to be a significant departure in subject and form from anything he had written before, or, for that matter, from anything others had written before. Yet his admiration for Wharton's stories and his experimentation with Wharton's style years before, along with the similarity in treatment between Paula and Mrs. Anerton, surely suggest that he regarded Wharton as a significant predecessor in mapping the tragedy of the muse—and that of the modern American woman who wears the muse's mask.

NOTES

I would like to thank Sara S. Hodson, Curator of Literary Manuscripts at the Huntington Library, for her generous assistance with the research for this essay.

1. Jay Williams, "Editor's Introduction: On Jack London's 'The House Beautiful,'" *Jack London Journal* 3 (1996): 35.

2. *The Complete Notebooks of Henry James*, ed. and introd. Leon Edel and Lyall H. Powers (New York: Oxford University Press, 1987), 33. "Miss Claremont" is Mary Jane, or, as she preferred to be known, "Claire" Clairmont, as Edel and Powers note. In "James, 'The Aspern Papers,' and the Ethics of Literary Biography" (*Modern Fiction Studies* 36, no. 2 [summer 1990]: 211–16), Gary Scharnhorst argues convincingly that "James clearly conceived Aspern as a type of the elder Hawthorne" (211) and that the novella's exploration of the ethics of invading Hawthorne's privacy emerged from James's own experience of writing *Hawthorne* and of the controversy over Julian Hawthorne's plundering of his father's legacy in creating his 1884 biography of his parents.

3. Henry James, *The Aspern Papers and The Spoils of Poynton*, introd. R. P. Blackmur (New York: Dell, 1959), 52. Instead of the text of the New York Edition (1908), this volume reproduces the text of the first book edition (1888); it is cited here since the earlier version would have what Wharton read before writing "The Muse's Tragedy" in 1899. In the New York Edition, Tita's name is changed to Tina, among other revisions.

4. Edith Wharton, "The Muse's Tragedy," in *The Collected Short Stories of Edith Wharton*, volume 1, ed. R. W. B. Lewis (New York: Charles Scribner's Sons, 1968), 73. Subsequent references are cited in the text.

5. Wharton to William Crary Brownell in *Letters of Edith Wharton*, ed. R. W. B. Lewis and Nancy Lewis (New York: Macmillan, 1988), 91. Reviews cited are as follows: Harry Thurston Peck, "A New Writer Who Counts," *Bookman* 9 (June 1899): 344–46; Review of *The Greater Inclination*, *Academy* 57 (8 July 1899): 40; "Recent Fic-

tion," *Critic* 35 (August 1899): 746–48; John D. Barry, "New York Letter," *Literary World* (1 April 1899): 105–6; all are reprinted in *Edith Wharton: The Contemporary Reviews*, ed. James W. Tuttleton, Kristin O. Lauer, and Margaret P. Murray (New York: Cambridge University Press, 1991).

6. Millicent Bell, *Edith Wharton and Henry James: The Story of Their Friendship* (New York: George Braziller, 1965), 229.

7. Jeanne Campbell Reesman, " 'The Deepest Depths of the Artificial': Attacking Women and Reality in 'The Aspern Papers,' " *Henry James Review* 19, no. 2 (1998): 148–65. Another approach to the implicit feminine violence of the Misses Bordereau is William Veeder's psychological reading in "The Aspern Portrait," *Henry James Review* 20, no. 1 (1999): 22–42.

8. The long excerpts from Johns's autobiographical narrative published in the last few years do not mention this story specifically. See Cloudesley Johns, "Who the Hell *is* Cloudesley Johns?" James Williams, ed., *Jack London Journal* 1 (1994): 65–108 and 2 (1995): 39–63.

9. *Letters of Jack London*, vol. I, ed. Earle Labor, Robert C. Leitz, and I. Milo Shepard (Stanford, Calif.: Stanford University Press, 1988), 60. The missing accent occurs in London's original letter. Subsequent references are cited in the text. In reproducing this paragraph for *The Book of Jack London*, Charmian London omitted only the sentence about Mrs. Anerton (*Book of Jack London*, vol. I [New York: The Century Company, 1921], 285).

London's enthusiasm for Wharton's work was apparently not reciprocated, for it seems that Wharton either never read or never commented on London's work. To date, extensive searches in her published and unpublished letters and essays, the books in her library, and other references have failed to turn up any mention of London's work even at the time of his great popular fame in 1903 when *The Call of the Wild* was published.

10. "Jack London's Letters to Cloudesley Johns," Jack London Collection, the Huntington Library, JL 12093. According to Sara S. Hodson, Curator of Manuscripts at the Huntington Library, no letters from Ernestine Coughran appear in the Huntington's collection (personal communication, 5 March 1999).

11. Jacqueline Tavernier-Courbin, personal communication, 9 October 1998, gives March 1899 as the date; a date of fall 1899 appears in Clarice Stasz's *American Dreamers: Charmian and Jack London* (New York: St. Martin's Press, 1988), 76. I am indebted to Sara S. Hodson for the reference to London's use of "Dear You" (personal communication, 5 March 1999).

12. Sara S. Hodson, personal communication, 5 March 1999.

13. Charmian Kittredge London's Diary—1905, Jack London Collection, the

Huntington Library. Both Wharton books are in the Jack London Collection at the Huntington Library. The first edition of *The Greater Inclination* (Scribner's, 1899) is unmarked. The first edition copy of *The House of Mirth* (Scribner's, 1905) is signed "Charmian Kittredge" and has passages marked with light pencil lines. The only written notation occurs at the end of the volume: "Did she die?" is written in pencil, a reference to Lily Bart's accidental or intentional death by an overdose of chloral hydrate.

14. "Study: a la Edith Wharton," JL 1277, Jack London Collection, the Huntington Library.

15. The dates of composition appear indirectly as first submission dates in Appendix A, "Publication History," compiled by Earle Labor, Robert C. Leitz III, and I. Milo Shepard in volume 3 of *The Complete Stories of Jack London* (Stanford, Calif.: Stanford University Press, 1993), 2497–545. Based on London' s *Magazine Sales Notebooks* and other sources, Jay Williams also has established a list of dates of composition in "Jack London's Works by Date of Composition" (available at http://sunsite.berkeley.edu/London/Essays/comp_date.html; date of access 30 June 1998). The stories written during the period from 30 March 1899 through 25 May 1899 include the following: "What Are We to Say?" (31 March 1899), "Strange Verbs" (31 March 1899), "In a Far Country" (17 April 1899), "The Children of Israel" (25 April 1899), "An Odyssey of the North" (24 May 1899), and "Their Alcove" (25 May 1899). The 27 May 1899 date for "The Unmasking of a Cad" does not appear in Williams's list, but Labor, Leitz, and Shepard give this as the submission date (2504).

16. "Their Alcove," *Complete Short Stories of Jack London*, I, 259. Subsequent references are cited in the text.

17. Quoted in George Woodberry, "*Alastor; or, The Spirit of Solitude* Introductory Note," *The Complete Poetical Works of Percy Bysshe Shelley* (Boston: Houghton Mifflin, 1901), available at http://www.columbia.edu/acis/bartleby/shelley/shel1120.html. London suggests a metaphysical poem by this name, but London's audience would surely have been more familiar with Shelley's version.

18. Clarice Stasz, *American Dreamers: Charmian and Jack London* (New York: St. Martin's Press, 1988); Robert Forrey, "Three Modes of Sexuality in London's *The Little Lady of the Big House*," *Literature and Psychology* 26, no. 2 (1976): 52–60.

19. "Jack London and 'the Sex Problem.' " I am indebted to Bert Bender for letting me read this work-in-progress.

20. Jeanne Campbell Reesman, "Irony and Feminism in *The Little Lady of the Big House*," *Thalia* 12, no. 1 (1991): 33–46; Andrew Furer, "Jack London's New Woman: A Little Lady with a Big Stick," *Studies in American Fiction* 22, no. 2 (1994):

185–214; Tony Williams, "London's Last Frontier: The Big House as Culture of Consumption," *Jack London Journal* 2 (1995): 156–74; and Susan Gatti, "Stone Hearths and Marble Babies: Jack London and the Domestic Ideal," *Jack London Journal* 3 (1996): 43–56.

21. In discussing the "masculinized" suicide of Paula in "The Little Lady with the Big Stick," Andrew Furer points out that no Wharton heroine ever shot herself, and Jeanne Campbell Reesman points out the parallels between Paula's plight and that of the "moment's ornament" Lily Bart of Wharton's *The House of Mirth.*

22. For an extended comparison of Dick Forrest and Dick Diver, see Stoddard Martin's "The Novels of Jack London," *Jack London Newsletter* 14, no. 2 (1981): 60–71.

23. Jack London, *The Little Lady of the Big House* (New York: Macmillan, 1916), 188. Subsequent references are cited in the text.

24. Stasz, *American Dreamers,* 261; Jonathan Auerbach, *Male Call: Becoming Jack London* (Durham, N.C.: Duke University Press, 1996), 236.

CONTRIBUTORS' NOTES

SAM S. BASKETT is Professor Emeritus of Michigan State University and was the first president of the Jack London Society. His publications include the 1956 Rinehart edition of *Martin Eden* and pioneering essays on London in *American Literature, American Literary Realism, American Quarterly, Modern Fiction Studies,* and *Western American Literature.*

BERT BENDER is Professor of English at the University of Arizona, where he has taught since 1971. He is the author of *Sea-Brothers: The Tradition of American Sea Fiction from Moby-Dick to the Present* (1988) and *The Descent of Love: Darwin and the Theory of Sexual Selection in American Fiction, 1871–1926* (1996). A third book, *Evolution and "The Sex Problem": Soundings of Life and Love in American Fiction,* is in progress. His essays have appeared in *American Literature, The Journal of American Studies, Nineteenth-Century Literature, Prospects,* and elsewhere.

LAWRENCE I. BERKOVE is Professor of English and American literature and Director of the American Studies Program at the University of Michigan-Dearborn. He was elected 2000–2002 president of the Jack London Society. His work on London includes essays on the short stories "An Unparalleled Invasion," "The Captain of the *Susan Drew,*" "By the Turtles of Tasman,"

"The House of Pride," and "The Red One." In addition, he has published extensively on Mark Twain, Ambrose Bierce, and Dan De Quille and other authors of the Comstock Lode. He has recently completed an edition of Comstock memoirs being published by the University of Nevada Press, and a critical study of Bierce's fiction to be published by Ohio State University Press.

DONNA M. CAMPBELL is Associate Professor of English at Gonzaga University in Spokane, Washington. She is the author of *Resisting Regionalism: Gender and Naturalism in American Fiction, 1885–1915* (1997) as well as articles on Frank Norris, Mary Wilkins Freeman, Sarah Orne Jewett, Edith Wharton, and other authors.

MARÍA DEGUZMÁN is Assistant Professor of English at the University of North Carolina at Chapel Hill teaching Latina/o literatures and cultures. She is at work on two books, *"American" In Dependence: Figures of Spain in Anglo-American Culture* and *Buenas Noches "American" Literature*. She is the author of essays on the Spanish-American War and on contemporary Latina/o writers Ana Castillo, John Rechy, and Floyd Salas.

SARA S. HODSON is Curator of Literary Manuscripts at the Huntington Library, where she administers all English and American literary collections, including the Jack London Papers. Her essays on literary and archival topics have appeared in *The American Archivist, Rare Books and Manuscripts Librarianship, California History, Dictionary of Literary Biography*, and the *Huntington Library Quarterly*. She prepared a major Huntington exhibition, "The Wisdom of the Trail: Jack London, Author and Adventurer," on view from September 1998 to January 1999. She is currently working on London's *People of the Abyss*, and her next exhibition will celebrate Christopher Isherwood in 2004, the centenary of his birth.

DEBBIE LÓPEZ is Associate Professor of English at the University of Texas at San Antonio. She has also taught at the University of Alabama at Birmingham, Birmingham-Southern College, and Harvard University. Her teaching and research interests involve British and American Romanticism, nineteenth-century British poetry, late-nineteenth- and early-twentieth-century American novels, and ethnic minority literature. The author of numerous essays in her field, she is at work on a book manuscript, *Adam's Nightmare: John Keats's Legacy to Nathaniel Hawthorne and Herman Melville.*

JOSEPH R. MCELRATH JR. is the William Hudson Rogers Professor of English at Florida State University. He is the author of seven books on Frank Norris and three treating another of Jack London's contemporaries, Charles W. Chesnutt. The essay published in the present volume is based upon extensive textual, bibliographical, and biographical research that he conducted in collaboration with Kenneth Brandt.

JEANNE CAMPBELL REESMAN is Ashbel Smith Professor of English at the University of Texas at San Antonio. Her books include *No Mentor But Myself: Jack London on Writers and Writing*, coedited with Dale Walker; *Trickster Lives: Myth in American Literature and Culture*; *Jack London: A Study of the Short Fiction*; *Speaking the Other Self: American Women Writers*; *Rereading Jack London*, coedited with Leonard Cassuto; *Jack London, Revised Edition*, coauthored with Earle Labor; *A Handbook of Critical Approaches to Literature*, with Wilfred Guerin, et al.; and *American Designs: The Late Novels of James and Faulkner*. Her essays on London and other writers have appeared in such periodicals as *Europe, American Literary Scholarship, American Literary Realism, Renascence, The Henry James Review, Western American Literature, Resources in American Literary Scholarship*, and *The Kenyon Review*. She serves as Executive Coordinator for the Jack London Society.

GARY RIEDL and THOMAS R. TIETZE teach English at Wayzata Middle School in Plymouth, Minnesota. They have received several grants from the National Endowment for the Humanities, most of them in support of their research on Jack London. They have published several articles on London's Pacific fiction and are the editors of *A Son of the Sun: The Adventures of Captain David Grief,* to be published by the University of Oklahoma Press. They are currently at work on two other books on London's fiction. Mr. Tietze has also published on the history of psychical research, the films of Alfred Hitchcock, and the non-Sherlockian fiction of Arthur Conan Doyle, and is the author of *Margery* (Harper & Row, 1973).

JACQUELINE TAVERNIER-COURBIN is Professor of English at the University of Ottawa, and has published over fifty articles on the writers of the Lost Generation, in particular Ernest Hemingway and F. Scott Fitzgerald, and on the Realists and Naturalists, including Stephen Crane, Theodore Dreiser, Frank Norris, and, most extensively, Jack London. Her work has appeared in journals such as *American Literary Realism, The Jack London Journal, The Southern Literary Journal, Studies in Canada, Symbiosis,* and in scholarly books. Her own books include *Ernest Hemingway: L'education de Nick Adams, The Making of Myth: Ernest Hemingway's* A Moveable Feast, *Critical Essays on Jack London,* and *The Call of the Wild: A Naturalistic Romance.* She is also editor of *Thalia: Studies in Literary Humor,* now in its twentieth year of publication. She is at work on a new book on the women in Jack London's life. From 1998 to 2000, she served as president of the Jack London Society.

INDEX

Academy, The, 196

Adams, Henry, 130

Aiken, Conrad, 156; *Great Circle*, 156

Ainslee's, 190

Alger, Horatio, 99

Aligieri, Dante, 22

Anderson, Sherwood, 178–79; *Dark
    Laughter*, 178–79

Applegarth, Mabel, 3, 15, 23, 106

Arena, The, 5

Atlantic Monthly, The, 2, 5, 190

Auerbach, Jonathan, 136, 207

Austin, Mary, 11, 15

Baskett, Sam, 8, 19

Bell, Millicent, 196

Bender, Bert, 19

Bergson, Henri, 149, 156, 161–62, 171;
    Creative Evolution, 149, 156, 161

Berkeley, George, 84

Berkove, Lawrence I., 18, 48, 143

Bierce, Ambrose, 195

Black Cat, The, 2

Bliss, Leslie, 10

Bohr, Niels, 143–44

Bookman, The, 196

Bourget, Paul, 195, 196

Boylan, James, 28, 36

Browning, Elizabeth Barrett, 113

Browning, Robert, 22, 113, 208

Buck, Philo M., Jr., 93

Burbank, Luther, 149

Byatt, A. S., 127

Byron, Lord (George Gordon), 191

Campbell, Donna M., 19

Cassuto, Leonard, 8, 9

Century, 190

Chaney, William, 26

Chase, Richard, 142

Chopin, Kate, 78, 83, 91, 119–20, 150–
    51, 163, 167; *The Awakening*, 78–80,
    119–20, 150, 163, 167

Christy, Howard Chandler, 163

Coleridge, Samuel Taylor, 110

Collier's, 190

Conrad, Joseph, 15, 115, 142, 208;
    "Heart of Darkness," 66; *Lord
    Jim*, 115; *Victory*, 142

Coughran, Ernestine, 197, 210 n.10

Crane, Stephen, 80, 91; *The Red Badge of Courage*, 80
Critic, The, 196
Crother, Rachel, 100; *A Man's World*, 100
Crow, Charles L., 179

Dante. *See* Aligieri, Dante
Darwin, Charles, and Darwinism, 19, 22, 65–67, 71–72, 127, 147–82, 186–87 n.45, 189, 203; *The Descent of Man and Selection in Relation to Sex*, 147–48, 162, 173, 181–82; *The Expression of the Emotions in Man and Animals*, 162, 172–73; *Influence on Freud*, 172; *Origin of Species*, 152, 82
Davis, Robert Con, 51
De Casseres, Benjamin, 13
DeGuzmán, María, 19
DeLillo, Don, 140; *Underworld*, 140
Dickinson, Emily, 137
Dijkstra, Bram, 100, 113; *Evil Sisters*, 100; *Idols of Perversity*, 100, 113
Donoghue, Denis, 133
Dostoevsky, Fyodor, 137
Dreiser, Theodore, 85
Dyer, Dan, 8; *The Call of the Wild, by Jack London, with an Illustrated Reader's Companion*, 8

Eliot, George, 151
Eliot, T. S.: *The Waste Land*, 182
Ellis, Havelock, 147–48, 153, 155–58, 160–62, 167, 176–78, 181; *Analysis of the Sexual Impulse*, 157; *Man and Woman*, 162; *Sex in Relation to Society*, 148; *Sexual Selection in Man*, 148, 152; *Studies in the Psychology of Sex*, 148, 155, 161, 167, 176
Emerson, Ralph Waldo, 18
Erbentraut, Edwin, 203

Faulkner, William, 125
Fiske, John, 113
Fitzgerald, F. Scott, 150, 182, 204, 207; *The Beautiful and the Damned*, 207; *The Great Gatsby*, 150; *Tender is the Night*, 204
Flaubert, Gustave, 79; *Madame Bovary*, 79
Fleming, Becky London, 31
Foote, Mary Hallock, 195
Ford, Alexander Hume, 58 n.5
Forel, August, 155; *The Sexual Question*, 155
Forrey, Robert, 203
Freud, Sigmund, 114, 123, 148–49, 156, 158, 165, 167, 170, 171–78, 185 n.36, 186 n.41; *Civilization and Its Discontents*, 165; *Essays on the Theory of Sexuality*, 148; *The Interpretation of Dreams*, 159; *Selected Papers on Hysteria*, 167, 172; *Three Contributions to the Theory of Sex*, 172
Furer, Andrew, 203

Haeckel, Ernst, 22, 148, 189; *The Riddle of the Universe at the Close of the Nineteenth Century*, 148
Hamburger, Anna Walling, 42 nn.6, 23
Hamilton, Frank Strawn, 21
Hassan, Ihab, 127–28, 142; "radical innocence," 127–29, 135–36
Hawthorne, Nathaniel, 96–97

Hegel, Georg Wilhelm Friedrich, 136–37, 140; *Phenomenology of the Mind*, 137

Hemingway, Ernest, 136, 154, 163; *The Sun Also Rises*, 163

Henley, William Ernest, 118

Henry, O. (William Sydney Porter), 199

Hodson, Sara S., 210 n.10

Holt, Edwin B., 156, 157; *The Freudian Wish and Its Place in Ethics*, 156

Howells, William Dean, 147, 169

Huntington, Henry E., 10

Huntington Library, 9–17, 211 n.13

Huxley, Thomas, 148; *Man's Place in Nature*, 148

Ibsen, Henrik, 140; *The Wild Duck*, 140

Ingram, Cordie Webb, 4

Ishi, 179–81

Jack London Journal, 8

Jack London Research Center (Glen Ellen, California), 13

Jack London Society, 8, 14

Jackson, Helen Hunt, 195

James, Henry, 82, 147, 150–51, 190–91, 193, 198; *The Aspern Papers*, 190–91, 194, 196, 198; *The Portrait of a Lady*, 150; *The Tragic Muse*, 196

James, William, 123, 139–40, 187 n.45; *The Varieties of Religious Experience*, 140

Johns, Cloudesley, 3, 6, 11, 15, 134, 190, 195, 196, 210 n.8

Jones, Gail, 75 n.5

Jung, Carl Gustav, 11, 48, 60, 71, 123, 128, 142

Kafka, Franz, 137

Kamehameha I, 45

Kant, Immanuel, 23

Keats, John, 106–13, 119; *Lamia*, 106–13

Kershaw, Alex, 9; *Jack London: A Life*, 9

King, Cameron, 28, 35

Kingman, Russ, 9; *A Pictorial Life of Jack London*, 9

Kipling, Rudyard, 22, 83, 195, 208

Kisch, E. Heinrich, 167; *The Sexual Life of Woman*, 167

Krutch, Joseph Wood, 137, 142

Labor, Earle, 8, 9, 18, 142, 183 n.5; *Jack London: Revised Edition*, 9, 73

Lacan, Jacques, 48–49, 51, 55

Lawrence, D. H., 96, 177

LeConte, Joseph, 84, 151

LeGallienne, Richard, 195

Leitz, Robert C., III, 8

Levinas, Emanuel, 133–34

Lewis, Austin, 21

Lewis, Sinclair, 15, 207; *Dodsworth*, 207; *Main Street*, 207

Literary World, The, 196

Lombroso, Cesare, 49

London, Becky. *See* Fleming, Becky London

London, Bess Maddern, 13, 24, 26–31, 35–38, 40, 41

London, Charmian Kittredge, 10, 11, 12, 13, 16, 25–26, 35–39, 41, 58 n.4, 134, 137, 154, 161, 197, 211 n.13

London, Jack
    advice to writers, 6–7, 11
    and alcohol, 7, 138, 140–41
    and Beauty Ranch, 10, 11, 16, 155

biographical context, autobiographical content, and "myths"
of London, 5, 7, 15, 80, 90, 98,
123–44
credo ("I would rather be ashes
than dust"), 13, 17
critical and scholarly reception and
reputation, 4–5, 7–10, 19, 60–63,
84–85
death of, 60, 137–38
and depression, 83, 93–95
and eugenics, 26
and fatherhood, 50–58
and the feminine, 48, 66, 71, 74, 101,
103–19, 132, 134, 181–82, 200,
207–9; Lamia figure, 106–15
and gender and race, 119
and Hawaii, 45–58, 74–75, 143
and heroes, 83
irony, use of, 63–64
Klondike (or Northland) fiction of,
2, 61, 71, 74
letters of, 8, 11–13, 28
and love and sex, 24–33, 40, 46–50,
52, 56, 101, 114, 135, 137, 147–82,
206
marriages and divorce, 26–28, 35–
37, 40
and masculinity, 70, 116
as naturalist, 132
and "the Other," 49, 100–101
parents of, 26
and philosophical contradictions,
4, 7, 83–84, 93–95
and photography, 12, 16
and race, 7, 50, 100–101, 102; treatment of African-Americans, 100–
101; treatment of Asians, 62–65;

treatment of Mexicans, 113, 118;
treatment of Pacific Islanders, 47–
58, 61, 66, 87, 101, 117–18
and readers, 18, 83, 87, 91
and religion (esp. Christianity), 44–
47, 50–51, 53, 54, 66–68, 78, 99;
Adam and Eve and the Garden of
Eden, 106–10
and the Romantic, 81–82, 110, 120
and sexuality, 24, 47, 50, 54–55, 101,
114, 147–82, 204–9
and sincerity as philosophy of life,
honesty as feature of writing, 4,
6–7
and Social Darwinism, 80, 113
and socialism, 7, 11, 21–22, 80, 82,
89, 92, 93–96, 130, 146
style, 7
and success, 2
and "White Logic," 139–41
works: *The Acorn-Planter: A California
Forest Play,* 179; *Adventure,* 12; "All
Gold Canyon," 15; *Burning Daylight,* 69, 92, 135; "By the Turtles
of Tasman," 71; *The Call of the
Wild,* 3, 11, 12, 15, 16; "The Captain of the *Susan Drew,*" 69–72;
Cherry (unfinished manuscript), 11;
"The Children of Israel," 211
n.15; "The Chinago," 64, 75 n.3;
The Cruise of the "Snark," 16; *A
Daughter of the Snows,* 149, 151, 169;
"Eyes of Asia," 64 (*see also* Lon-
don, Jack, *Cherry*); "Getting Into
Print," 6; "Goliah," 65; "The
Grilling of Loren Ellerbey," 199;
"The House of Pride," 18, 47–58,
71; "In a Far Country," 211 n.15;

"The Inevitable White Man,"
64; *The Iron Heel*, 15, 39, 95, 146;
John Barleycorn, 90, 96, 124, 135,
136, 138–42, 146; "The Kanaka
Surf," 74, 186 n.41, 187 n.51; *The
Kempton-Wace Letters*, 11, 13, 25–28,
35, 40, 152–53, 168; "Koolau the
Leper," 64; "The Law of Life,"
66; "Like Argus of the Ancient
Times," 74; *The Little Lady of the
Big House*, 16, 19, 135, 149–83,
202–9; *Martin Eden*, 11, 15, 16, 19,
78–144, 197–98; "Mauki," 64;
"My Castle in Spain," 190; "An
Odyssey of the North," 2, 211 n.15;
"The Night-Born," 71–74; *The Peo-
ple of the Abyss*, 3, 16; "The Proper
'Girlie,'" 199; "The Red One,"
66–71, 124, 143, 146, 187 n.51;
"Samuel," 71; *The Scarlet Plague*,
69; *The Sea-Wolf*, 3, 11, 16, 17, 69,
94, 152; *A Son of the Sun*, 71; "The
Son of the Wolf" (short story),
199; *The Son of the Wolf* (collection),
2, 5, 16; *The Star Rover*, 15, 16, 168;
"Strange Verbs," 211 n.15; "Their
Alcove," 190, 199–202, 211 n.15;
"A Thousand Deaths," 2; "To
Build a Fire," 11, 12; "To the Man
on Trail," 2; "The Unmasking
of a Cad," 199, 211 n.15; "The
Unparalleled Invasion," 62–65;
The Valley of the Moon, 135, 153, 157,
168, 170, 178, 180, 182, 183 n.5,
204; "The Water Baby," 15, 74–
75, 143; "What Are We to Say?"
211 n.15; "When the World Was
Young," 69; *White Fang*, 15; "The
Wit of Porportuk," 73–74; "Wonder of Woman," 73; "The Yellow
Peril," 63–64
and writing, career, and self-
identity, 2–5, 7, 11–12, 15, 60–62,
80, 82, 123–24, 130–33, 137, 140,
190
London, Joan. *See* Miller, Joan
London
López, Debbie, 19

Macmillan Publishers, 90
Mansfield, Katherine, 124
Markham, Edwin, 195
Mauberret, Noël, 76 n.12
McClintock, James, 142
McElrath, Joseph R., Jr., 19
Mellor, Anne, 109
Melville, Herman, 44, 80, 87, 91, 96,
101, 116–17, 123, 136, 141; *Billy
Budd*, 123; *Moby-Dick*, 80, 116–17
Miller, Joan London, 27
Moll, Albert: *The Sexual Life of the
Child*, 186 n.41
Morris, Wright, 142

Nietzsche, Friedrich, 85–87, 91, 95–
96, 99–100, 119, 121, 136; *Beyond
Good and Evil*, 100; *On the Genealogy
of Morals*, 100
Nordau, Frank, 148
Norris, Frank, 79–80, 91, 151, 195; *The
Octopus*, 79–80
Nuernberg, Susan, 7, 9; *The Critical
Response to Jack London*, 8–9

Ouida (Marie Louise de la Ramée),
208
Overland Monthly, 2, 5, 13, 90

Pacific Monthly, The, 90, 101
Paget, Violet, 140; *Vital Lies*, 140
Pagnard, Christian, 76 n.12
Partington, Blanche, 38
Peacock, Thomas Love, 202
Phillips, Roland, 154, 203
Picasso, Pablo, 138
Poe, Edgar Allan, 78, 96
Powers, Stephen, 179–81; *Tribes of California*, 177–81

Ragland-Sullivan, Ellie, 55
Ragnor, Beatrice Barrington, 186 n.45
Reesman, Jeanne Campbell, 4, 8, 9, 18, 75, 131, 139, 194, 203; *Jack London: Revised Edition*, 9, 73; *London: A Study of the Short Fiction*, 9; *No Mentor But Myself: Jack London on Writers and Writing*, 9; *Rereading Jack London*, 8
Review of Reviews, 5
Reynolds, Joshua, 196
Riedl, Gary, 18
Ritvo, Lucille B., 172–73; *Darwin's Influence on Freud*, 172–73

San Francisco *Bulletin*, 36
Schopenhauer, August, 85–87
Scribner's Magazine, 191, 196
Shakespeare, William, 88
Shaw, George Bernard, 165; *Man and Superman*, 165
Shelley, Percy Bysshe, 202, 211 n.17; "Alastor; or, the Spirit of Solitude," 202
Shepard, Eliza London, 11
Shepard, I. Milo, 8, 10
Shepard, Irving, 10

Sinclair, Andrew, 9; *Jack*, 9
Sinclair, Upton, 11, 15
Smart Set, 199
Sonoma State University (Jack London Collection), 13
Spencer, Herbert, 22, 84–85, 89, 113, 140, 189, 208
Stasz, Clarice, 203
Stein, Gertrude, 100; *Three Lives*, 100
Sterling, George, 11
Stevenson, Robert Louis, 70–71, 115, 118; *Dr. Jekyll and Mr. Hyde*, 70
Stoddard, Charles Warren, 2, 13
Stone, Herbert, 190
Stopes, Marie, 115; *Wise Parenthood*, 115
Strunsky, Anna. *See* Walling, Anna Strunsky
Sulloway, Frank, 176–77
Sutherland, John, 138
Swinburne, Algernon, 22, 80, 99, 101, 113

Tavernier-Courbin, Jacqueline, 4, 8, 18; *The Call of the Wild: A Naturalistic Romance*, 8
Taylor, Harvey, 12–13
Tietze, Thomas R., 18
Transcontinental, 90
Trilling, Lionel, 130, 142

Utah State University (Merrill Library, Jack and Charmian London Collection), 13

Walker, Dale, 9; *No Mentor But Myself: Jack London on Writers and Writing*, 9
Walling, Anna Strunsky, 11, 13, 18, 21–41, 41 n.1, 42 nn.10, 18, 19, 134,

139, 152, 197–98; and *The Kempton-Wace Letters* (*see* London, Jack, works); and *Violette of Père Lachaise*, 33, 43 n.26

Walling, English, 32–33, 34, 38, 40–41

Watson, Charles, 124, 136

Wave, The, 5

Weininger, Otto, 113–14, 155, 167; *Sex and Character*, 114, 155, 167

Wharton, Edith, 19, 147, 189–209, 210 n.9; *The Decoration of Houses*, 190; *The Greater Inclination*, 191, 196–97, 199, 208, 211 n.13; *The House of Mirth*, 211 n.13; "The Muse's Tragedy," 19, 190–209; "The Pelican," 196; *The Reef*, 193

Whitman, Walt, 119

Wilcox, Ella Wheeler, 195

Williams, James, 8, 211 n.15

Williams, Tony, 203

Wilson, Robert, 32

Wolfson, Susan, 106

Woman's Home Companion, 199

Wordsworth, William, 22, 110

Youth's Companion, 5, 12, 190

Produced by Wilsted & Taylor Publishing Services

    Copyediting: Caroline Roberts

    Design and Compositon: Melissa Ehn

    Project Management: Christine Taylor

Text Typeface: Monotype Baskerville

Display Typeface: Poplar

Paper: Glatfelter Supple Opaque

Printed and Bound by Thomson-Shore, Inc.